FROM THE PEN OF
J. B. WADLEY

FROM THE PEN OF
J. B. WADLEY

Selected and edited by Adrian Bell

From the Pen of J. B. Wadley

Introduction © Adrian Bell 2002
A Tribute to Jock © Neville Chanin 1981

First published in 2002 by
Mousehold Press
Victoria Cottage
Constitution Opening
Norwich, NR3 4BD

Photographs: front cover – Bernard Thompson/Photosport International
back cover – Ron Good/Photosport International

ISBN 1 874739 22 6

Printed by Barnwell's Print Ltd., Aylsham, Norfolk NR11 6ET

CONTENTS

Publisher's acknowledgements:

The publishers gratefully acknowledge the publishers of *Cycling Weekly* for permission to reprint material originally published in *Coureur* and *Sporting Cyclist*, Fretwell Print and Design for permission to reprint material originally published in *International Cycle Sport*, and Mrs Mary Wadley for permission to reprint material originally published in *The Bicycle* and the extract from *My 19th Tour de France*.

Editor's acknowledgements:

A number of people have helped considerably in the production of this book both through the loan of materials, and through giving me their time to share their memories of J. B. Wadley. I am particularly grateful for the help received from: Richard Allchin, Martin Ayres, Peter Bryan, Neville Chanin, David Duffield, Roy Green, Phil Liggett, Fergus Muir, John Pierce, John Wilcockson and Les Woodland. Most especially, I would like to thank Mrs Mary Wadley for giving the project her blessing.

FOREWORD

J. B. Wadley – A Man in Full

A few years ago, the celebrated American author Tom Wolfe wrote a novel he called *A Man in Full*. It tells the story of an opinionated, sometimes cantankerous gentleman farmer, turned property developer from the Deep South of the United States, who was having a hard time adjusting to the realities of the late-twentieth century. He was a man of many lives, hence the novel's title.

The subject of this book is J. B. Wadley. He, too, was a man of many lives who was sometimes opinionated and perhaps a little cantankerous (in a playful way) and, although he lived in a totally different society, this very English writer on cycling, in all its aspects, was very much a man full of life.

Wadley, as he often referred to himself, got married late in life and so had no children, but he was a father figure to many, including me. My own father also was a cyclist. He enjoyed cycle touring and English-style time-trialing, and rode his bike everywhere. Just like Wadley. They never knew each other, as my Dad died unexpectedly at the age of 49, when I was 18. His racing bike was all I inherited, and I couldn't have asked for something more life-changing. It opened up my own world, which until then had centred around a grammar-school life of 'A' Level studies, playing cricket and football, and cross-country running. And, although I went on to complete a degree course in Civil Engineering, it was the bike that gave me a true education. It was a crimson-coloured made-to-measure Frederick, built by local frame builder Fred Pratt, who once did the skilled work on the frames that bore the Claud Butler imprint.

That bike took me away from home for the first time, to long tours around England, Wales and up to Scotland. I started reading the *CTC Gazette* that my Dad received as a member. I progressed to *Cycling* magazine, then discovered some back issues of *Coureur – the magazine for the Sporting Cyclist*, edited by J. B. Wadley. Inspired by his tales of people and travel, I grew fascinated with the world of cycling 'over there'. So, then a university student, I applied for a summer job in Switzerland and planned to get there by bike – taking in the Tour de France on the way. It was July 1963, a first-ever trip abroad. My first view of the Tour was from the roadside in Picardy.

Shay Elliott was wearing the yellow jersey he'd won the previous day in Roubaix. I was hooked.

That first trip saw me riding 120 miles a day, staying at youth hostels and campsites – across to Angers to see Anquetil win the first time trial, down to the Pyrenees to see Bahamontes in a lone break over the Tourmalet, traversing the long, hot, lonely roads of the Massif Central, and ending up in Chamonix to see Anquetil take the yellow jersey from 'Baha' in the Alps' toughest stage. I was more than hooked.

That trip became the subject of a piece, called 'The Modern Touriste Routier' that Wadley accepted for publication in *Sporting Cyclist*, as his magazine was then called. That was the start of my career as a writer. And it was the beginning of a father–son kind of relationship we enjoyed for the following two decades. When *Sporting Cyclist* was folded into *Cycling* by IPC, Wadley asked me if I wanted to give up my then profession of civil engineering to help him start a new cycling magazine. I accepted, of course. Wadley had been contacted by a firm of printer in Keighley, Yorkshire, owned by three brothers, the Kennedy Brothers, who offered to publish the new mag, which we called *International Cycle Sport*.

It was the first English-language cycling magazine with a four-colour cover, and a few more colour pages inside. We were thrilled with the first issue that came off the presses, even though the colour reproduction was pretty awful. The contents of that first issue were those that would have been the next issue of *Sporting Cyclist*. But a new cycling season was starting, and Wadley needed lots more stories. He told me to go the Continent on my bike, with a notebook and camera, and 'don't come back until you've got lots of stories.' It was March 1968.

I could go on and on, but it's enough to say that Wadley taught me to be a cycling journalist. We sublet a tiny basement office from Milk Race organiser, Maurice Cumberworth, in Kingston, Surrey. Wadley rode his bike down from Richmond each day; I rode up from Dorking; and we typed stories, subedited copy, laid out pages, and sent everything off to the bike-crazy Kennedys each month. It might have continued like that, but Kennedy Publishing was having a hard time financially; a Receiver was brought in, and the firm's assets (including *ICS*) were transferred to another Yorkshire printer who was also in difficulty, but had a more modern printing press. The owner, Peter Fretwell, was a tough-minded businessman – the antithesis of the mild-mannered Wadley. The two men didn't get on. For added 'efficiency', Wadley asked me to move to Yorkshire and put the magazine together at the printers, while he went on the road once more to write the stories he loved writing.

The arrangement worked for a while, but Fretwell soon decided he could do without Wadley. I was prepared to go too, but my 'father' said no. He reasoned that I had just married and that I couldn't jeopardise my life, and anyway, he'd rather see *ICS*, his baby, continue with me at the helm. Well, within a year, I was fired, too. I found work in London, editing trade magazines, but still wrote about cycling on the side.

Wadley began collecting stories, too, and began publishing his own books, besides doing his annual stint covering the Tour de France for the *Daily Telegraph*. He asked me to read his manuscripts, to suggest changes and edit the copy. Wadley had a wicked sense of humour. He loved telling funny stories, and his articles were laced with puns and wicked plays on words. You'll find them in the stories chosen here by Adrian Bell that make up this wonderful book.

I continued visiting Wadley (I called him by his real name, John) and his beloved wife, Mary, whose Welsh hospitality always showed through in the sandwiches, cakes and pots of tea that magically appeared as soon as she had guests at their place in Kew, where they had moved to. Her husband, who spoke with so much enthusiasm and urgency, had a raucous laugh that punctuated the tales he would tell. He loved being a mimic, imitating the voices of famous cyclists. His Queen's English sometimes flowed into Gallic French, and he even loved telling jokes in 'their' language. His company was so admired and enjoyed by the French that he was inaugurated into the famous wine-tasters' fraternity in Burgundy – the Chevaliers de Taste-vin.

Wadley and I went on trips together. Once, on a trip I believe to the Grand Prix des Nations, where the organisers had accepted his suggestion to allow Beryl Burton to ride against the men, I got stopped for speeding near the motor race track at Montlhéry. Wadley joked with the *gendarme* in French, saying it was only natural that his young friend [me] should want to drive fast near the most famous race track in the world. The *gendarme* laughed and waved us on our way. He loved what was typical Wadley humor.

With more time to ride his bike than ever before, he decided to compete in the North Road CC's 24-hour time trial and asked me to be his *directeur sportif*. As always, he rode in Hush Puppies – he couldn't stand leather cycling shoes. He used the red Lejeune he received for riding with the Audax club in Creteil, France. (Typically, he titled the chapter of one of his books, 'Arces-Aix' – pronounced 'Arse Aches' – to describe an Easter Audax ride with his French club, starting in Arces, near Paris, and ending at Aix-en-Provence). Wadley duly completed his first '24' when he was approaching 60, and when he stopped for food or a toilet stop in the night, he always had a joke to share. Although the race was making him suffer with cramp and stomach problems, his sense of humour never left him. Even on one of my last visits to see him, when he was in Kingston Hospital, fading from a terminal illness, he still raised a smile with his words.

John Borland Wadley was a man who enjoyed life to the full. A man in full. And now his words come to life again in this book dedicated to his memory.

Read on.

John Wilcockson

J. B. WADLEY
'Our Man on the Spot'

Although I never met J. B. Wadley*, except through his writing, like many of my generation who had any sort of interest in bicycles, it was he who first sparked, and then fuelled, my love of cycle-racing. The earliest acquaintance was with his dispatches from the Tour de France printed in the *Daily Telegraph*. I can still remember my father's look of curious amusement when I asked him to add that paper to our newsagent's order, just for three weeks every July. Later, of course, I came upon *Sporting Cyclist*, although I didn't for one moment realise, at the time, what a unique and significant achievement it was in British cycling journalism.

Others did. Writing in 1974, the French cycling journalist René de Latour suggested that just as the initials H.D. (for Henri Desgrange) used to be embroidered on the yellow jersey, British cyclists would do well to recall the initials J.B.W., together with W.J.M. (for Bill Mills, founder of *The Bicycle*). 'Without their written word,' he argued, 'there would have been no Rainbow Jersey for Tom Simpson in 1965, no World Championship at Leicester in 1970, and certainly no Tour de France at Plymouth in 1974.' Even allowing for French generosity, and for the fact that he was writing those words in an introduction to J. B. Wadley's final book, it would be difficult to dispute his conclusion. If he were writing today, he would, of course, have so much more to add to that list.

As a French man, de Latour perhaps instinctively recognised the power of the written word since, in its Continental heartlands, cycle-racing was a product of newspapers, or rather of the commercial drive to sell them. Cycle-racing was thus born umbilically tied to the written word. The world's first long-distance road-race, from Paris to Rouen, was sponsored by *Vélocipède Illustré* in 1869. Then, in 1891, *Véloce-Sport* organised the 600-kilometre Bordeaux–Paris, and *Le Vélo* the 1,200-kilometre Paris–Brest–Paris. Indeed, most of the great single-day road-races that we have come

---

*He was universally spoken of as 'Jock' by those who knew him, although he only ever wrote under the byline J. B. Wadley. This was the convention when he began his career in the 1930s and he never deviated from it, apart from the occasional reference to himself in the text as JBW. Since I never met him, I will stick with those conventions.

to define as the 'Classics' began as no more than a glint in the eye of an ambitious circulation manager. In their bid to outdo each other, they devised ever longer or more strenuous routes that demanded ever more heroic exploits (and extended the paper's circulation area), until, finally, in 1903, Henri Desgrange, on behalf of *L'Auto*, trumped them all with a race that would encompass the whole country.

All of this was in an age before radio or television, and when print photography was still in its infancy; so the unique coincidence of the development of mass-circulation newspapers and the bicycle, which produced the sport of cycle road-racing, also generated an epic language that was designed to match the deeds of those pioneer riders – and sell more newspapers. This, for example, is Desgrange, himself:

Their legs, like giant levers, will power onwards for sixty hours; their muscles will grind up the kilometres; their broad chests will heave with the effort of the struggle; their hands will clench on to their handlebars; with their eyes they will observe each other ferociously; their backs will bend forward in unison for barbaric breakaways; their stomachs will fight against hunger, their brains against sleep. And at night a peasant waiting for them by a deserted road will see four demons passing by, and the noise of their desperate panting will freeze his heart and fill it with terror.

This was not even remotely the world that the fourteen-year-old John B. Wadley met when he first joined the Colchester Rovers Cycling Club in 1929, for on this side of the Channel 'massed-start' racing on the open road had been outlawed by cycling's own authorities since before the turn of the century. That brashness, the extravagant public enthusiasm, and above all the blatant commercialism of professional Continental cycle sport, not to mention the over-blown, mock-heroic language that accompanied it, was simply not our way. In Britain, cycle-racing meant the purity of the track, or the crack-of-dawn discipline of the time trial, with riders cloaked in the self-effacing uniformity of their black alpacas and the ever-present threat of disqualification should they break the strictest of amateur codes. Despite the huge growth in cycling clubs in the 1920s, Continental road-racing went almost unreported here, and its spectacle was virtually unknown to British club cyclists.

Ironically, it was by courtesy of *Cycling*, which had so consistently and vehemently disparaged Continental cycle-racing, that JBW was to get his initiation into how they did things over there. In 1933 the journal organised an excursion for its readers to see one afternoon of the World Track Championships in Paris. Nineteen-year-old Wadley went and, enthralled though he was by the sprinting and the motor-paced riding at the rebuilt Parc des Princes track, his most significant discoveries were those large-format, sepia magazines which told, in dramatic photographs and equally evocative text, the story of the Tour de France which had ended only the previous week. He returned with an armful, and immediately placed a daily order for *L'Auto* with his Colchester newsagent, who must have thought him a most extravagant young man. But now he was hooked. Over the next couple of years he regularly made his own way to Paris, to the indoor meetings at the Vélodrome d'Hiver and to the Parc des Princes to see the conclusion of the Tour, and he soaked up all the information on Continental cycling that he could get hold of, from the French magazines and from avidly listening to the sports reports broadcast each evening by Radio-Paris.

Then, in February 1936, *The Bicycle* was launched. Here, for the first time in more than a quarter of a century, was a serious weekly rival to *Cycling*. And it was a rival in every sense: its founder and editor, W. J. Mills, was one of the very few British cyclists who had any direct experience of road-racing abroad – for two years he had even secured a small contract with a Paris-based professional team – and, with the founding of his paper and the promotion of 'massed-start' races such as 'The Bicycle 100' on the Brooklands track, and the first Isle of Man races, he set about opposing the conservative views that *Cycling* had persistently championed. It was a mission to open the eyes of British cyclists to the full extent of the Continental programme of road-racing. Wadley, desperate at the time to get away from the family wholesale fruit business, must have written to Mills to ask for a job almost immediately because within a month of the first appearance of *The Bicycle* he had been interviewed, and appointed as editorial assistant. His career in cycle journalism had begun.

His primary task was race reporting: British races, of course, but also he was to compose reports of Continental races culled from French and Belgian Press, and from the cuttings posted by their contact at *L'Auto* – it was always Mills's intention that *The Bicycle* would have an overtly educational function. 'Should I use the word *peloton*, since nobody will know what we're talking about?' the cub-reporter once asked his editor. 'Yes, use it,' was Mills's immediate reply. 'What *The Bicycle* writes today, the cycling world will be talking tomorrow.'

Working for *The Bicycle*, Wadley also encountered another peculiarly British form of cycle sport – the place-to-place record. In 1939 the Hercules cycle company assembled a group of talented riders to attack record after record. Scarcely a week went by throughout that season when one record or another was not rewritten, and JBW followed and reported many of them – Marguerite Wilson on the A30 between Portsmouth and London, one week; Richard Kemps on the A4 between Bath and London the next. It was an experience that was to lead to a life-long affection for the lonely vigil of the long-distance rider, particularly over that most romantic of routes – Land's End to John o'Groats. This was, perhaps, the closest comparison Britain could offer to those marathon stages in the early years of the Tour de France that called forth the kinds of heroic exploits that would have appealed to the young JBW. Years later he was able to confess:

> I find an End-to-Ender's weary climb over lonely Berriedale after 800 miles in the saddle every bit as inspiring as a solo by a continental mountain king on fan-packed Galibier.

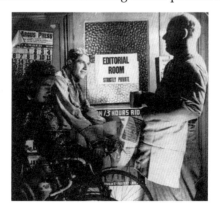

Christmas party 1937 in the office of The Bicycle.
J. B. Wadley (centre) with colleagues.
(Photo: courtesy Peter Bryan)

4

This encounter with the 1939 Hercules record-breakers also led to a new job: after two years with *The Bicycle*, JBW left to join the advertising agency that handled the company's publicity, but this venture was soon to be truncated by the outbreak of war. By the end of the year he had been conscripted, and was on his way down to the West Country for basic military training. It would be another ten years before he returned to full-time journalism.

After the war, Wadley went back to the family business in Colchester, but he was never far away from cycling. He was one of the three British Press officers for the UCI at the London Olympics in 1948 and, as a freelance, he continued to write about all aspects of cycling.

Also during these immediate post-war years JBW renewed his acquaintance with Continental cycling and began making regular trips abroad, particularly to Belgium, both during the road season and for the winter six-day races. The mere fact of there being an Englishman in the Press box, at the Ghent velodrome, for instance, would have been enough to attract attention, but J. B. Wadley was more than that – he was a thoroughly well-informed enthusiast, as knowledgeable and deeply steeped in the sport as any French or Belgian journalist he would have met. It was almost certainly during this interlude in his own professional career that he started to establish the contacts, with riders, promoters and foreign journalists, that were later to provide him with such a rich source of material.

In 1951 he was persuaded back into full-time journalism by Peter Bryan, who had recently succeeded W. J. Mills as editor of *The Bicycle*. They had first met in late 1939 when Bryan, then still at school, had been evacuated to Colchester. He recalls one occasion when he signed up for a hard-riders' section club run with the Colchester Rovers, without fully realising what he was letting himself in for:

> We stopped for tea in Braintree, and I was wet through. It was pitch black and snowing outside and I didn't have any money. Jock adopted me. He paid a shilling for what was my first club tea.

Partly on the strength of Wadley's introduction to W. J. Mills, Bryan was invited to join the staff of *The Bicycle*, and in 1950 was appointed its editor. He soon concluded that the journal needed a 'foreign correspondent'. Who better than J. B. Wadley? And what better way of repaying that shilling?

So began a pattern of working life and, with it, a unique style of writing about cycling that Wadley was to maintain, to a greater or lesser extent, for more than twenty years. When not required for race-reporting duties in England, he would load the panniers of his bicycle – spare clothes and maps in one, a portable typewriter in the other – and take to the roads of France, Belgium, Holland. Whatever the route, it was of his own choosing. And back would come the reports – of major tours, French Classics, frenetic kermesses over the Belgian *pavé*, or six-day dramas on the steep banking of indoor velodromes – or interviews with current riders or with those whose exploits had once made cycling history, or simply touring features that depicted the appealing variety of the terrain through which he travelled. During one two-month tour in the spring of 1954 he was submitting 3,000 words a week; there was simply nothing else like it in the English cycling Press. 'Man on the Spot' he was known as in the office of *The Bicycle*, and JBW liked that label.

He could be said to have been British cycling's man on the spot in another sense. Inspired by his vivid accounts of the road-racing programme of criteriums and kermesses in Flanders, a small number of British racing cyclists were beginning to venture abroad to pit their strength against foreign opposition in the heartland of road-racing. Often he was on hand with advice, and encouragement of course, but also with helping them sort out their seemingly mundane but vital domestic arrangements. This was a role he was increasingly to play, especially when that advance guard of professional British and Irish riders, headed by Brian Robinson and Shay Elliott, began to make a serious impact on the Continent. Then his travels frequently included detours that enabled him to interview and write home about those pioneers. It was a role that received some formal recognition when he was invited to contribute to Francis Pélissier's Simplex training camps in the South of France. Like Mills before him, Wadley was no advocate of the development of a programme of professional open road-racing in Britain; on the contrary, he insisted, if a talented young rider wanted to break into the professional circuit, he had no serious alternative but to board the ferry and head for the Continent. JBW's support for those who tried was born not simply from patriotism, but out of a recognition of the depth of challenge that it entailed.

In 1955 Wadley, himself, faced a challenge of similar proportions: *The Bicycle*, whose financial position had always been somewhat precarious, was sold to Temple Press, publishers of its arch rival, *Cycling*. In the merger, no one on the staff of *The Bicycle* was offered a job. Working for *The Bicycle*, Wadley had been largely his own boss, reporting what he thought was worth reporting, and paid for doing what he loved doing. He could see no way that he was going to be able to continue that unless he was prepared to go it alone – literally – unless he was willing to set up his own journal. But he had no experience of the mechanics of producing a journal, nor of how to sell one, and even if he had, the portents were not exactly propitious: the post-war cycling boom had ended, and the circulation of specialist journals was dipping. His market research was discouraging: 'There is no room for another magazine about cycle sport,' the cycling trade advised him. 'Try a magazine about touring.' Set against that voice of Cassandra was his own evidence – the countless letters of condolence he'd received in the weeks following the demise of *The Bicycle* from readers who told him how much they'd appreciated those reports from the 'Man on the Spot'.

Perhaps Wadley's idea of an independent magazine of his own was given further, unanticipated encouragement the following month at the National 24-hour Championship; in spite of being unemployed he wrote a report of the championship race. It began:

'You've got a great story to write this time, Jock,' was an observation made to me many times from eighteen hours onwards in this year's Catford '24' hour. But most of these friends immediately realised the situation and added, 'But what are you going to write for?' – to which I replied, '*The Catford Gazette*'.

No doubt the editor of the club's magazine was delighted – here was an unexpected bonus to cap a particularly exciting race which saw the championship record broken. But you can't make a living writing cycle-race reports for *The Catford Gazette*. At some point during the summer of 1955 J. B. Wadley made up his mind to chance all and to follow his instincts.

Two weeks after the Catford '24' he was off to France: it was in 1934 that he'd caught his first glimpse of the Tour, and now, 21 years later, he was to follow the entire Tour from the seat of a Press car.

Also for the first time, he was to see a British team competing. Only two of those ten hopefuls would finally arrive in Paris, but for JBW the fact that a full complement had started was a 21-year-old dream realised. Then, in September, he was back in France for his own post-Tour circuit of the final races of the road season (including Millie Robinson's historic victory in the Tour Féminin) and the opening of the winter track season in the Vélodrome d'Hiver.

When he returned to England after this 'late-season tour de plume' as he called it, not only was his mind made up – he would start his own journal – all the material he would need for the first (and perhaps the only) issue was already there in his notebooks.

The first issue of *Coureur* was published in the winter of 1955; Wadley had written every word, and taken most of the photographs himself. It was produced in Peter Bryan's dining room – his antique mahogany table serving as a make-up desk – with further practical help from photographer Bill Lovelace, and designer Glenn Steward – all three of them former colleagues from *The Bicycle*. The title was a last minute inspiration: Steward telephoned to report that the cover was ready, apart from the lack of a title – what was it to be called? Wadley wasn't sure, but mentioned a few possibilities, among them, *Coureur*. That was good enough for Steward, and so *Coureur* it was.

W. J. Mills wrote encouragingly: 'It's as good as the *The Bicycle* was in 1936.' But the question remained – would it sell? In fact, it was sold in much the same volunteer fashion by which it had been produced, by friends or enthusiastic well-wishers on the gates at Herne Hill, and in specialist cycle shops up and down the country. Then came the tension of awaiting the response. Three months later JBW was able to report:

Having bought it, hundreds of readers sat down to write their appreciation of the publication which had been produced with the help of my little band of supporters. Those letters settled it. *Coureur* was no longer an experiment in cycling journalism. There had to be a second issue.

In fact, there were four issues, coming out quarterly. One measure of the success of the experiment could be gauged from the advertising revenue it generated: in the first issue there was none; in the second issue, six pages of advertisements, and this had more than doubled by the fourth issue. A second measure was the fact that after four issues the new journal attracted a publisher. Charles Buchan's Publications agreed to take on Wadley's venture and to publish it as a monthly, although the title had to be changed. The newsagents W. H. Smith had refused to stock *Coureur* because, so they claimed, it could too easily be confused with another of their titles – *Courier* (a glossy, general interest magazine!). So, *Coureur* became *Sporting Cyclist*. It arrived on the news-stands in May 1957, and continued to do so for the next eleven years, every month selling some 11,000 copies, apart from September, when the figure was substantially higher, because that issue was always given over in its entirety to the J. B. Wadley account of the Tour de France.

This decade marked the zenith of J. B. Wadley's career. Under Charles Buchan's patronage *Sporting Cyclist* was no amateur, one-man operation conducted from a dining room with the help of a group of loyal and willing friends: it had a Fleet Street office, an art editor, an advertising manager and, above all, guaranteed financial stability. Nevertheless, it remained a small enterprise. JBW no longer wrote every word, of course, nor did he take most of the photographs, but only when Roy Green was recruited as assistant editor in 1960 was there any addition to the editorial staff. That was to prove a wise appointment, for Roy Green was to play an essential role in holding the fort when, as so often, the Editor was away from the office.

The only other professional journalist who regularly wrote for *Sporting Cyclist* was René de Latour who contributed articles on the Continental racing scene, and also many of the historical pieces that the journal carried. These would undoubtedly have been dear to Wadley's heart: one of his first assignments on *The Bicycle* – an article about W. J. Pett, a cycling gold medallist at the 1906 Olympics – had invoked the irritation of one reader who had written to demand more about contemporary riders. 'Don't take too much notice,' Bill Mills had advised him. 'Provided you don't overdo it, the real cyclist laps up the historical stuff.' It was advice he remembered; after all, hadn't he set out to cater for that person he saw as the 'real cyclist'?

And real cyclists of every persuasion, what's more, because, as Roy Green points out, *Sporting Cyclist* had a uniting influence upon British cycling. There was no aspect of the sport that did not feature in its pages: Continental road-racing and British time-trialling; track and cyclo-cross; six-day races and six-minute hill-climbs; record-breaking on two wheels or – that most English of enthusiasms – tricycles. 'Cannot we rejoice in the extraordinary variety of our sport instead of refusing to be interested in the other man's speciality?' he asked rhetorically in one earnest editorial plea for liberalism.

As for the rest of the copy, much of it came from his extensive network of keen amateur cyclists, each one with a personal story to tell, and whom Wadley could induce, by his gentle persuasion, into print. It says something for his skill in identifying talent that for some this was the first step in a professional career: Alan Gayfer and Martin Ayres (both destined to become Editor of *Cycling*) wrote their first cycling articles for *Sporting Cyclist*; so, too, did John Wilcockson (currently Editor of *VeloNews*); and an enthusiastic article Wadley himself wrote for *Amateur Photographer* about the first British photographer on the Tour de France was the launch of John Pierce's career. But the key attraction was invariably the article that carried the J. B. Wadley byline.

'Jock was not really a journalist; he was more an essayist,' explains Peter Bryan. To illustrate the point, he cites an occasion when, as editor of *The Bicycle*, he asked Wadley to cover for him and provide a 200-word report of the Isle of Man race to a national newspaper for which he was also cycling correspondent. The conversation apparently went:

'How many words, did you say?'

'About two hundred.'

'Two hundred? I can't possibly write the story of that race in two hundred words; I'll need at least a thousand.'

'They only want two hundred, Jock. They'll only print two hundred.'

'You just can't *do* it in two hundred words.'

'Yes, you *can*, Jock. And you bloody well will.'

And, of course, he did, perfectly adequately, for his first lesson in reporting, when he joined *The Bicycle*, all those years before, had been in reducing a story to its essentials, and beginning with the essential fact. He could write like that when called upon, and indeed did so throughout those years when he was sending back his daily Tour de France dispatches to the *Daily Telegraph*. But it was not something he enjoyed: it ran counter to his natural style which was always more discursive, with a slower, often intriguing 'lead in' that could keep the reader in suspense precisely because he didn't yet know the essential fact – the style of an essayist, if you like.

But what kind of essayist? He did not have the literary eloquence of a Geoffrey Nicholson, a writer whom he admired enormously and who, even in his daily column, could mint phrases that still ring in your memory thirty years on. Wadley's was a more homely style of writing. In his introduction to the very first issue, he spoke of *Coureur* as a 'diary – the diary of a clubman'. Well, yes, a diary in that it was written throughout in the first person, and it chronicled what he did, what he saw, and whom he met. But in no sense was it private like a diary; on the contrary, it was written with a very clear sense of audience, an audience that he referred to collectively as 'the clubman', and for which he always showed the greatest respect. To me, his essays were not so much a diary as letters home, and home was the world of the clubman – the keen, specialist cyclist.

This consistent use of the first person in his articles is crucial to understanding the appeal of his writing. Regardless of whether he was composing an account of a race, interviewing an old-time, retired cyclist, or describing a leisurely tour, he always used this technique. Events were not reported as if they were simple objective facts, nor were they sensationalised; always we saw them through his eyes and ears. He offered us his thoughts, his emotions and his immediate impressions at the moment of their happening, and if those impressions needed to be revised in the light of later revelations, he did that, too, and explained why. But it was that immediacy, that sense of the author's own involvement and proximity to the action which the first-person style provides, that enriched his descriptions of the terrain, or the riders, or conveyed more vividly the drama of the occasion. Sometimes it could give the article the appearance of not having been very carefully constructed – just like a letter, in fact – but it invariably made for a highly accessible report. Good letter-writers, so they say, are basically good conversationalists, and, by all accounts, J. B. Wadley was certainly that.

That discursive, first-person style which carried his letters back home to the clubman looks simple, but the simplicity is deceptive. 'Yes, it looks easy,' says Martin Ayres. 'I tried to copy Jock's style once or twice when I was editor of *Cycling*, but when I did it, it just seemed like name-dropping.' From the pen of J. B. Wadley, somehow, it never did. Perhaps it was his natural modesty that prevented the continual use of 'I' from seeming like a form of self-aggrandisement. Perhaps it was that when he spoke so matter-of-factly about, for example, what Bobet had said to him or what Anquetil had told him you sensed the genuineness of it. JBW – an English gentleman – had earned the respect and affection of many of the key figures in the world of Continental cycling – a fact which sometimes saw affectionate acknowledgement in their references to 'Sir J. B. Wadley'.

So often the richness of those first-person accounts lies in the little details they afford. For instance, a riveting account of Charly Gaul riding the entire French team off his back wheel on a bitterly cold, rain-drenched ascent of the Luitel is brought to life by the incidentals his eye had picked up – the 'tier after tier of umbrellas under the dripping pines' that formed the 'corridor' through which Gaul passed. The Angel of the Mountains – and we know that he climbed in a lower gear than any of his rivals, but Wadley is more precise: here was Gaul 'twiddling his 45 x 23 gear, hands on the tops, eyes fixed straight ahead'. The whole story is enriched by that final, prosaic detail of the exact gear ratio.*

Or consider a different example. Everybody knows the bare facts of Christophe's broken forks on the Tourmalet in 1913 – the story has been retold often enough – but it is through the minute specifics in the very first lines of JBW's interview with him, nearly 50 years after the event, that we start to picture the man. And we haven't even met him yet, nor heard him speak:

> I rang the bell of No. 26 in a street at Malakoff which, although only 20 minutes on the Metro and bus from the centre of Paris, is, officially, a country town. There was no answer. I enquired at the butcher's next door.
> 'M. Christophe?' said the friendly tradesman. 'I don't think he can be far away – but wherever he is, you can be sure he'll be on his bicycle. Even if he goes 200 metres down the street to post a letter, he takes his bike!'

As with any good letter, the apparent absence of structure rarely matters, because, so often, the interest lies in the detours. It is these that seize the reader's attention. So, in the course of a long article detailing a cycling tour JBW made through Brittany, taking in a couple of races, glimpses of the organisation behind the racing scene

---

* A sign of the times, perhaps, that this should have been considered an unusually low gear.

in that bicycle-crazy region, and interviews with current aspirants and past champions, he describes a brief encounter on the road with a *cyclotouriste*. 'Un peu de cyclo?' this short, stocky man had inquired as he came up alongside our editor, and then for two full paragraphs we ride with them. We never learn his name, only that he had once raced with the C.V. Nineteenth in Paris. Suddenly the exhuberant ex-racer turns off the main road, leaving editor Wadley 'still doing evens from the impetus of our brief encounter'. An inconsequential encounter, perhaps, and yet, without ever labouring the point, it is a perfectly drawn miniature on the importance of the bicycle in French culture.

When it came to reporting a race, however, Wadley never forgot its essential narrative. For all the detours – the excursions into cycle-racing's history or into riders' psychology, or the verbatim snatches of conversation in the Press car in which he was travelling or the live news they heard over Radio Tour as the action unfolded – you, the reader, always knew what was going on. And if what was going on was especially complicated, as it can be when the peloton breaks up in the high mountain stages, he would freeze the action if necessary so as to explain it. He knew how to reveal the coherence of the main story in the midst of its developing sub-plots, whether it be the short story of a one-day Classic, or the 21-chapter novel of a Tour de France. That skill at 'reading' a race, which made any of his race reports so compelling, received official recognition during the 1970 Tour when he was awarded La Medaille de la Reconnaissance du Tour de France. It was also, incidentally, one of the reasons why British riders, trying their hand on the Continent, would often seek him out on the start line to ask his advice.

By 1970, however, his own professional life in England had changed irrevocably: *Sporting Cyclist* had ceased publication. In its eleven-year life it had happily survived a number of Fleet Street mergers but, when its publishers were bought out by the IPC media empire, which had little interest in a scarcely profitable monthly magazine, its title was merged with *Cycling*. J. B. Wadley's *Sporting Cyclist* – and it always was very much a personal chronicle – became an insert within the pages of the weekly. This time he was offered a job, but turned it down. Despite the resigned tones in which he explained the change in his 131st and final *Sporting Cyclist* editorial in April 1968, he was deeply disappointed. 'It was,' says Peter Bryan, 'the only time I ever saw Jock really angry. He felt badly let down.'

He also felt convinced, nonetheless, that there remained a place for a monthly cycling journal which could carry its stories and race reports in depth. Furthermore, when news of the demise of *Sporting Cyclist* began to circulate everybody seemed to be confirming that opinion. 'You simply *must* start another,' they said.

This time he did not have to search for a publisher: Kennedy Brothers, run by three keen cyclists, approached him with the proposal that he should edit a new cycling monthly which they would publish. Thus, *International Cycle Sport* was born. The change gave the impression of being almost seamless, the first issue of *International Cycle Sport* appearing on the news-stand just one month after *Sporting Cyclist* had disappeared from it. 'Return to the Independent Class' heralded its first editorial and, just as the first edition of *Sporting Cyclist* had contained a lengthy article from René de Latour about Fausto Coppi, so, too, did the inaugural edition of the new journal.

Yet, so the saying goes, you can never walk the same road twice: *ICS* was not *Sporting Cyclist* in full-colour guise. In the first place it never had the same breadth of coverage. Secondly, not only was it more narrowly focused, it contained fewer articles, and they were mainly written by professional journalists. In its text and use of full-page colour photography it was closer to a contemporary monthly cycling journal; it was never a diary written by clubmen for clubmen. But above all, it simply did not seem to bear that unmistakable stamp of J. B. Wadley which ran through any issue of *Sporting Cyclist*, even those in which he may have written no more than the editorial. With *International Cycle Sport* you sensed that there were more hands than his alone on the editorial tiller.

In addition to that, his publishers were soon experiencing the financial difficulties that eventually led to *ICS* coming under new ownership. But the new relationship was not a happy one, and Wadley, who was not a businessman – and probably not much interested in the commercial side of producing a cycling magazine – parted company with *International Cycle Sport* in May 1971.

The next few months must have seemed like a re-run of 1955. After the Tour de France (which he continued to report for the *Daily Telegraph)* he stayed on for another cycling venture, before returning home to write up the story which he would eventually publish under his own name. This time, however, it was no leisurely 'tour de plume', but a plunge into the deep end of the world of *cyclo-*

sportif. Just a few years previously he had begun to acquire a first-hand relationship with this form of cycle sport which, hitherto, had scarcely figured in his work.

Having successfully negotiated a 12-hour comparatively easy *randonneur* event during one of his Continental trips some years earlier, he entered, with some trepidation, the 1971 edition of the Paris–Brest–Paris. He completed the ride in 83 hours 22 minutes, and published his account of it the following year, under his own imprint, in a volume entitled *Old Roads and New.* More directly, perhaps, than anything else Wadley wrote, that publication illustrates the impact that his written word had on British cycling. His account generated a considerable interest among sporting cyclists here and led to the formation of Audax UK, an organisation which now numbers close to 4,000 members.

Two years later, again under the imprint of J. B. Wadley Publications, another book appeared. Having had his contract with the *Daily Telegraph* to cover the 1973 Tour (as he had been doing since 1962) cancelled at the last moment, he took the decision to follow it anyway, by bicycle. This, after all, was what he had been advocating to British club riders for the best part of 40 years. It is not difficult to see *My 19th Tour de France* as the culmination of a life's work: his preface hints at just that:

> I had practised and thoroughly enjoyed what I had for so long been preaching. Instead of lazing 3,000 miles in a Press car, I had pedalled 1,750 on a bike. Instead of scribbling 400 words a night and phoning them through to Fleet Street, I have taken my time in writing 90,000 and sent them to the printers.
>
> Nearly 200 pages of prose will look dull stuff to the enthusiast who judges cycling journalism by the number of big close-up action photographs per issue, but I am confident the book will be enjoyed by those ready to draw their own mental illustrations from a broader appreciation of our sport.

So, here he was, back once more on the Tour route just as he had followed it in the early days of *Sporting Cyclist*, with nothing planned in advance, arranging his own accommodation every evening, and mixing easily with cycling enthusiasts of every level – from *cyclo-sportifs* to ex-World Champions. And the book? A 200-page Wadley letter vividly full of his own perceptive observations and all the usual detours, such as an account of his own ascent of the Galibier, from which, of course, all kinds of memories of other, more illustrious epics on that most famous mountain came flooding back.

I spoke at the beginning of never having met J. B. Wadley. Those whom I have spoken to who did know him speak of him with one, affectionate voice. He was a gentleman; an enthusiast who always made time for others; a man who invested in others. But also a very private man. He died that way, suddenly and unexpectedly in March 1981: few even knew of his illness.

One who perhaps knew him better than most was Neville Chanin, who carried his ashes to the Alps. He recalls being at his house in Kew one day when Mary, his wife, reminded him that they were out of eggs. Would he run out and get some? Like Monsieur Christophe, who never went beyond the postbox on foot, J. B. Wadley took his bike. He returned two hours later with half a dozen eggs, having ridden almost to Guildford and back. His excuse? 'I knew where there was a nice little farm shop.' The truth, of course, is that he simply loved being on a bicycle. And, fortunately for us, he loved writing about it, too.

Adrian Bell

CLUBMEN AND GENTLEMEN

'Clubman' was a word J. B. Wadley used throughout his life, even when it had come to acquire a somewhat dated ring, echoing that period of the 1930s and '40s when, up and down the country, cycling clubs were at their zenith. To JBW the word always signified the serious cyclist who maintained a keen interest in cycling as a sport as much as a form of recreation. This was the reader he always had in mind: *Coureur* might well have been called 'The Clubman'. 'There will be no "writing down" to the reader,' he promised, in its maiden issue; and there never was.

Often the stories in *Sporting Cyclist* were contributed by clubmen, themselves, and when JBW had coaxed one into putting pen to paper, he ensured that his club was mentioned in the by-line.

Wadley, himself, was a frequent guest at club dinners, and used to report them for *The Bicycle*. This was something the clubs greatly appreciated and so, too, his editor – in the winter, they could be short of copy. Often he rode there, despite the weather and the time of year – attending the 1966 Wessex Road Club dinner, for instance, involved a 100-mile slog to Bournemouth into the teeth of a south-westerly gale.

'Called Up North' is an account of his visit to the West Pennine R.C. annual dinner; this time he went by train, but those clubmen who had invited him ensured that he was out on the road with them on the Sunday. His affection for that world of the English club rider, and his respect for those who made it what it was, is evident in every line of his report.

The core of club racing was, and is, the time-trial, and Wadley would have none of that bickering between time-trialists and roadmen which had so blighted the sport in this country. His editorials appealed for tolerance, and more than once he pointed out how that first generation of British road-racing professionals then making their presence felt on the Continent had all enjoyed their first successes on the domestic R.T.T.C. circuit. Brian Robinson's 19-minute Tour de France stage win, had been, he suggested, inspired by those 100s and 12-hours he had once ridden in Yorkshire. Personally, he loved the time trial, especially in its lengthier version, and persuaded himself, at the age of 59, to ride the North Road Club's 24-hour. He failed by just a few miles to reach the coveted 400-mile mark.

Such was Wadley's fascination with the sheer variety of the club world that he even confessed to a sneaking regard for the tricycle. The two coincided – the trike and the 24 hour – with his report of John Arnold's valiant ride in the 1953 National Championship.

J. B. Wadley was probably not the first Englishman to ride in a Grand Prix des Gentlemen – that delightfully French affair whereby an over-40-year-old is teamed with a current professional or leading amateur in a sporting 20- to 30-kilometre time trial – but his account of riding the Marseille event, partnered with Jean Bobet, younger brother of triple Tour de France winner Louison, brought 'Gentlemen' to the attention of British veterans.

One consequence of his report in *The Bicycle* was a series of phone calls from eager veteran time-triallists. So began an annual stream of English Gentlemen to a small village outside Paris to be paced by some of cycling's leading professionals of the day in the Grand Prix Parisien des Gentlemen, organised by the *Club des Vétérans et Ancêtres* (the French equivalent of the V.T.T.A.).

Called Up to the North

On November 14, 1940, when called up to the West, I was ordered to take my civilian gas mask with me. On November 14, 1964, I was called up to the West Pennines. "Bring your cycling stuff with you," I was instructed. "We'll go for a ride on the Sunday and blow some of the overnight cobwebs away."

The order was signed by J. Spencer, and I must say that in every respect my welcome to the North at Bury was much warmer than that awaiting me in the West at Yeovil 24 years ago. I was up for the most enjoyable W. Pennine R. C. dinner, and the plan was for me to stay the night at Jack Spencer's at Clayton-le-Moors. However, his spare rooms being full of bikes and equipment for the Christmas trade, he had to book me in the local hotel, a very swish place indeed. Harry Aspden has reported in "Cycling" how I carried one of Jack's spare bikes up the marble stairs to my room rather than leave it out all night. In the morning Jack came to collect me and got equal pleasure by carrying it down!

Clayton-le-Moors is, of course, the home of Alan Ramsbottom, and normally the "Demon" would have been home and joined us on the run. But business kept him in Belgium, so there were just three of us who set out from Clayton at half-past-ten on the Sunday morning, the third being Harry Aspden. Harry had, in fact, only left us in the early hours of the morning on his way home from the dinner. Then, he was appropriately dressed and riding a flat-barred bike with built-in luggage racks. This morning he looked much more formidable on his Harry Quinn.

When, at the W. Pennine dinner, I had told the president, Harry Benson, that I was riding one of Spencer's own bikes, he told me to be careful because it certainly would go sideways! This was not to imply the machine was badly built, but that "Sox" rides such big gears that all his bikes progress in a series of Randall-like jerks from force of habit!

This, in fact, is what the bike did, but for a different reason. When we left *chez* Spencer and headed north, the strong westerly hit us in a series of jerks as it whistled between the houses. All right for Harry and Jack, part and parcel of their bikes, which knew every inch of the road anyhow, but a bit upsetting for me at first with the light front tub skating about on a wet surface.

In Whalley, my guides led the way through the back streets to show me the ancient Abbey, and soon we were flying down into the Ribble Valley for a five-minute spell in Yorkshire before climbing back into Lancs. Until then I had been at the front with Jack, but I was glad to let Harry take over and then endeavoured to hang on to two of the most remarkable vets. in the country. Harry had had a quiet year, he told me, his 1964 best efforts being only 1-3, 2-13 and 4-39. I should be more than happy to improve to those times in three years when I reach his present age of 53.

As for "Sox", of course, he holds the vets.' absolute best "25" record with 58-23 ridden in 1963 at 45 years of age. Would he have beaten that time this year? Well an unsigned reporter in the October issue of "Slush", the West Pennine R.C. club magazine, writes:

Guess who finished third in a Vets.' "25" with 1-3-41, having been stopped by a policeman for riding furiously, held up twice by traffic lights and finally puncturing. Your guess is as good as mine as to whether we would have had a new competition record or not, but the aforementioned offender apparently had a witness for each of the delays!

No shame, then, in occasionally being dropped by such men. They had plenty of breath to talk about the great countryside through which we were passing. That bleak high point back over our right shoulders was Pendle, home of Nick o' Pendle, the hill climb test; that long ridge to our left was, in fact, Longridge Fell; behind it the Trough of Bowland.

The road we were on, I learned, was that to be used in the W. Pennine open team time-trial next year. Having tried a 50-km. "three-upper" in my club's own event on E7 in September and suffered on the few tiny hills, I should hate to ride in that. There are too many ups and downs in it for a puffing vet. brought up on the East Anglian flats.

Modern young speedmen with their eye on the top rewards of the sport should welcome the chance to ride on such a course. It was round these roads that Alan Ramsbottom used to chase in his club days, developing all the while into the *routier complet* that he is today.

We followed the curve of Longridge Fell for a few miles before branching off to the right. The signpost said Chipping, and I remembered that it was here we had a rendezvous with another friend. Earlier in this week-end story, after talking about Harry Aspden, Harry Benson and Harry Quinn, I almost said that the place was full of Harrys. There waiting for us in the Sun Inn at Chipping was yet another, if you will forgive the liberty – Reg Harris!

To see Reg out on a road bike is nothing unusual these days. He often joins "Sox" in runs through the district, and although ostensibly social, the aggressive urge of each occasionally takes over. One day, 45-year-old Reg suggested he should lead out a sprint to see if "Sox" could come by.

"I was howling fit at the time," Sox told me, "but I just couldn't get near Reg. That is why I think Reg would make the ideal national track coach. He can still get up there on the track with prospective riders and show how it should be done."

On this ride I had not the slightest difficulty in dropping Reg Harris – when I wanted to get on ahead to take pictures of the distinguished little bunch. We plugged on into the wind to Longridge village, then turned east to be blown along to our lunchtime stop at Hurst Green. Spencer won the sprint, but the judges are still considering a protest from Aspden that he was pulled back by a hand grasping his windcheater.

Our table at lunch, where we were joined by two more friends, was a lively one. On the road I had been surprised at Reg's simple enjoyment at riding the bike. Like many others, I suppose, I always regarded the fivefold world sprint champion as a man who would not have much interest in cycling after his competitive days were over.

We were wrong. Over lunch, Reg talked a little about Maspes, Coppi and various tracks in Europe – and a lot about his early days of riding with the Bury section of the C.T.C. when he used to go touring, pot-holing and hostelling just like any other young fellow. In that section was an older member, Jimmy Battersby, who got him interested in racing – and every sporting cyclist will be glad he did. Now we are happy to find Reg back in the touring saddle again – a mere figure of speech; he is still on a B17 narrow – and enjoying the freedom of the Lancashire roads. Perhaps the wheel will turn full circle, and Reg will find his successor out on a Sunday morning run.

Over the coffee I tried to persuade the three of them to come down to the Whitewebbs "10" the following Sunday; all three were eligible to ride under the conditions published in "Cycling" – Aspden (journalist and official); Spencer (cycle dealer); Harris (former rider*). That would have pushed me down three places in the list!

On parting, Reg rode west, we three back to Whalley, where Harry peeled off for home at Langho. I somehow hung on the "Sox" back to Clayton-le-Moors, the large lunch not talking kindly to the exercise. I looked forward to the tea that Mrs. Spencer said she would have ready for us on our return. A nice cup before getting the bus back to Manchester Central station – just the job.

Which shows what a simple Southerner I am. The "tea" referred to was not a cup and biscuits, but a feast. Mrs. Spencer readily understood my embarrassment, and from the pick of the table made me a packet of sandwiches. These I ate somewhere towards Derby, then settled back in my corner seat and followed the day's ride on a map. Those hills couldn't have been all that bad; perhaps I'll ride in that team time-trial after all.

* I have now realised that, as an ex-pro., Reg would not have been eligible.

Sporting Cyclist, January 1965

The two men on the right look pleased with themselves, having just beaten their friendly rivals on Cycling *in the Whiteways 10 miles t.t.*

Times were (l. to r.) Mike Duffield (27-33), Alan Gayfer (29-31) and Roger St. Pierre (27-8), and for Sporting Cyclist, *J. B. Wadley (27-0) and Roy Green (25-26). The photograph was sent to* Sporting Cyclist *by the Editor of* Cycling *with the generous invitation that they might care to print it. JBW was happy to oblige.*

Arnold's "Unbelievable" 24 Outshines Carter's Championship Win

It meant missing the finish of the Tour de France. It meant missing H-Day. It meant missing two nights' sleep. But I swear by all the gods of the winds that howled across the Wirral on Saturday and Sunday that I saw something greater than even the Parc des Princes or Herne Hill has ever staged, something far more fantastic than could have been pictured in a cyclist's wildest dreams. Scores of clubmen making for the finishing circuit of the R.T.T.C. National Championship 24 just would not believe that tricyclist John Arnold had been all the way round the course. It was 402 miles to this point for bicyclists; Arnold still had 3 hrs. 2 mins. 36 secs. to go. He *must* have omitted at least one of the detours.

In their place I would have been a doubter, too. But we had not just arrived on the scene. We had been out all this afternoon and morning, all last evening and night, and we knew that Arnold had been every inch of the way. We had seen him go "mad" from Time-keeper MacQueen's "Go" at 5.37 p.m. on Saturday. We had seen him catch and drop his great friend, and rival and occasional part-ner, Albert Crimes (who started 22 minutes in front), with an inci-dental 4hrs. 47mins. 100 to show for his pains.

He would "crack", of course, but if he didn't (we said) then he might beat some of the established bicycling stars. That was early on. Now, there we were at the start of the finishing circuit at 402 miles, looking at our watches, doing sums and saying, "You know – Arnold has an outside chance of beating Carter." And Carter was the man who had caught and dropped the 1952 champion Eddie Mundy by 12 minutes and was the actual race leader.

The race leader, on a bicycle, and only 13 mins. 1 sec. faster than a tricyclist after more than 22 hours of riding. Anybody who can deal with Mundy – as Carter had done – in a 24 is a great rider, and I invite you to choose your own superlative to describe a three-wheel merchant who can throw out a challenge like that.

This was a 10m. 3f. circuit, and the Carter (No. 61) versus Arnold (No. 37) pursuit was terrific, with Arnold first on the road as he had been since the 12-hour mark – and despite the dozens of corners and twisting lanes and a westerly that literally howled, the honours went to Arnold. On the first lap, which occupied 34 mins. 6 secs., he took two minutes out of Carter, and successfully set about repeating the process in the second. Just as Carter completed his first lap, Mundy entered this giants' arena, well down, but full of fight. The Addiscombe man – just recovering from a bad patch – immediately re-caught and dropped Carter, who began to have a rough time of his own. Not so our astonishing Arnold; he crashed his way round that circuit, grabbing every drink he could lay his hands on and munching miles, miles, miles.

After completing the four-course circuit meal, during which he had put away 41m. 5f. in 2-15-30, and beaten Crimes's 422 competition record with 1hr. 55 mins. to spare, the menu-of-miles directed him on supplementary roads to the west. He had covered

443.5 miles and still had 47 mins. 26 secs. to go – and when Carter completed his own fourth lap his lead over the tricyclist was reduced to a bare five minutes!

In a car with R.T.T.C. judge Frank Slemen, I followed that last three-quarters of an hour of a day in the life of a superb athlete, admiring for the hundredth time in this championship, the purposeful way his body swayed from side to side to the rhythm of his pedalling. Yet how still the arms that guided the trike, how strong the legs that thrust it forward – how perfect the communion of muscle and machine.

That finishing stretch was hilly and bumpy and exposed to the wind, but Arnold battled on. Coming back from the last turn but one he crossed Carter, who called, "Sorry, John," for he knew that, barring a last-minute accident, the honour of the two-wheeler had been saved. Arnold turned for the last time with about three minutes to go … a sprint down hill … the long blast of a klaxon as Slemen's watch went up to 5.37, and he free-wheeled to a halt looking more as if he had done 257 in two days than 457 in one.

The interview-cum-autograph-signing session was interrupted by the arrival of Nick Carter on the way to the last turn, and John got up from his grassy resting place to join in the applause. Nick was soon back, with five minutes still in hand, and with friend Slemen I followed him to the end – stylish, 79-fixed, sprinter-saddled Nick, with his white cap, smart club jersey, white socks, immaculate as when he started 459.25 miles ago.

Eddie Mundy, whose time was up, was sitting by the roadside, and cheered his championship successor when he still had a minute to go. I saw Eddie finish last year and Gus Andrews in 1951, and remarked on their freshness, but compared with friend Nick they were tired men.

It was of Nick that an ordinary club-man said to me very early in the trial: "There is not a finer sportsman in the North – unless it is John Arnold."

The Bicycle, 29 July 1953

Wadley – a Gentleman and a Champion

Towards the end of one of the biggest meals I have ever eaten, one of my fellow diners rose from his seat and came along to see me.

"I am disgusted with you. Black coffee and a liqueur – that should be cut out of your regime!"

My critic was friend Jean Bobet, and, of course, he was pulling my leg, and I was also pulling his when I replied, "It's only for today; tomorrow I start training for next year, and we'll jolly well make sure we beat Louison."

What nonsense were we talking there at Marseille on the first Sunday afternoon of February? I will explain.

During Jean's visit to London with his World-Champion brother in November,* I happened to ask when his first race of 1955 was likely to be, as I would probably be down on the Côte d'Azur at that time. The answer was that the opening competition wasn't really a race at all, but a bit of a stunt. "We've promised Mr. Coupry at Marseille to take part in the Grand Prix des Gentlemen. As you know, many well-known racing men take part, and each paces a 'gentleman' cyclist. The gentlemen are local business people who have never raced, but there are other categories, such as former riders, champions of other sports, and journalists …"

That did it! At the mention of the word "journalist" Jean and I were both struck with the same idea, and there and then in a restaurant on Western Avenue the Jean Bobet–J. B. Wadley contract was signed for the 1955 Grand Prix des Gentlemen at Marseille.

We had a bit of fun together looking through the menus and making a list of all the things I ought not to eat, and although I defied them there and then in some matters, I must confess that I subsequently adopted part of the regime which was substantially the same as laid down by Charles Pélissier at the Simplex training camp.

The thought of going into training again at 40 years of age rather tickled me. I had a couple of full seasons of time-trialling after coming out of the army in 1946, but since then I have ridden only three end-of-season 25s and an old-time's-sake 12 hrs. of 212 miles on my 37th birthday.

*Louison Bobet was guest of honour at the 1954 Champions Concert in the Royal Albert Hall.

As readers will know, I have undertaken many long-distance tours since then, but owing to journalistic travels by land, sea and air, my 1954 cycling mileage was probably the lowest in 25 years of club life. I was tickled with the prospect of training again because I felt I was just the fellow to put Pélissier's method to the test.

Please do not think I am losing my sense of proportion. I was not training for a world championship, but for a silly little race of 20 kms. But basically the principle was the same, and I am now convinced that the right way is to build up strength gradually, and not to flog oneself silly. *Si j'avais su ...* If only I'd known when I was young.

For my two months training I had rides of about 60 miles on a Sunday, pedalling the gear of my derailleur which I imagined to be 63, but which on examination on the last week turned out to be 58! (the tyres were fairly heavy wire-ons). During the week I did two evening runs of about 20 miles each, each ride just slightly faster than the last, endeavouring to keep the same pedalling rhythm going on the hills, but giving up and recuperating if it began to hurt. I don't blame a clubman for laughing at the improbability of a 58 gear hurting anyone on the Harrow road, but if he reckons in terms of 66 for his own use, then he can take the principle seriously. I did all these evening rides having had nothing to eat since lunch but a cup of weak tea and a chocolate biscuit. I cut down my bread consumption by a half and chipped potatoes by two-thirds.

I was thus able to reply truthfully in the affirmative when Jean Bobet wrote to me just after Christmas saying, "I do hope you are training eagerly." I also told him that I had spent the holiday riding from Biggleswade to Lincoln and back, still on the 58.

Snow and smog interrupted my progress a bit, but following the Pélissier advice, I refused to try to make amends by subsequently doubling the mileage, or rushing it. The Grand Charlot says that on the contrary, you should not overdo the reopening run.

Higher gear

In the last fortnight in January I stepped up the pace, using 68 for normal, and flicking into 76 for the easy bits. On the last run I felt good. I knew that I was in good enough shape not to be in any danger of hurting myself, and I had arrived in this condition without once having had an aching pair of legs.

When I reached the Côte d'Azur and got mixed up with the

Simplex camp trainees I was reminded that I was fit by "Gentleman" standards only. Two 30-mile rides with them did, however, give me an idea of the difficulty of hanging on to the back wheel of a fit young racing man.

The plan was to strip down my touring bike of all its odds and ends, borrow light wheels and tyres from some of the boys and use it for the Gentlemen. A visit to my friend, M. Urago in Nice, however, spared me the bother. During a look around his busy factory with Shay Elliott (and others from the Simplex camp) we came across a pukkah racing job which was just my handwriting, and it was placed at my disposal.

"I rode the Gentlemen two years ago," said M. Dominique Urago. "The wind at Marseille is terrible!"

Ferri's machine

Next day, the Saturday, I went by bus into Nice from Monte Carlo, taking with me only the saddle from my own bike. While the position was being fixed we were joined by two young men in cycling garb. I knew the shorter of the two very well – he was Jean Dotto, ace climber of the Tour de France and record-holder of the Mont Agel hill-climb which was being held the following morning. I regretted not being able to see the "Agel" again, but I was held by my Marseille contract!

His companion was particularly interested in me and my borrowed bike for the very good reason that he had raced on it all last year.

"This is Ferri," said M. Urago. "On that bike last year he was third in Marseille–Nice." And the rider remarked that the bike had been raced so many times in Marseille that it would not need any steering. (Of the two, Ferri did much better in the Mont Agel, finishing fifth; Dotto retired.)

*   *   *

So off we went, then, to Marseille on the Paris-Rapide from Nice. *Dinner on the train.* An aperitif for monsieur? *Non!* And for wine? Why, Bordeaux red, of course. Cheese, Monsieur? *Oui,* some of that non-fermented stuff. Ice-cream, coffee, liqueurs? *Non, Non, Non!*

At the hotel. Monsieur Wadley? Yes, a room has been reserved for you by Monsieur Coupry. You are the first gentleman to arrive.

We are expecting M. Vietto and Marcel Bidot shortly.

In the street. I buy a copy of *Le Provençal*, the local paper, which has full details of the big race. "Many champion cyclists, headed by Louison Bobet, will be seen in action tomorrow on the Prado," say the headlines. There is quite a lot about Louison and a piece on Jean: "He will have the task of pacing an English journalist, Monsieur Wadley, of *Cycling*." Tut, tut, *tut*.* Forty entries. First pair off at 9.30 a.m. via the following route … This place Prado seems to figure largely on the course. What is it? I find a big map of the city at an Enquiry Post and sort it out. At least I try to sort it out, because this seems even more complicated than the evening section of the Mersey Road Club 24.

Back at the hotel. Breakfast for Monsieur at eight hours? But certainly. You are English and doubtless would like cornflakes, bacon, eggs and sausage, strong tea, bread and butter and marmalade. Monsieur would not. He would like at 8 a.m. (because he is due to start at 10.15) one omelette, a little bread and butter and jam and *café au lait*.

In the bedroom. Monsieur le coureur does an English crossword and glances at the horoscope of the local paper which says, "Health: do not overdo it." He sleeps on and off from 23.00 hours until 07.30 hours. Under his plus fours he puts on the racing shorts that Shay Elliott has lent him (they are the shorts that won the Tourmalet stage in the Route de France) but as yet has no racing jersey, so keeps on his pyjama top under his thick pullover. At 08.10 hours the breakfast arrives, as per order, with the addition of an enormous plate of ham. The *coureur* protests. The waiter says, "The manager does not think an Englishman would really refuse a plate of ham for breakfast." But evidently this manager has never met an English gentleman bike racer, and the ham is not touched.

Down the stairs. "Good morning, Mr. Wadley. I am one of your opponents. I am a journalist from Algiers. My name is Stampa. I am 48 years of age. Shall we ride to the *Départ* together? (M. Stampa doesn't really talk like that; I have merely quoted his answers to my questions.) M. Marcel Bidot is here, too, and says, "No, I am not riding; originally I should have been paced by Louison Bobet, but I have been ill recently and it is wiser not to risk it." A pity; it would have been a grand sight to see the double Tour de France cum World

---

*Monsieur Wadley was, of course, of *The Bicycle*.

Champion pacing the French team manager who was Champion of France nearly 30 years ago. "Marcel is still very good," Jean Bobet had told me in London.

In the street it is raining and M. Stampa and I get quite wet and shaken on the *pavé* on our friendly ride to the start.

*   *   *

Headquarters for the race were in a huge garage on the Prado, which is a fine, wide boulevard. The garage was completely clear of cars and I was able to amble round it at leisure on the bike and try out the gears, which were 46 x 50 x 15-17-18-19. Then I signed on, just like the real Tour men. I was given my number, nine, and four pins. Some of my opponents looked formidable – fitter than the professionals who were to pace them, in many cases! Not all were taking it seriously, though. One tall character in racing garb was running round in false beard and whiskers.

Though it was raining steadily, there was a big crowd outside in the Prado – a typical gathering of race-goers, with the kids pressing their noses against the big windows and some of them trying to sneak through the doorman's legs into the sacred presence of such stars as Francis Anastasi, Raoul Remy, Charles Coste, René Vietto and Apo Lazarides. But the man they were really looking for did not turn up until the first pair were making for the start-line: a scamper of feet and cries of "Bob-et, Bob-et" announced the arrival of the World Champion in his big maroon Pontiac.

He drew into the main part of the garage and four *gendarmes* immediately spread out across the entrance to keep the fans outside. But I, the racer, was permitted to go in and renew acquaintance with the Bobet family, who were accompanied by Raymond Le Bert, the famous trainer. Louison looked in great shape after his winter rest, all trace of the tiredness so noticeable at the Albert Hall having disappeared.

Jean handed me the family jersey which I was to wear and a pair of shorts which – with all due respect to Shay – were probably more famous than the ones I was already wearing. Why, they might even have been first to the top of l'Izoard in the Tour de France …

The contest was now in progress. The Jean Bobet method before a race is always to ride up the road briskly for a few kilometres to warm up. Today, in the rain, it was different. Together we rode steadily for a kilometre to inspect the nasty tram-lined patch of *pavé* at the first roundabout. "The road is very good and fast, on the whole," said Jean. "But it was not fast enough last year for my 'gentleman', who hardly knew how to ride a bike; I pushed him most of the way."

During our amble a couple of pairs went off, roaring down the road at thirties. I began to feel slightly ill.

At last it was time to start, pullovers off and handed to Mme. Jean. On the line. One minute to wait (early starters were off at one minute intervals, the later pairs at two minutes). Behind us was a motor-cycle with a painted board on the front – J. Bobet-J. B. Wadley. Fame at Forty. "*Dix seconds*," said the time-keeper. "*Cinq, quatre, trois, deux, un – partez!*"

We were off. I had started on the left of Jean, but he signalled me to move over to the right to get better protection. "*Allez Jeannot*," yelled the crowd. What the devil did they want Jeannot to "go" for? He was "allezing" fast enough already … That corner we had reconnoitred had been difficult at a slow pace, but now at 35 k.p.h. it was really nasty. We got round safely and tore along the Prado. The rest of it I don't really know much about. The map says we did a three-kilometre stretch along the shore, but I saw no sea!

There were a couple of turns, as at home, a lorry parked in the middle of the broad promenade marking the spot.

Coming back from the second turn Jean eased, calling, "We're doing fine; now get your second breath." Back along the Prado it was not so bad, but then the road began to rise and my speed began to fall and there I was re-thinking the thoughts of every British time-trialist that ever was: "Will that last turn ever come?"

The last 500 metres were a little steeper, but laughingly simple to my pace-maker, who dropped back and gave me a welcome push for a couple of hundred metres. Just as we made the last turn there was a swish and a whirl and we were caught by the local champions of this sort of thing – Mirando–Pedrali. Ambitious Jean was after them, but almost immediately one of the pair punctured. Down hill, a good road, feeling pretty good, top gear in ready for a grand-stand finish. But ouch! Suddenly the left calf seizes up with cramp and we finished at no more than evens.

On the last kilometre we met the last pair off – Louison Bobet– Lavergne. The two brothers cried out a greeting. A score of local cyclists seemed to be keeping up with the World Champion so easily that I got the wrong impression that we were beating them comfortably.

I did not know the result until a couple of hours later at the banquet given by the local cycling club "Pédale Joyeuse de Marseille", a really hilarious affair attended by all the riders and officials. Leading light of this club is Georges Coupry, a 17-stone giant who had been paced in the morning by little René Vietto.

"I rode at Herne Hill against Bill Bailey once," he remarked to me. I replied that I remembered it well – Good Friday, 1929, the meeting I watched as a 14-year-old from the top of a tree.

My neighbour at lunch was Raymond Le Bert who imparted much valuable training advice during the meal. "The basis of Louison Bobet's drink is rice," he said. "Boiled rice mixed with fruit juices and water, well sugared. In 1951 Louison and Pierre Barbotin finished first and second in Milan–San Remo with two bidons of that and nothing else to eat or drink."

The banquet, as I have said, was one of the biggest I have met. All kinds of wine and succulent dishes. Along the table Louison Bobet was not taking everything that came his way, but strictly following the regime. So was Jean. But not J.B.W. and that was why Jean came and said, "I am disgusted with you …"

After the meal the prizes were presented. I won the journalist's cup – a tremendous performance considering that M. Stampa was my only competitor and his pacemaker, Borlinelli, had punctured, leaving him to ride five kilometres on his own! But my 34 mins. 45.6 secs. was the twelfth fastest of 31 finishers, and we had been beaten by Louison Bobet–Lavergne by 6.6 seconds.

My time works out at 1-9-30 for a 25. I was paced – perhaps a little too fast at the start – and I reckon on the morning I could have done a 1-11-30 on my own. I am pretty sure that in my old haphazard way of training, riding big mileages at week-ends when not really ready for them, and bashing away aimlessly during the week and not watching my diet, I would have had a job to beat "evens". I hope my experience will have been of some help to others who are now preparing for the coming season.

Breton pipers

I had the honour of being driven back from Marseille by Louison Bobet, but first we paid a visit to a local celebration by the "Bretons de Marseille" – an organisation similar to Welsh, Scottish and Irish gatherings in London – to which the Bobet family had been invited to look in. Over the entrance to the hall there was a big banner – "Welcome to our World Champion" – and Louison, Jean and their wives were played in by kilted pipers to the Brittany anthem, "Bimou", which is the same tune as the Welsh national anthem, "Land of My Fathers".

There were presentations to the guests of honour, short speeches, dances by men and women in the picturesque costumes of Brittany, the girls' lace head-dresses being exquisitely beautiful. After Louison and Mme had joined these kindly costumed folk in a waltz, it was time to go.

Out on the open road at 5 p.m., heading for Toulon, the World Champion was soon recognised by car and bus passengers. But we agreed that he had partly been spotted at the outset by my bike on the top. I was therefore called *Le champion*.

The Bicycle, 16 February 1955

RECORD-BREAKING

J. B. Wadley's undisguised affection for the place-to-place or out-and-back record attempt stemmed from his early days on *The Bicycle*, and in particular from 1939, the year in which the Hercules Cycle Company assembled a team of professional riders to attack just about every record in the book. The group included Marguerite Wilson and the Belgian Richard Kemps, and was managed by Frank Southall, of whom the young Wadley already had strong memories: as a schoolboy he had watched the track battles between Southall and his rival (and JBW's own hero) F. J. Wyld, from his perch on the branch of a tree at Herne Hill.

Wadley followed and reported most of those record-breaking rides, and the experience left its mark. It was Kemps, he said, who really taught him how to ride: 'I never knew what trying was until I watched him beat Hubert Opperman's London to Bath and back record.' A few weeks after that close-up observation of sustained effort, JBW bettered his own 100-mile time by almost half an hour in what he came to regard as the best ride of his racing life.

More than personal tuition, though, this intimate association with Southall's stable, breaking record after record through the summer of 1939, left him with the highest regard for those who set out on those long solitary journeys. Most abiding was the memory of Marguerite Wilson's End-to-End and 1,000 miles which, after three days, finished in the black-out at Wick, quite literally, in the dying hours of peace time.

In the early 1950s Wadley travelled over those same roads in similar circumstances, first following George Laws' successful London–Bath ride, which prompted the affectionate 'Open Letter to Richard Kemps' which is reprinted here. Then came that memorable long weekend which saw Eileen Sheridan and the Albert Crimes/ John Arnold tricycle duo break their respective End-to-End records. JBW reported them for *The Bicycle*, and later wrote:

> I have seen nearly all the Continental classics, followed the Tour de France from start to finish, almost set up camp at the major six-day races, yet I think Crimes and Arnold gave me just as big a thrill on those lonely epics as some of the highly paid stars of peloton and path.

It was precisely the epic quality of such rides, their hour-after-hour heroic narrative, that would have appealed to J. B. Wadley. Years later he spent a day with Eugène Christophe – no stranger to epics, himself – during the course of which he told the French *coureur* about record-breaking in Britain. It is not difficult to imagine JBW being silently pleased to hear Christophe replying that the End-to-End 'sounded just up his street', and he would have loved to have had a crack at it.

The final article in this section, originally published during the last week of the war, is an account of JBW's own liberation, of getting back on to a light-weight bicycle for practically the first time in five years. His route took him away from the barracks in Exeter to the hotel that had been used by the Hercules team in 1939, and back along the route that Marguerite Wilson had followed during her record-breaking rides that had begun at Land's End, just before the outbreak of war. He might almost have prefaced it with the phrase famously used by the *Daily Mirror* columnist, Bill Connor: 'As I was saying before I was so rudely interrupted.' It was a piece which celebrated not just record-breakers, but his love of the bicycle, and of the particular perspective on life that is acquired from the saddle of a bicycle – themes that were to characterise much of his later work.

Kemps Breaks Bath and Back Record – in last 11 miles

Hercules Rider Takes 7 Minutes Off "Oppy's" Time

Richard Kemps, the Belgian member of the Hercules team, broke the coveted London–Bath-and-Back record on Sunday by 7 mins. 6 secs. The previous record was put up in 1935 by Hubert Opperman, and has withstood many attacks by first-class riders.

Kemps began fast and gained on schedule, but a puncture at about 60 miles started a loss on schedule which gradually accumulated to ten minutes by the time he turned at the Bath G.P.O. It seemed at this stage that a beating of the record, however slight, was impossible.

The tough-as-nails Belgian, however, had other ideas on the matter and "trying" as if his life depended on each thrust of the pedal, he fought back to such effect that he had got back level with record at Reading, eleven miles from the finish.

From that point onwards he simply sprinted to the finish, gaining no fewer than seven minutes on the record in the process.

The start

Kemps was despatched at 1 a.m. from the twenty-eighth milestone, a mile of so west of Maidenhead, by timekeeper Mr. B. W. Best. Conditions seemed ideal, the air being practically calm.

Pedalling rapidly along the well-lit Great West Road, Kemps reeled off twenty-three and a half miles in the first hour, and after a clear ride through the London streets he turned at Hyde Park Corner (28 miles) in 1 hr. 12 mins., or four minutes better than schedule.

Kemps had started very fast, and although he did not move quite so smoothly on the first few miles of the return journey, he was maintaining his lead over the schedule and the 40 miles went by in 1 hr. 46 mins., and forty-six and a half miles in the first two hours.

Reading (66 miles) was reached in 3 hrs. 58 mins., or six minutes better than schedule, but seventeen miles further on his helpers were surprised when he arrived a minute behind his time. A puncture at Woolhampton accounted for most of this surprising loss, but at the same time Kemps was not moving quite so well as earlier on. Eight miles further down the road to Bath, at Hungerford, he had dropped back again with 4 hrs. 17 mins. against the required 4 hrs. 14 mins.

First hundred

Over the next ten hilly miles to Marlborough, Kemps worked very hard indeed to catch up again, and the first hundred went by in 4 hrs. 45 mins., but he was still fighting a losing game with his time-table. However, at Calne (114 miles), he had got back a minute of it with 5 hrs. 26 mins., only to lose it again at Chippenham, where he was clocking 5 hrs. 45 mins. for the 120 miles, whereas the tell-tale "white paper" wanted him there five minutes beforehand.

According to schedule, Kemps should have got to the Bath G.P.O. (133 miles) at 7.17 a.m., but it was 7.25 before he got there, and another two minutes had slipped by before he started the homeward trek, because he took on supplies of food and drink. He thus started from Bath with a ten minute deficit on schedule, and 5 mins 18 secs.

outside Opperman's record time.

Conditions so far for the homeward trip were exactly the same as for the outward – a complete calm, and any improvement that the rider made was the result of his own effort entirely, for there was no wind to give any help at all.

At 50 miles to go, Kemps still had 2 hrs. 24 mins. in which to equal the record. Another half-minute gain was Kemps' effort over the next 13 miles to Marlborough, and at the top of the notorious hill outside the town he took a couple of feeding-bottles, a packet of sandwiches, and, with the hilliest part of the ride over, he prepared for the final stages. At Hungerford (175 miles) he was back to seven minutes outside, with 8 hrs. 30 mins. and at Newbury he was still in the same position in 8 hrs. 53 mins.

Kemps then passed through Theale, where a crowd of club folk – the remnants of the Bath Road 50 – was gathered to see the rider pass through. Their cheers seemed to act as a tonic to "Le Belge", so accustomed to racing to the plaudits of the public, that he put in probably the most magnificent effort of his ride to reach Reading (200 miles) in 9 hrs. 41 mins. Now only four minutes outside his schedule and at last inside record!

The last miles were a revelation of the finishing powers of a really great rider, for with powerful lunges on his 86 gear, he gained handfuls of seconds as each of the final eleven miles went by.

Just a slight breeze had sprung up by this time, and the last eleven miles were rattled off in 26 mins., Kemps eventually passing Mr. Best at 11 hrs. 7 mins. 36 secs., having beaten Opperman's record by 7 mins. 6 secs.

The Bicycle, 27 May, 1939

J. B. Wadley Follows George Laws on "Bath-and-Back" Record, and Writes an Open Letter to Richard Kemps

Dear Richard,

I am writing with news which you have probably been expecting for some time. One of your two R.R.A. records was broken this afternoon – the Bath and Back. But don't you worry, *mon vieux*, it was beaten by a very great English rider named George Laws, and you can feel proud that though Richard Kemps no longer holds one of the toughest records on the R.R.A. books, his name will long be remembered in our cycling world. In some ways I feel that "my" Bath and Back record has been broken, too, because you will remember that you used my handlebars on your ride!

George's actual time was 9 hrs. 50 mins. 7 secs. for the 210 miles. That is over 17 minutes better than your ride in 1939, but that is nothing to be ashamed of. The standard of our riding here has increased enormously – why, even our modern girl champion, Eileen Sheridan, is not only beating Marguerite's* records by hours, but last week was faster than your old friend, Frank Southall, over the Liverpool–Edinburgh trip!

Laws is a fine, big lad, who will be 30 next month; he weighs around about 80 kilos and is 1metre 85 tall. A *coureur complet* you would call him, because less than three weeks after breaking the "out and home" 24-hour record with 741 kms., he rode a one-hour unpaced on the track, covering 41.9 kms.

It was on the night of that track ride that George told me he was going for your London–Bath–London record in another three weeks' time, on a Sunday. (He is an amateur, and can only race at weekends.) Judging from my experience of records, it seemed impossible that he could pick a good day so far ahead, whereas full-time professionals often have to wait months for the right conditions.

On the Saturday the wind was blowing quite strongly from the north and the position looked hopeless, but Sunday dawned still

---

*On the weekend when Kemps broke the Bath-and-Back record, Marguerite Wilson reduced the W.R.R.A. London–Portsmouth–London record by a huge margin. It was her sixth record since turning professional, and the twelfth Hercules record-breaking success in a period of seven weeks.

and calm, and when I picked George up at Hyde Park Corner he was already four minutes inside schedule.

I cannot compare your own times with George's, because whereas you started at Maidenhead, and then rode 28 miles to London, he preferred starting only 15 miles from London.

When he had turned at Hyde Park Corner and began the long trek to Bath, we noticed that the wind was beginning to have a north-easterly drift in it, and was, therefore, at times, slightly behind. Consequently he was up on his schedule all the way down, this schedule, by the way, being made for a 10-hour ride. Looking back on my notes I found you had taken 4 hrs. 45 mins. for the first 100; but Laws was 18 minutes faster.

Watching the rider in his shorts and racing vest, I remembered those terrible old tights and alpaca of yours. I remembered, too, the desperate way you used to fling your bike from side to side as you climbed the hills. George climbed the English way, the bike upright and his body swaying.

The funny thing about this ride was the fact that Laws knew the first half of the course like the back of his hand, but had never been beyond Savernake! All those long, tough climbs beyond Marlborough were new to him, all the tricky descents into the towns through which he had to pick his way by watching the A4 signs. We gave him a drink near Box, where he was nearly 10 minutes up on schedule, and then waited for him to come back. But he was a long time coming, and was only five minutes up when we spotted him in the distance, tackling the difficult climb on his 76. We learned later that he had got hopelessly lost in Bath, and had to ask lots of people the way to the Post Office! Pity you weren't there – you could have shown him. You can guess that during this time he felt like retiring.

When he did get going again the wind was troublesome, at times right in his face, but he held on to his lead, and once the hills were over, drew still further ahead of your record, which was now well and truly lost. A puncture with about 50 miles to go cost him a minute or two changing bikes, and then back to the first when the tyre was changed.

You will, of course, be interested to know what gears he rode. He used a *double-plateau* (we call it a "double-clanger") giving him 76, 79, 81, 84, 86, 90, but the ones he used most were 76, 81 and the 84. I think you used 76, 81 and 86.

George doesn't worry about food (except tea, which makes him sick), and ate sandwiches, plums, oranges and rice pudding. He drank fruit drinks, was envious afterwards when I told him you had had a pint of beer handed up to you, but agrees with you that probably the best drink of all is cold water.

Well, Richard, *mon vieux*, I told you at the start of this letter not to worry. Hubert Opperman, I am sure, did not worry when you beat his record by 7 mins. 6 secs. in 1939; he accepted the inevitability of progress, and was content to know that Richard Kemps, of Belgium, was a worthy successor. Now you can take it from me that you have been followed by a man of whom, had you seen him in action on Sunday, you would immediately have said: "*Voilà un as.*" Yes, George is an ace, all right. You must come over and meet him some day.

Yours, very sincerely,
Jock Wadley

The Bicycle, 20 August, 1952

A Cornish Comeback

Today I report with pleasure that I am once again really riding a bicycle; riding, that is, in the more complete sense, because since being called up in 1940 there has usually been some opportunity to cycle in a basic kind of way. You may recall how last year when I had an urge to ride a "50", speedy bars and shoes were rushed down to the South Coast in readiness. D-Day stopped any ambitions.

Early this year – nine months behind schedule – my bicycle gradually became transformed to match my renewed enthusiasm. In February the Maes bars at last were fitted; March brought forth the toe-clips; and under April showers the gear grew four inches in no time. Each of the ultimate benefits first produced alarming pains – chiefly the 'bars. I thought I never could stoop so low again after three "flat" years. Victory came one night when I made myself ride 32 awful miles from Taunton to Exeter without sitting up once. After that it was easy; I even wished the frame half an inch smaller so that the 'bars would be that much lower.

The machine got changed; the machine got lighter. And although I got lighter as well, I didn't dare change out of khaki on the grounds that if the difference between Army clothes and civvies was so great at that time of the year, then battle-dress to shorts direct would be a short cut to the M. I. Room. Not until mid-May, then, did I emerge nervously from my second home at Exeter clad in the battle-dress of 1939 – ankle socks, shorts, pullover – and rode to Barnstaple 40 minutes faster than my previous best in khaki. Tea, then to Bideford, Torrington and back for supper in Exeter at 10 p.m. Ninety-two miles in eight. A satisfactory un-dress rehearsal.

A week later I was due for a short pass, starting on the Sunday about 10 a.m. until 23.59 Monday. I wanted to cycle somewhere special, but was still uncertain whether I was ready to tackle such a trip. On the Saturday night I telephoned the friends I wanted to see, chatting only about this and that almost until the second set of pips; then came the leading question: when was I going down to see them? I said, wildly, "to-morrow", and there was no getting out of it after that.

"Mad," said Mrs Bartlett at Exeter when I left her house next morning at 11 o'clock to ride to Penzance. "My, what a long way," said the lady at Launceston, 41 miles further on, where I stopped for a meal. "Bravo," said Betty and her mother when I got to Penzance at 7.30 p.m. after 110 miles into the wind on a 70-fixed over one of the toughest main roads in the whole country. You see, they thought me neither crazy nor having come "a long way" because before the war the Hercules team used to stay at their hotel, and one day at 10.30 a.m. Marguerite waved to them as she rode by (she having started from Land's End) and was nearly in Norwich 24 hours later. A month passed: she waved again, this time off to John o' Groats and 1,000 miles in less than three days. In the circumstances their "Bravo" comment was very condescending for a mere bagatelle like 110 miles…

This was indeed a flying visit; a very big supper and a chat over old times, then to bed, highly pleased with the progress of the job that was now half-done. Would I take an awful bundle on the way back next day? From my window I looked out on to Mount's Bay, a story-book glimpse of the harbour, the mount and the moon, by whose light I saw something more comforting still – a Victory flag blowing perkily towards Redruth. There would be fair sailing on the way back home.

Flags that have become soaked by rain during the night are not blown out full stretch next morning by anything but a strong wind. This one was, but it had about-turned! My dramatic pen sees in this incident the chance to introduce a stormy scene with stamped feet, frayed tempers and despair. As a reporter, I am bound to say I took it in the same way as most people do when their leave gets cancelled at the last minute. There was nothing much I could do about it. I sought sympathy at breakfast when someone said it had started raining again. "And the wind will be against me too," I ventured. Nothing doing. Marguerite had started from Land's End with the wind against her and had beaten two records. That girl – she takes the very sympathy out of people's mouths.

And so I started off inside a cape, and banged away to Hayle, over Connor Downs into Camborne and on and on, taking peak punishment over Bodmin Moor. And yet … hard as it was, I was the Boss at last! For more than four years hills had frightened me, for I knew only too well that they had defence and to spare against my weakened attack. Sometimes they would lead me up the garden – let me, for instance, plod to the top of Long Ash Lane on the Dorchester–Yeovil road and think myself a rare fellow, only to be brought sadly back to earth with a forced march up the normally easier Evershot climb a little further on. Yet here I was beating Bodmin Moor on points and coming out of it ready to knock the stuffing out of Launceston–Exeter as well. A grand and glorious feeling.

I stopped again at Launceston; the meal on the outward journey and the one I got this time and many since have made it in my eyes the Girtford of the West, although I have never seen any other cyclists there. Three Yankee transport drivers were hard at work with their forks when I arrived; they wanted to know what kind of time we "bike-riders" could make over a stretch. The answer (my own current performance) shook them, but they believed it because they had roared past over the Moor. I should have left it at that instead of starting to tell them about Marguerite. "What … a dame ride a bike all dem moiles to London!" They had no use for fantasy and went on to discuss the price of gasoline. That girl – she makes people call me a liar.

Through Lifton, a little way after Launceston, another storm broke, necessitating the unravelling of the cape for the umpteenth time. I was joined under the shelter of a high hedge by a local. Ha, here was Credence; unsolicited Credence! He told me that many times while working on fields adjacent to the main road he had seen the stars go by – Rossiter, Opperman, Innes-Thompson, Southall, Kemps, Ferris, Heppleston, Wilson, and "the girl was the fastest of them all". Ah, that would be that 90 top.

Balanced up, this chat cost a good half-hour, saved a Dartmoor saturation, and, as a compromise, gave an uncomfortable cold shower from the laden roads as I swished the last 15 miles from Whiddon Down to Exeter. Two hours down on the outward journey. "Mad," said Mrs B., and fed the maniac. I rode back to barracks in khaki, well aware that I possessed a pair of legs, planning my riding for the following week: rest until Saturday, then 40 or 50 easy miles and another rest from cycling for a few days. An attempted comeback after so long an absence from strenuous riding needs careful handling.

Cycling, 1st August, 1945

Less than 50 miles to go. After the eight-mile drag out of Helmsdale, a quick freshener for David Duffield on his 1960 Land's End–John O'Groats record.

Sporting Cyclist, February 1961

THE CLASSICS

At one time or another J. B. Wadley was present at all the major classic road-races (although he rarely attended World Championships). When it came to reporting them, however, it is clear that he had his favourites: the second issue of *Coureur* was devoted largely to just two races – Paris–Roubaix and Bordeaux–Paris – and this was a bias that would be repeated over the years. Perhaps this should come as no surprise, since these were the one-day classics which, in their quite different ways, displayed most vividly the old-time epic qualities that were dear to his heart. The 'Hell of the North' had the worst cobbles and usually foul weather; the 'Derby of the Road' had its mammoth distance and – another echo of the past – its pacing Dernys.

For the most part, JBW's focus on road-racing was confined to France (especially the area of northern France that he knew best) and Belgium. His visits to Italy were comparatively rare and, despite his unbounded admiration for the great Spanish climbers of his day, Bahamontes and Jiménez, Spain was entirely off his route. No doubt one practical reason for this was proximity – his travels abroad to take in the races that he would later write about were frequently undertaken by bicycle. The result was that he often found himself writing about routes that he had, himself, ridden, which must have given him some insight into what the riders were experiencing. He knew those roads, and he knew them as a cyclist.

In each of the three reports of Continental Classics reprinted here we see the characteristic Wadley style: the story is told through his own moment-by-moment responses as he followed the race – what he was thinking and feeling as the action unfolded. It was a particularly vivid kind of eye-witness account which, as Roy Green remarked, 'put you in among the peloton'. It was also a style which naturally highlighted the fate of the British (and Irish) cyclists who were then beginning to venture to the Continent, and in whom he took so keen an interest.

Shay was King of the
Flemish "Mountains"

It is Gand to the French, Ghent to the British and Gent to the Belgians themselves. It is the capital of Flanders, and one of the unofficial capitals of the cycle-racing world. Every day of the year there is something going on of interest to the enthusiast: in the winter you will find the *pistards* racing or training on the saucy little 150-metre wooden track; then, as spring approaches, there is a steady exodus of the city's roadmen towards the windswept country roads. In spring, road-racing begins and quickly builds up to an intensity unknown anywhere else in the world.

Already at Easter this year the season was well under way. The previous week-end Germain Derijk had won a memorable Tour of Flanders, with action from the dropping of the starter's flag in Ghent to the finishing-line at Wetteren, a few kilometres out of the city itself. And on Easter Sunday morning the big square facing St. Pieter's station was again alive with the activity such as only a road-race can produce.

There were rucksack-laden roadmen riding their own bikes towards the start; roadmen sitting in cars with their bikes on top; roadmen lounging in cafés and hotels; pillion-riding roadmen shouldering their machines. Roadmen everywhere, all of them bound via various routes for Wevelgem.

Ghent–Wevelgem was, for many years, a privately promoted early season road-race. So was the "Het Volk", organised by the flourishing local newspaper of that name. With an ever-increasing number of events to crowd into the opening weeks of the season, the publicity department of *Het Volk* ("The People") took a leaf from the book of *Les Sports* who had taken two old-established events (Flèche Wallonne and Liège–Bastogne–Liège) and lumped them together under the title of the Weekend Ardennais. *Het Volk* were running the 224-km. Ghent–Wevelgem on Easter Sunday, and Wevelgem–Ghent (204 kms.) on the Monday, each being a separate race, but with points awarded as well as prizes. Best points scorer for the two races would earn another good prize and the *Trofee van Vlaanderen* – the Flemish Trophy.

And now, just to confuse you a little more, I have to explain that in addition to this arrangement confined to professional riders, *Het*

Volk were also putting on a Ghent–Wevelgem for debutants (94 kms.), a Ghent–Wevelgem for amateurs (155 kms.) and a Ghent–Wevelgem for Independents (169 kms.) You will see from the map that the direct route from Ghent to Wevelgem is only just over 30 miles, and the routes of the different races wound their various ways over the plains of Flanders. (On Monday there would be four separate races back to Ghent.)

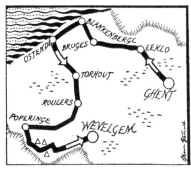

Ghent-Wevelgem (224 kms.)

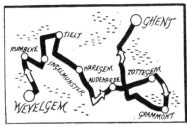

The "Het Volk" (204 kms.)

When the journalist is equipped with a helicopter he might be able to cover all four races in one hop. As it was, I had to be content to follow the professional event in a car kindly provided by the organisers of the race. Mr. Jerome Stevens, the man behind it all, was not surprised to see me there: "You have come to see Robinson and Elliott achieve another exploit?" he said.

All Flanders remembers the riding of Brian and Shay in the 1957 Het Volk. The two of them were involved in a two-up break which failed near the finish, though not before they had collected a haul of town and hill primes that came to something like £150 apiece and a washing machine to divide between them! Their earnings amounted to something more: they earned the respect of the cycling-mad Flemish public, who had no quarrel with the newspapers which this year put them in the short list of visiting riders most likely to trouble the Belgian stars, De Bruyne, Van Looy, Derijk, Foré and Vlaeyen.

I knew, however, that so far as Brian was concerned, he was un-likely to be prominent. The Yorkshireman was still in his "easy" period of riding himself in ready for mid-season fitness. On the other hand, Elliott could hardly be said to be having an easy time. By nature he is a puncher and seems incapable of sticking in a bunch shadow-pedalling when there's the chance of starting a fight or joining in someone else's. His aggressive riding had brought him into the prize list or the headlines in every one of his 1958 races. By the look of his rosy cheeks at the start of this Ghent–Wevelgem, the boy was still full of fight.

"Well, Shay," I greeted him, "are you going to have a go today?"

"I hope so," was the reply, "but with a field of 200 riders a lot depends on how you get away. Can you spare that newspaper?"

The Dubliner did not want the newspaper to study the list of starters, of whom he knew the danger-men well enough; nor to check the itinerary which was roughly the same as last year; nor the location of the principle hills and primes of the day. Elliott has a reputation not only for being a *puncheur*, but a *penseur*, a man who always lines up in a race with a pretty good idea of what lies in front. Shay wanted the 24-page *Het Volk* newspaper to stuff under one of his three jerseys as additional protection against the bitter cold.

At midday the 205 riders to sign the control sheet lined up for the start, their front wheels pointing northwards to the coast, with the prospect of a troublesome wind on their right shoulders all the way.

Although racing commands the roads of Belgium, the race organisation does not take complete control of the situation as in France, where the race director of a classic and his assistants control not only the riders, but the caravan of team and Press cars. In Belgium the motor-cycle police are in charge, and in those opening miles of Ghent–Wevelgem they kept the cars in one long line on the right of the road. With more than five hours racing ahead, the Pressmen could not complain, but it was hard on the team-cars forced to the back of the queue, as was quickly proved when a punctured rider had to wait much too long for his manager to appear with the new wheel.

As the road changed direction we could see, far in the distance, the giant field already split into three *bordures* staggered across the road in skilful shelter against the wind. Nevertheless, our speedometer showed a steady 40 k.p.h., and that despite long stretches of *pavé*. Still further ahead of the leading *bordure* we could faintly discern further small groups of riders. We learned from the motor-cycle black-board man (who chalks up details of what is going on) that a break was developing at the front of the field – and among the characters involved was No. 92, Seamus Elliott of Ireland.

Noting my impatience to get up to the scene of the battle, my driver said: "Don't worry. We'll get ahead at Bruges." And so we did, for after passing through the jam-packed centre of the historic jewel of Flanders, the field took to the dirt cycle-path, leaving the cobbled road free for us to speed ahead. The battle was now really on; as anticipated, Brian Robinson was sitting comfortably in the second of the three main groups – three long lines of riders wheel-to-wheel. And, again, as anticipated, there at the front of the front group of 23 riders was Elliott, his most noticeable companion being friend Géminiani.

In view of later developments of the race, it would be confusing to list the other members of the Shay–Gem group. It would be more helpful to the understanding of the situation to say that it did not include top favourites like De Bruyne, van Looy and Germain Derijk, whose team-mates were working hard at the front of the chasing groups to get them up to the break-aways.

To appreciate that it was not only a serious break, but an intelligently planned one, can be seen from a glance at the map. Once Blankenberghe had been reached, there would be a back-wind flyer all along the coast to Ostende, with the moral advantage clearly in favour of the first group. Even with the wind still on their sides, they were doing steady 26s – whether wheel to wheel on the paths, or staggered out in a *bordure* on the new cement road.

Then came Blankenberge, the turn due south-west, and a sixteen-mile sprint to Ostend along the dune-flanked road. With the 52 x 14s constantly in action and relays short and sharp, the score of scorchers were often doing 35 m.p.h. with the average for the stretch just over 30s. At Ostend, where the main group was two and a quarter minutes back, a small bunch led by Brankart, Schroeders and Adriaenssens had, nevertheless, kept within a minute of the Elliott group.

With a side-wind again, and on to bad roads with constant switches on and off cycle-paths, the rhythm of the leaders was broken, and at Turnhout they were caught by the strongest of the various chasing groups. On the face of it, it seemed that Shay & Co. had been hard at work at 27 m.p.h. for three hours, and all for nothing. In actual fact, their efforts had knocked out at least half the starters, who were grouped together at the back without any further ambition for the day. There would not now be long to wait for the vital attack of the day.

As so often the case, the feeding town was the key to the situation. A Géminiani–van Est inspired group of 20 made a vain dash to get first to the *musette*-men at Roeselale. The exit from the town was a fantastic sight as a long line of *coureurs* switched on to the narrow down-hill cycle-path, many of them riding hands-off and stuffing food and *bidons* into their pockets.

Suddenly, the familiar form of Jan Zaggers spurted his way to the front, snaffled a 500-franc (£3.10s) prime put up by a café owner, continued his effort to grab another 300 francs from a similar source, and taking with him six others in the process. One of those others was Elliott, whose powerful relays were largely responsible for getting the little bunch farther and farther away from the main group. Shay is no stylist, but how effectively those cranks go round under the impulse of those powerful thighs and supplementary beats of those solid shoulders.

For an hour or more the Dubliner was to give me one of the greatest treats of my race-following career as he and his five companions punched away over the worsening roads twisting and turning through hedge-less fields, dotted with pyramids of drying flax or heaps of farm-yard dung. Fields that in Autumn would be red with poppies, for we were now passing through such tragic villages as Passchendaele and Zonnebeke and were on the road to Ypres.

And after Ypres it was Poperinge, and at Poperinge it was Zaggers to the fore again to take the 1,000-franc prime. Shay knew the Belgian was only a danger as a prime-chaser, but took no chances and was quickly on his wheel. We eased to take a rough time-check, and sped back to give him the news: "A minute and a half up," we yelled.

"How far to go?" Shay called back.

"Fifty-seven kilometres. The first hill is ten kilometres ahead."

And looking up we could see the long range of wold-like hills which barely top 500 feet, yet loom up from the Plain of Flanders in a brave attempt to justify their title as the "Flemish Alps".

The Elliott group quickly came to the first of the tests, the one-and-a-half kilometres of the Mont Noir, with 1,000 francs to the winner and five points for the overall climbing prize for the two days. Elliott won it so handsomely that he could easily have sneaked away to a considerable lead, but the boy was not born yesterday. The help of the other five was needed to get him safely to the foot of the next hill – the Kemmelberg, twice as hard, twice as many points, and four times as many francs.

Kemmel is a real snorter, a freak road whose only workaday function is to take any necessary traffic to the observatory at the top, yet a boon to road-race organisers. It has hairpins like an Alpine pass, an average gradient of about 1 in 8, paved with unpleasant cobbles most of the way and flattening out on to a short plateau of sand and gravel.

Elliott first again.

His dropped companions regrouped on the descent, working desperately to keep ahead of a small group they could see chasing as the road doubled back towards Messines, and the last hill of the day. The news came up that the chasers included Van Looy, his great rival De Bruyne and Raymond Impanis; the situation was serious, for a time-check showed them to be only a minute behind, with the main group just over another minute further back.

What I dared to hope was that Elliott was still strong enough not only to win the Messines prime, but to get away on his own to keep clear of the chasers all the way to Wevelgem. But although he was still strong, one man was stronger. He was Noel Foré, and Foré flung himself into a powerful sprint on the modest hill. First Mertens lost contact, then Schroeders, Schepens and, finally, Elliott. The Flemish boy fairly flew on the following flat and, wildly applauded by the crowds, rode to a well-earned victory.

Caught by the van Looy–Impanis–De Bruyne group of ten, Elliott and Co. kept their company until the finishing sprint on the cold and windy Wevelgem air-field, where van Looy won from De Bruyne, with Elliott seventh.

Shay was well pleased with his day's work, as indeed he had every reason to be. With 19 points he was easily the best climber of the day. Would he add to his achievements next day and so succeed Brian Robinson as King of the Flemish Mountains?

Although by no means as animated a race as Ghent–Wevelgem, the return trip on Monday was still an interesting one, on which it would be easy to write another detailed report. But boiled down, it amounted to this: a few hundred yards after the start, the giant field were already strung out on the cycle-paths to escape the cobbles. Within five kilometres a group of seven were away, building up a lead which was soon three minutes. Just as the Elliott group had shared yesterday's hill primes, so today the new assault party of Adriaenssens, van Aerde, Demunster, Vandenbrekel, Planckaert, Everaert and Pascal were to do the same.

Shay was imprisoned in the *peloton*. He had tried to get with the break, but his legs were not yet ready for so rapid an effort. Moreover, van Looy, Foré and Co., recognising him as a possible two-day winner, allowed him no rope at all.

My anxiety for his 19–0 lead lessened on learning that only three hills were to count for the overall climber's prize. This meant that to beat his 19 points total, one man would have to win all three primes.

Adriaenssens took the first at Edalaere from van Aerde, and it was with a double interest that we sped on to the village of Grammont, doubled round a maze of side-streets, and roared to the top of a long, difficult, cobbled hill of about 1-in-7 gradient. But this wasn't the race hill! It wasn't hard enough. We parked the car and dashed along a rough, cobbled path no more than six feet wide to the top of the most notorious of all the Belgian hills, the Wall of Grammont. Length – half a mile; average gradient – 1-in-7, steepest 1-in-4; surface – rough cobbles; effect on a rider – so violent that even World Champion Rik van Steenbergen has had to get off and push his bike during a Tour of Flanders.

Together with the excited crowd, I peered down into the darkness of the tree-lined lower slopes for signs of the leaders. And there they were – and a black and white Carpano man in front with a clear lead! Too bad for you, Shay, if that's Adriaenssens – there's 10 points for this one, and that'll bring your lead down to 19–15.

But wait – it's not Adriaenssens. It's Planckaert – and he's welcome to that £70 for being first to the top of the Grammont, because he has saved the day for our lucky Irishman who now cannot be beaten in the two-day classification.

Not until five minutes later did the *peloton* top the Grammont, led by Meuleman, Elliott, De Bruyne, van Looy and Derijk. Sixty kilometres to go.

Planckaert's feat on the Grammont was a clear indication that he was the strongest of the leaders. After van Aerde collected the last of the hill primes at Varent – a miniature Alpine cobbled pass – Planckaert was clearly in command of the situation. And with the *peloton* now getting level in spite of the efforts of Planckaert's team-mates to hold it back, it was necessary to make a bold bid for victory.

The Belgian timed his effort beautifully when, only six kilometres from the finish, he left his two remaining companions, van Aerde and Demunster, to stamp on for a great solo ride to Ghent, finishing 55 seconds ahead of one huge bunch (all his erstwhile break-mates had been absorbed). Needless to say, Rik van Looy won the sprint and, with the best points total, took the two-day Flemish Trophy.

Brian Robinson finished quite cheerfully in the bunch, placed equal 12th with Elliott. Later that night Elliott drove his Peugeot back to France quite content with his two-day effort which earned him at least £150 clear – and still more respect from the Continental world of wheels.

Sporting Cyclist, June 1958

Incomparable "Derby"

Three days before the Epsom Derby – won by a French horse – Jacques Anquetil won the biggest gamble a cyclist has ever risked by taking the Derby of the Road, the 350 miles from Bordeaux to Paris. He set himself a sensational handicap, for whereas his opponents trained in the traditional manner behind Derny machines and slept and slept and slept, Anquetil's preparation was the Critérium du Dauphiné Libéré.

This eight-day race through the French Alps is always a tough one, and this time Anquetil was given a very hard fight by his great rival Raymond Poulidor. Yet Jacques not only beat Raymond in the time-trial on the penultimate day, but had previously twice outsprinted him for first place at the end of hard, cold, wet stages through the mountains where Poulidor often managed to get away on his own.

Anquetil was a certain winner of the Dauphiné on the Friday night, but there was the formality of riding the last 142-miles stage from Romans to Avignon on Saturday. Last days of stage-races are often promenades. On this occasion the Ford team made sure the pace was lively; their leader, Anquetil, had a plane to catch. All the same Jacques did have time, during the stage, to ride alongside the winner of last year's Bordeaux–Paris for a chat. Was he asking for a few tips? If so, I hope he didn't get them, because Nedelec is a team-mate of Tom Simpson!

At five o'clock the stage and the race was over. Twenty minutes later, all formalities – bouquets, interviews, laps of honour, etc. – were finished and Jacques was in the bath of his hotel. A quick meal took 20 minutes or so, and well before six o'clock with Géminiani driving, he, soigneur Vergani and mechanic Debruyckere were in a Ford Taunus car speeding towards Nîmes airfield with an escort of police car and motor-bikes. The 38 miles in 35 minutes.

Within 20 minutes of arrival the party were taking off in a chartered Mystère 20 Business-Jet plane on their 250-mile flight to Bordeaux where they touched down at 7.45 p.m.

This, then, was the astonishing preparation that Jacques Anquetil made for Bordeaux–Paris, the test that has frightened off so many champions, the "race that kills".

Nine out of ten experts questioned believed that the adventure would end in disaster. "You can't improvise Bordeaux–Paris," said Bernard Gauthier, who won it four times, and so did Louison Bobet, once a winner, once a runner-up. And what must dear old Francis Pélissier – the Wizard of Bordeaux–Paris – have thought up there in his castle in the sky, for on earth he shared this view? In 1953 Pélissier sacked Ferdi Kübler for insisting on riding a Critérium two days before Bordeaux–Paris.

Kübler won that Bordeaux–Paris "just to show him", and it was probably just to show everybody else that Anquetil won as well.

Some observers fear that Anquetil has killed the legend of Bordeaux–Paris as the race that kills, and that public interest will never be the same again. Some contend that other champions – van Looy, Poulidor, Janssen, Altig, etc. may be encouraged to ride Bordeaux–Paris although they will hardly be expected to sit down to an eight-day Dauphiné course as *hors d'oeuvre*.

It was not Anquetil, however, who made the 1965 B.P. such a splendid race. It was Tom Simpson. Had the Englishman not been there, Anquetil would probably have won all right, with Stablinski second and the rest nowhere. Instead of a furious Battle of the Chevreuse Valley we should have had a parade of honour by the two French friends and team-mates.

Although he would have won if he could, Stablinski is the man who helped Anquetil to win and caused Simpson to lose. Take him away, and Simpson would have won his second Bordeaux–Paris. But if the Dauphiné Libéré had been taken away and Anquetil started at Bordeaux fully rested and prepared, what would have happened then?

*   *   *

"Monsieur Jean Bobet has just left for the Hôtel Continental," I was told when I arrived at our rendezvous in Bordeaux at about 7.30 on Saturday evening, May 29. "He asks that you join him there."

I found Jean in the restaurant of the hotel, and he suggested that before I ate, I might like to go to the other side of the partition to see a friend. And there he was in a Ford track suit with his name, Vin Denson, embroidered on the top. With him were a pal or two, a trainer, and one distinguished team-mate, ex-World Champion Jean Stablinski. They had already begun their meal because the third member of the Ford team entered for Bordeaux–Paris might be a bit late. We chatted a bit while Stab and Vin munched away, and then at eight o'clock one of the party facing the window exclaimed – "There he is."

A Ford had drawn up outside, and the first to emerge was the missing third man, Jacques Anquetil. He came into the restaurant, shook hands all round sat down beside Stablinski, said he wasn't tired, but was hungry, and readily accepted his team-mate's offer to get cracking on his own substantial steak. Jacques normally looks a little bored on such occasions, but this night he was obviously excited at the adventure that lay ahead.

What he ate, what he said, during the full meal that followed, I don't know, because we went to our part of the restaurant to eat, and when we had finished, the riders' table was cleared. But Jean Bobet did get up between the cheese and *la suite* for a few minutes, taking a little leather bag with him. The bag weighed the same when he came back, yet in it, on tape, was now an interview with Anquetil that Jean put out during the 10 o'clock news.

It was a typical Anquetil interview: clear, concise, with no humming or ah-ing, and with direct replies to Jean's questions. He said he had no illusions about the magnitude of the task ahead. It wasn't his idea, this fantastic dash from the Dauphiné Libéré to Bordeaux–Paris, it was Géminiani's. But he was his own master and could have rejected the plan completely. The part of the course he feared

53

the most was the early morning unpaced section. The man he feared was Tom Simpson.

Jean and I went back to our own hotel for an hour's sleep, and then drove over to the splendid Bordeaux velodrome where the ceremonial start of the race was to be given. It was 1.15 a.m. when we arrived, yet some 5,000 spectators were still in the stands, the super enthusiasts of the much larger crowd which, from 9 p.m., had been watching a floodlit meeting.

After a few minutes the first of the 11 riders emerged from the tunnel, pedalled out of the gloom on to the ribbon of bright cement and up to the control table for the usual formalities, and examination of bicycles, which in this case included measurements to see that no ultra-short wheelbases were being used. Tom Simpson was one of the first arrivals with his team-mates Camille Le Menn, Claude Valdois and Francis Pamart. They were well wrapped up in black and white woollies for the night was cold – the coldest, an old race follower told me, he has ever known for Bordeaux–Paris.

Tom was in good spirits, yet I don't suppose he was entirely carefree since, as now was generally known, he was not on the best of terms with his *marque* or the *Directeur Sportif*, Gaston Plaud. Indeed, he had not been on the original list of entries for this Bordeaux–Paris. But he was fit and confident he told me, the London–Holyhead having done him a power of good last week.

The first Ford Bordeaux–Paris rally rider to the control was Vin Denson; he received a good hand, but the crowd had not come to see this Bon Vin de Bordeaux–Paris, but his colleague from the Château-Ford, Jacques Anquetil. When Jacques arrived at 1.30 his reception was enthusiastic and an indication how this Dauphiné–Derby double gamble was appealing to public imagination. Even last year when Anquetil was *maillot jaune* in the Tour and within a few days of his fifth victory, here at the Bordeaux velodrome a large part of the 20,000 crowd were, for reasons best known to themselves, booing him. Yet tonight 5,000 spectators cheered him heartily for merely starting in a race.

The answer to the question of the hour: "How long did you sleep?" was "One hour."

At 1.45 the riders did a lap of honour, and five minutes later, rode out of the track for a slow neutralised stretch to the official start just over the Pont St. Jean where, after a brief halt, they were sent on their way at 2.30 a.m. In the case of Anquetil one might say that he was launched, for he was embarking on an adventure into the unknown, not as dangerous, obviously, as that of the early space-men, but involving incredible risks to his health, prestige and pride.

Two years ago when I went down to Bordeaux to follow the "Derby" from start to finish, many Press colleagues could not understand why. "Nothing happens for 160 miles," they said. "Why not have a good night's sleep at Châtellerault and then see the real race behind the Dernys?" Yet there those same colleagues were, droves of them, down at Bordeaux, and of course they had come to see how Anquetil would fare during the night. There were record early morning crowds by the roadside, too – and I spotted one whole family, father, mother and three children all in dressing gowns and sheltering under umbrellas, for a light rain was beginning to fall.

They bowled along at a good pace, those 11, sharing the lead, and looking something like a gaudily dressed club run, and even more so when Annaert caped-up in a rather heavy looking yellow oilskin. The other *marques* were using lighter, nylon capelets. Everybody in the bunch looked cheerful enough except Anquetil. I won't say he looked miserable, but rather self-critical that he had been daft enough to embark on such an adventure.

"How is it going Jacques?" Jean Bobet called out from our car.

"So-so. My legs are aching, and I'm not breathing any too well. If the rain continues I'll pack."

Nobody would have blamed Anquetil if he had quit there and then. When the astonishing plan was first announced those who knew Anquetil best believed that he could pull it off, but only on condition that everything went his way – an easy Dauphiné Libéré, at least three hours sleep, a warm dry night, a back wind.

So far, everything was going wrong! Poulidor had really extended him in a hard, wet and cold eight-day stage-race, he had slept one hour, he was feeling rotten, it was cold and wet, and the forecast was that if and when the rain stopped it would be replaced by a head wind all the way to Paris. But Jacques stuck it out. Forty-five miles were covered in the first two hours.

In writing my story of the 1963 race, I told how the sun came up over the town of Angoulême (115 kms.) like a great orange. This time there was no such comforting scene. The rain was falling heavily. When it stopped an hour later the riders began stopping, too, for the various little (or big) needs that face all of us from time to time. It was necessary, too, to pull off those sodden lower woollen garments, for they were no longer leg-warmers, but leg-freezers. Riders were hopping on and off bikes, over hedges (though not always!), trainers running along with towels and changes of clothes.

At one point we were right alongside the only three riders still on their bikes: Anquetil and the two Merciers, Melckenbeek and Annaert. The two latter spotted a place to suit their own convenience – and then there was only one: Anquetil! At first Jacques did not realise what had happened, until he moved over to let his relief through. It was a comic situation, really, and a bewildering one to the spectators who found the world's greatest cyclist pottering along at about 12 m.p.h. looking back anxiously to see how long his rivals would be finishing their various toilets.

It highly amused Jacques, too, and he chatted more cheerfully to the crews of the various cars which drew alongside to take advantage of this unexpected chance of an interview. Things were a little better it seemed, and he had not lost his sense of humour: "I'm racing up near the Belgian border tomorrow afternoon," he said. "Do you think I will have ridden myself in by then?"

This was perfect material for Jean Bobet who was to put out the first of his string of broadcasts on the race at 7.10 a.m. speaking direct from our car as we drove along. He put over a perfect little piece of radio-reportage which went out from us on short waves to a Radio Luxembourg "platform car" a mile or two behind on the road which in turn passed it on to another vehicle at Angoulême, the "the fixed point" from which post-office land lines took the signals through to Paris and on to Luxembourg.

After five kilometres the Anquetil "break" was over, Tom Simpson leading the reformed group up with a little sprint. It was now quite light and the *bornes* showed a gradually decreasing number of kilometres to Poitiers, the traditional wash-and-brush up town of Bordeaux–Paris. A few kilometres before the town all but one stopped for three minutes to strip for the real action that was now only an hour away, and some to change on to bikes with higher gears. The exception was Claude Valdois who found himself on his own, though not unexpectedly as in Anquetil's case, for this was obviously a tactical move planned in advance.

Valdois is not a dangerous man by any means, and I was surprised when the little *peloton* had emerged from the roadside Gents and cloak-room, to find Anquetil and Stablinski leading a quite lively pursuit after the Peugeot break-away, with Tom Simpson happily tacked on the back. Perhaps the trio would have *rouled* just as forcefully even if Valdois had not been away, because with leg-warmers and sweaters off, it was not really cold. The threatened north-easter had arrived. The Fords had another reason, though, for wanting to bring Valdois back. They had plans of their own, and after Valdois had been caught the field were soon on the outskirts of Châtellerault where, in the Boulevard de Blossac, 11 chief pacemakers and 11 reserves were waiting with their Dernys to do their best to shelter the men all the way to Paris.

Suddenly a Ford sprinted into the lead, weaved through the narrow streets and sharp corners leading to the take-over point where he connected nicely with his pacemaker and settled down to work. An Englishman, Vin Denson, had taken the centre of the stage in the second act of the drama of the Derby of the Road.

*   *   *

And what a drama it is to be, watched by excited roadside grandstands all the way from Châtellerault to Paris, 300 kms., with no more thoughts of roadside stops, for anybody off-stage now for only a few seconds may have missed his cue to glory at the Parc des Princes.

Normally Bordeaux–Paris is a pleasant open-air performance watched by lightly-clad spectators basking in the sun. Today, all the way up, they have been looking decidedly chilly, and nips of cognac rather than beer and cold drinks have been keeping the café tills busy.

Good warm weather in these parts means the wind is blowing somewhere from the south, or maybe there is no wind at all. This will mean that chasers after break-aways have to make some effort to reduce the margin, but they will not be worn out in the process. Today, however, with that north wind, it is different. You can see its strength from the ripples flowing at us down the great cornfields on either side of the road (the wine country is now behind), and flags, trees and plastic bird-scaring strips are even surer evidence. This means that while the rider is getting some shelter from his Derny, another "tandem" placed intelligently behind is going to get a much easier ride, while a third pair will obviously be even more favourably placed.

Tactics today are going to play an important part, and this opening move of Denson's provokes an immediate reaction, and he is soon caught by Lefebvre and Pamart and Annaert – one from each of the other *marques* in the race. There is a general regroupment, the missing members being Mahé, Simpson and Anquetil who are at 45 secs.! Already the Simpson–Anquetil "marking" has begun, and Jacques is not too happy with his form nor with Denson's early stirring of the pace. Not that he reproaches his English team-mate for this, for Vin is only carrying out his orders. Anquetil has already threatened to pack several times, but "Gem" persuades him to go on. Then when Anquetil comes it again, his manager says: "All right – pack then!" And from then on he is no trouble at all!

Eventually all are together again and Mahé breaks away. He doesn't know it, but that break is going to last 200 kms.! The good team-mate Denson is there, too, but of course this time doesn't lead, and the Breton and the Briton pass through crowded Tours with a two-and-a-half minutes lead, a lead which is built up to five and a half minutes in the next 45 miles. In between the pair and the *peloton* is Pamart, a young good-looking boy considered No.1 man of the Peugeot entry this year until the late decision by Tom Simpson to contest the Derby.

At the moment though, he is riding Tom's race, because behind, Anquetil has been stirred into action. Simpson follows his acceleration, with Stablinski trailing him, but almost immediately Jacques has to stop and change a wheel. Needless to say Tom does not wait for him; far from it. We pull up in our car a few hundred yards ahead, but instead of seeing Tom in the lead it is Stablinski sprinting behind his Derny with Tom sitting up and cursing. His Derny has broken down, and the spare machine is not immediately behind as it should be. Looking behind we can see the cracked-up Derny "going backwards", and the spare one sprinting up like mad. Tom takes the incident with commendable calm. He latches on to the spare Derny and goes off in pursuit of Stablinski.

Our car is on the move again and we get a close-up not only of a splendid Simpson–Stablinski pursuit in front, but of a remarkable Anquetil effort behind. On changing his wheel, the stragglers had caught up with him – but not for long. In the same way that Peter Post goes to the front of a dozen men in a Derny-paced race on an indoor track and simply burns them off to the other side of the straight in no time at all, so does Anquetil treat the four or five men who are lucky enough still to be with him.

He comes steaming down the wide straight road, eyes fixed on the Derny mudguard, with but an occasional glance ahead to see what is going on. Tom has caught his man, who immediately eases, and this somewhat lessens Anquetil's task in getting up. Once Jacques is there, Tom goes to the back and has a quick munch and drink, the pace slackens and before long up pant the stragglers to rejoin again, much to their own surprise.

Again, it seemed to me, that an indoor track analogy is apposite. Simpson, Stablinski, Anquetil and their pacemakers are like three top teams in a six-day race who are head and shoulders above the rest of the field. When they "go", the others are soon laps behind. When the three teams ease, the others struggle back. This is now happening in Bordeaux–Paris, but there the analogy ends, for whereas in the wings of the velodrome an impresario is maybe lurking, script in hand, with signals to his leading men when to start and stop their star turns, here the struggle is fair and square.

Meanwhile, Mahé – riding in his fourth Bordeaux–Paris – is plugging on steadily into the wind. Newcomer Denson, though, is beginning to have his first bad time, and eventually goes back very rapidly into the bunch, along with Pamart who has proved no more than a useful apprentice lad in this Derby of the road. The race, clearly, is going to be between the three odds-on favourites and the 34-year-old outsider, Mahé, still five minutes ahead on the road. Difficult to say at what point it happened, but somewhere after Vendôme with 100 miles to go, we no longer consider Anquetil as a possible packer, but a certain finisher.

Then suddenly it seems that this promised battle is going to be a wash-out after all. Stablinski goes into an attack, his team-mate Anquetil eases with Simpson in behind. Are we going to see the opportunist "Stab" pushing on to Paris, passing Mahé and going on to take the Derby, while Tom and Jacques play silly so-and-so's behind? The onus is on Simpson, and during a period of hesitation during which the pair ride at no more than evens, Tom's thoughts can be imagined. At the base of his recent differences with Peugeot is their allegation that he did not "defend his chance" at the end of Paris–Roubaix. What would they say now if he let Stablinski off without resistance? What would the public think if he no longer rode to win, but simply to make Anquetil lose? Tom accepts the challenge, and takes up the chase after Stablinski who is now half a minute ahead, while Mahé has profited from the slow tactics behind and is a further five and a half minutes ahead of the champion of France.

Five and a half minutes lead over Stablinski, with 55 miles to go, six over Anquetil and Simpson ... Cannot old Mahé from Morbihan make it an outsider's Derby after all? Those who do not know their bikes might think it possible, and so might some who do, provided they have never heard of the Chevreuse Valley. Ironically the valley is only touched now and then; it is the getting out on to the plateaux that is the trouble.

All the way up from Bordeaux we have been on Route Nationale 10, and my little dream is that this is an omen for a Simpson victory, for his race number is 10. Then after Chartres I notice that the kilometre-stones are no longer simple affairs, but the larger, prouder monuments indicating that we are on La Route de la Liberté, the road the Allies took in 1945 on their advance towards the East.

While 20 years ago we were proud to be associated with our French friends in that victorious push, today our battling Tommy is fighting for nobody's liberty but his own. First there is the Tricolor itself, worn by national champion Stablinski, to be lowered, but what's the good of that, since Anquetil would simply pass into the attack leaving our Tommy soldiering on in his pursuit while "Stab" recuperates behind?

The chance comes on the rise out of Le Gue de Longroi where the crowd first cheer a tiring but still gallant Mahé, then two minutes later Stablinski, and third, on his own a minute behind, Simpson! Tom has found Anquetil's weak spot, for he has been left almost standing by the slick break of his Peugeot rival.

But we are not jumping to the conclusion that Jacques is beaten, for the signposts to Albis remind us that this was the half-way point on the old Grand Prix des Nations course and he knows the chosen route from here to the Parc des Princes as nobody else, rises, falls, direction, shelter, surface. And so steadily he pedals after Tom, and we begin to realise the odds now facing Simpson, the unfortunate English filling of a French-bred Anquetil–Stablinski sandwich.

Tom makes the junction, pauses in Stablinski's wake whereupon the Frenchman eases the pace, and in no time Anquetil is up with them. We look down at our race schedule. Thirty-five miles to go, the next town Dourdan, and although we are now off Route 10 at last, our Tom's chances are still good despite the buffeting he has been taking in these into-the-wind chases provoked by the two Ford men. It has been a tremendous battle so far, but it has all been kid-glove stuff to the fight to the finish that lies ahead.

*   *   *

I have never known anything like the atmosphere of this tremendous last hour – not even the Poulidor clash on the Puy de Dôme in the Tour last year, nor their subsequent showdown on the Versailles–Paris time-trial. Both those encounters were contested by men meeting, so-to-speak, on a "home and away" basis: Poulidor on his home ground on the mountains with Anquetil defending, so as to lose as little ground as possible; Poulidor the "visitor" in the time-trial section, already down on aggregate, striving with all his might to draw level and then score the winner.

Here in Bordeaux–Paris it is different. Anquetil has had 14 hours since Bordeaux in which to retire, hundreds of miles in which to pick a deserted spot and climb into the comfort of a car – and, as I have said, nobody would have blamed him.

But there is only an hour to go. If he packs it will not just be because he feels like it, but because he has collected the *defaillance* of his career – and how ironical that's going to be if he cops it in the Valley of the Chevreuse, the district in which he has ridiculed the world's greatest time-trialists in so many Grands Prix des Nations. We are now nearly at Dourdan, and those in the cars in front are looking back, and those behind peering forward so as not to miss a second of the fight, for nobody cares a jot that Dourdan is a *cité historique*. Its attraction today is that the cobbled, narrow streets play round-the-shops-and-houses for 200 metres, then straighten out into a reasonably surfaced road shooting up to the woods in a mile-long hill. You northerners wouldn't call it a hill at all, but Bordeaux–Paris men from G. P. Mills to Nedelec have found it a hill all right and, coming as it does after 14 hours of comparatively flat riding, it often feels like a mountain.

Jean Bobet – who is directing the whole of the three-hour all-round sports programme, football, basketball, motor and horse racing, athletics, swimming, etc. from our car as we travel along – orders Paris to clean the air for what he believes will be the vital five minutes of the race. Behind Anquetil, Stablinski and Simpson is Jean's colleague Guy Kedia, and the arrangement is that he shall "launch" this phase of the broadcast from his motor-bike leaving

Jean to take up the story ahead of the field.

Guy does, in fact, launch into as vivid a bit of radio reporting as he has ever undertaken, but, unfortunately, down there in the valley the signal does not get through to the platform-car, and Guy is for a minute or so talking to himself instead of the waiting millions.

Good old-fashioned eyesight therefore has to come to the aid of the Radio Luxembourg party, and from 100 yards ahead of the field, on the lower slopes of Dourdan hill we have to peer down through the crowded streets – and instead of three riders, there is only one – SIMPSON! "SIMPSON SEUL EN TÊTE" the cry goes up the hill as Tom tears after pacemaker Wambst in the most desperate sprint of his career, and right on his tail is race director Jacques Goddet's car with the red flag flying – the signal that a break is officially on and that Anquetil and Stablinski have been dropped.

What do the hillside crowds think of that? My thoughts go back to Hubert Opperman's talk at the Pedal Club ten days earlier when he said that he found French road-racing spectators the most sporting in the world. A pity you are not here now Oppy, because not only would you find that they are still the same 40 years on, but you would see just how great is our Tom, the man who has taken the yellow jersey in the Tour which caused you so much suffering, and now is tearing off perhaps to his second victory in the Derby of the Road.

Through that sporting, cheering crowd Tom is continuing the mighty effort, and gaining with every thrust of the pedal. Has Simpson pulled off the same masterstroke that won him the 1963 Bordeaux–Paris?

When we reached the very top of Dourdan in 1963 there wasn't any doubt about it at all, for he just sailed away from the worn-out opposition and gained five minutes in the last hour. Today, however, the opposition is very, very different. Anquetil and Stablinski have been dropped all right, but not knocked out, even though the timekeeper half-way up Dourdan gives them a count of 10 seconds, and his colleague at the top, twenty.

Are you there in the crowd John Fisher of the East Surrey Road Club and your C.T.C. friends? I met you training round Richmond Park one night, and you told me you would be seeing something of the Dauphiné Libéré race in the first week of your holiday, then moving over to the Valley of the Chevreuse for the finish of Bordeaux–Paris. You've chosen a great day for it, and I'll bet your little party is a popular one with the crowd, many of whom will have their regular annual roadside stations for this race. If you've never seen anything like the crowds, the excitement, well neither have they, and neither have I seen anything like the excitement in the Press caravan. Chany, Bastide, de Latour, Leulliot – men who have seen Bordeaux–Paris a hundred times between them – are as keyed up as if this were the first big race they had ever seen.

We keep forgetting, though, that Mahé is still ahead! He's great, this old campaigner, today adopting something of a stayer's position on the bike, his body doing a kind of twist as he pedals. He is now in sight in front, while behind us a slight drop on the road reveals the full drama as if on a tilted stage – Simpson battling on, but creeping gradually nearer is another man, he with the lightish jersey and cap with the turned-up peak. Jacques Anquetil is doing a Derny-paced time-trial pursuit after Simpson, and in so doing has dropped the man in the French championship jersey, Stablinski.

Not until later do we learn that "Stab" lost ground when his pacemaker fell on Dourdan, and it seems to us that here the two mighty men of the race are at grips at last, for this battle of the Ford and the Peugeot is an epic Grand Prix of Courage. And, not the least courageous is Mahé, who is finally caught by Tom, but all too soon by Anquetil as well, and with 18 miles to go he wins his pursuit, the pace eases and Stablinski is with them again.

It is not surprising to find that Simpson is beginning to look tired, even more astonishing that Anquetil looks far better than at the start … There is a brief period of "observation", but then on the Limours hill, Simpson flings himself into another attack which we somehow feel will not succeed, and it doesn't. Anquetil is dropped by ten metres or so, but gradually gets back. We begin to realise that Anquetil, with the wise old head of team-mate Stablinski to back him up, is riding a very intelligent race. He is, in fact, "doing a Dauphiné" here in the Derby; just as he refused to be bustled into trying to stay with Poulidor on the cols, so here he is taking his time in neutralising the Simpson attacks. His knowledge of the terrain is, of course, a priceless asset now.

Before the race Stablinski and Anquetil said they would each try to win Bordeaux–Paris, but would not, obviously, fight against each other so that a rival might win. Now it is Stablinski's turn to attack, on the St. Rémy hill; it doesn't come off, but it is another punch at Simpson's failing strength, and I wish more than ever that you British sports writers could be here, for Tom is now fighting not one man, but two.

We are now on the narrow roads leading down to the viaduct at Buc and in the cars we have to scream down the slopes to get there first because Simpson, Stablinski and Anquetil are dropping down at 50s, and Jacques has the old 55 x 13 engaged and is on the attack. It is extraordinary, the intensity of this clash. You can understand men having a go at each other after 350 miles riding, but this clash has more the look of a Gaignard v Reg Harris one-lapper than Anquetil v Simpson in a 15-hour affair. And a sprint, moreover, which Tom wins, and the three are together again.

Versailles. Once again, I wonder. This time, how many British tourists are in the city, puzzled that hundreds of thousands of French citizens are turning their backs on the royal palace of Louis XIV and cheering three commoners playing around on bicycles? If it's history you want, leave the French Kings alone for the moment – there were 16 Louis anyhow – and have a look at Jacques Anquetil, the First Man of world cycling. At any moment now he is going to strike an historic blow, and if the man who falls is an Englishman, don't hold your head in shame, for the gallant warrior has fought like a hero all the way.

I am roused from my dream by Jean Bobet, who is on the air again. "We are now on the Côte de Picardie. It is 1,200 metres long, and the crowds are tremendous either side of the road. The situation is extraordinary here with 11 kilometres to go. The three are now side by side, now one behind the other, jockeying for positions like sprinters. Anquetil is in front. He leans over to pull up his toe-strap. His Derny accelerates, Jacques follows steadily. He glances back at Tom Simpson, who is not so steady. His head, in fact, is on one side and he looks in trouble. Anquetil is five metres ahead. Simpson tries to counter, but loses his pacemaker. Anquetil is away!"

Yes, Jacques is away, I'm afraid. Afraid for Tom, that is, though I'm full of admiration for his victor, who has weathered fourteen and a half hours and now has landed his one real punch. Yet he does not soar away, for Tom is full of fight. But Jacques knows the way home from here to the Parc des Princes, and he seems to have another pair of legs. The ovation all along the descent to the Seine, over the Pont de Sevres, along the Avenue de la Reine is fantastic. He has won Bordeaux–Paris, achieved the impossible. But he has done something else which verges on the miraculous: he has at last won the hearts of the public, and he speeds through the tunnel on to the cement of the Parc des Princes to a tremendous chant of "Anker-teel - Ank-er-teel - Ank-er-teel".

Fifty seconds later, the two other leading men in this cycling drama most wonderful appear on the track, Stablinski beating Tom in the sprint for second place.

"Simpson third in Bordeaux–Paris" I shall find after some searching in Monday morning's English papers, as if he had put up a poor old race. Tom is worth the whole back page, and an editorial story, too, for he has been twice as great in defeat as in winning the Derby two years ago.

Sporting Cyclist, July 1965

Jean Stablinski Shows the Way from Paris to Roubaix

Just before ten o'clock on the morning of Sunday 7th April, 1968, I was a passenger in one of the long line of Press cars cruising slowly in front of a field of 135 riders making their way from the assembly area to the official start of a road-race. On looking back at the brightly coloured pack I noticed the sign welcoming travellers to the pleasant town we were now leaving: "Chantilly, City of the Horse" it said.

Race horses, of course. Chantilly might be called the Epsom of Paris. But the entries about to come under the starter's orders were today engaged in the greatest of all single-day cycling Classics, Paris–Roubaix, the race which starts like a Derby on the fine flats roads of the Oise and the Aisne and ends with a Grand National slam over the vilest roads that can be found in French Flanders.

In the old days Paris–Roubaix, logically enough, used to start in or very near Paris, the route making for the Franco–Belgian border by the shortest possible route. If any diversion was made it was to take in stretches of good road to avoid the dreadful cobblestones. Since the war this *pavé* has gradually disappeared and in recent years the organisers have literally been looking for trouble to give Paris–Roubaix its traditional character. If they did not do so, they said, the race would become the easiest in the world instead of the toughest.

But as new stretches of cobbled roads were discovered and included in the ever-changing route of Paris–Roubaix, so did the local highways departments take umbrage at the resulting publicity and quickly transformed the corrugated purgatory into smooth bands of concrete, and therefore useless for the following year's race.

"Within two years there will be no more *pavé* in northern France, and Paris–Roubaix will not be worth running."

So said the pessimists. Others had different ideas.

"Don't you believe it. If you want to see real old-fashioned *pavé*, just follow me."

The speaker was Jean Stablinski, the ex-World Road Champion who lives at Valenciennes. In the winter Jean is a great man for shooting, and he said he knew dozens of roads through the woods as bad as any that had been used since the first Paris–Roubaix was held in 1896.

And so Stablinski was invited to join the organising committee of the 1968 race, and from what we had heard and read in the newspapers, he had not been kidding. "Only 30 at the most will finish this race," said one newspaper. "Even less if it rains." Another quite seriously said that a rider changing on to a bike with a sprung saddle, well-padded handlebars and fat wired-on tyres, at the start of the "northern hell" would stand a good chance of finishing in the first ten. One official even thought that if the weather was really bad, no rider would finish at all …

None of these forebodings had any effect.

All the stars were there just behind us, riding slowly in a pack, waiting for M. Jacques Goddet to set them on their way. And one of the 135 was the villain himself, Jean Stablinski, the man whose research would be bringing so much pain and suffering to his companions on the road – and joy to the man who was destined to win the most coveted of all classics.

M. Goddet drops the flag, and they are off …

When I report Paris–Roubaix I like to be on the job the day before the race itself, picking up all the gossip and generally soaking in the atmosphere. This year, however, it was not possible. I did not arrive in Paris until mid-night Saturday, and only got to Chantilly half an hour or so before the start. But my colleague Jean Payen of

Lille, whose guest I was in the *Nord Éclair* car, put me in the picture.

"Most interesting point was yesterday's draw by the *Directeurs Sportifs*. Antonin Magne, the Mercier boss, drew No.1. That means he will be first in the line of team cars. On these wide roads we are now on, of course, that doesn't mean a thing. But in the 'northern hell' it will be a priceless advantage. I have been over the roads and some of them are just beyond words and wide enough for only one car. So if Poulidor punctures in the leading group Magne will be right behind to change his wheel. Hard luck on the fellow puncturing whose car is in 12th position!"

"Good for Poulidor," I said. "But what about Barry Hoban? He's a Mercier man, too, you know!"

"Yes, of course," my friend apologised. "I admire Hoban very much. He was 12th in last week's Tour of Flanders and any rider who can finish in the same time as Merckx, Janssen, Altig, Poulidor, etc. in such a tough race is quite capable of winning Paris–Roubaix where chance plays such an important part."

"So Poulidor is in luck before the race starts," put in our driver. "But Anquetil can't be so happy. His race number is 13!"

We were now on wide open roads, dipping and climbing gently so that at the crest of one little rise we could see the field spread out for our inspection two to three hundred yards behind. Just before Senlis, five miles from the start, we saw a lone rider sprinting out in front.

A condition of following Paris–Roubaix is that every Press car must be fitted with a short-wave radio capable of picking up the 51-metre transmissions from the same technical organisation that is used in the Tour de France. Into our note books went the first "break" of the day: "Rider No. 103, De Pra, Italy, has a lead of 100 metres," the radio announced.

Within two minutes, as we sped through Senlis itself, came the curt announcement *Echappée terminée* (break over). The little incident was not without significance, though, for De Pra is a teammate of Gimondi, Paris–Roubaix winner in 1966, and this might have been part of some ambitious plan for another victory.

One advantage of "following the race from the front" and joining the procession of cars ahead of the field, is that it is possible to slip handily behind any real break that forms. A disadvantage is that you can't see what is going on behind the main groups, although thanks to Radio-Tour you soon know about it. The next announcement was:

"Puncture to Claude Guyot. He is waited for by three of his Pelforth team-mates, including Bernard Guyot."

I remarked that it was a nice brotherly act, but M. Payen did not agree. "A stupid thing to do," he exclaimed. "Bernard Guyot has a tiny chance of winning Paris-Roubaix. His place is at the front, not to stooge around acting the *domestique* to his brother who hasn't much chance of finishing."

I argued with friend Jean that today was different, on account of the head wind. Those who have travelled the roads of Europe with me over the last 30 years will have noticed that I have a "thing" about wind and its influence on road-racing. On this occasion, when I first saw the flags and smoke blowing from the north, I sensed that the average speed would not be high, not just because of the physical influence of that wind, but because of its effect on the minds of the riders.

Had there been a back wind blowing – as in 1964 when Peter Post won at the record average speed of 28.25 m.p.h. – then Bernard Guyot would have been plain crazy to have stayed behind for Claude. They would have got back on, all right, to the back of the bunch that is, but during their chase a break would certainly have formed in the front.

With a head wind there was little risk in the Guyot exercise. That wheel was changed slickly, and the Pelforth quartet cunningly but quite legitimately used the shelter of the following Press cars (on the left of the road) and the team cars (on the right) to ride comfortably back to a still compact bunch.

This incident began at the hamlet of La Roue Qui Tourne (The Turning Wheel) soon after which we passed through the town of Compiègne where the 1918 Armistice was signed. Here in Paris–Roubaix the battle had not even begun, and in the first hour only 23.5 miles were covered. There was protection enough from the forests on the right side of the road, but the wind was blowing hard over the open wheat fields to the left. Just the weather for Dutchmen! One, Harings, indeed was out for a minute or so with a 200-yard lead perhaps in the hope that reinforcements would come up to form one of the *bordures* at which the Lowlanders excel (a *bordure* is what we in Britain call an echelon).

The fact that no reinforcements came did not mean that the *peloton* was lethargic. The opposite, indeed was the case. Stars and team-men alike were very much on the alert for any such surprise build-up.

Another announcement over Radio Tour:

"The commissaries have decided that the following must submit to an anti-doping control after the race at Roubaix: The first, second and third finishers, the 13th and the 17th. It is the responsibility of the *Directeurs Sportifs* of the riders concerned to see that this is carried out."

And so the second hour went by, slower even than the first. There had been skirmishes, but without any real result. One little group of eight or so managed to get a 30-second lead, the instigator being Jose Samyn, a North of France boy who obviously meant to be in evidence on his home ground. De Pra there again, too, with another Salvarani team-mate. But behind, all eyes were on Gimondi lest he should attempt to get up with his two hard-working slaves.

Then at Mericourt (75 miles) the first real build-up of the race began when the Dutch-born Frenchman in the Peugeot colours, Van Der Linde, was away pursued by Haeseldonckx (Mann-Grundig), Neri (Max-Meyer, an Italian team managed by 1960 Tour de France winner Nencini), Leblanc (Pelforth) and Casalini (Faema).

These five rapidly gained on the main group, partly because none of them was all that dangerous, and partly because their team-mates were giving them some measure of protection. Then when the quintet had a 30-second lead out shot the familiar figure of Roger Pingeon, a crash-hat over his racing cap, pedalling powerfully after them. Van Der Linde glanced back, saw his team captain coming up, dropped back a few yards, and in no time the junction was made. Six men in the lead, including two of the Peugeot team who proceeded to the front to force the pace and take the break further and further from the field.

When the lead was one and a half minutes we stopped by the roadside, let the break-aways pass, just at the moment when an incident was taking place: two riders were slightly off the back, Haeseldonckx blocking and chopping and generally trying to get rid of Casalini who was obviously not a working member of the party, but simply there to make a nuisance of himself on behalf of his own leader Eddy Merckx.

The presence of Pingeon at the front turned the break from being just an interesting passage of arms, to something more serious. Of all those who had been training on the course during the past few days, Pingeon was the one who had created the biggest impression. His intentions were now obvious. He meant to be well clear of the main group at the "gates of hell" at Solesmes where the real rough stuff started. Pingeon had said in interviews that he believed that if it rained, the 70 miles from Solesmes to Roubaix would be an individual time-trial, with the advantage to the man in the lead.

At Solesmes the Pingeon group had a lead of four and a quarter minutes and with a big black menacing cloud looming up ahead!

You will see from the sketch accompanying this article that the *pavé* comes in sections, big black hunks of cobbles sandwiched between slices of white concrete. In some ways this is worse than having the stuff all the way, so far as comfort is concerned. But from the point of view of progress the concrete provides an opportunity to ride fast. The "white portions" certainly contributed to an eventual downfall of Pigeon, for while on these stretches he was at the front doing practically all the work, the main bunch behind were gradually reducing his lead.

I wonder if Pingeon appreciated the irony of the road sign just outside Solesmes, which said "Solesmes thanks you for slowing down. Good luck!"

But still Pingeon battled on. The roads were narrow, without shelter, a rough dirt path besides the cobbled stretches. It was a do-or-die effort by the 1967 Tour de France winner. Off the back of his leading group went first Haeseldonckx, then Le Blanc, then the Faema man who lately had at least been going through when his turn came. The three dropped men teamed up together, and when they were 30 seconds behind Pingeon and the other two, we went by them in our car, the chosen moment being on a nasty downhill stretch of cobblestones strewn with gravel chippings. In the space of 50 yards all three were off their bikes with punctures.

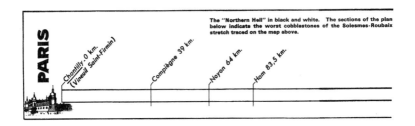

The "Northern Hell" in black and white. The sections of the plan below indicate the worst cobblestones of the Solesmes-Roubaix stretch traced on the map above.

"Behind in the main group, now at two and a half minutes from Pingeon, Bracke has fallen but is not seriously hurt. Gimondi has punctured and five of his team-mates wait behind for him," came news from Radio Tour.

Then, almost immediately, "Punctures sustained by De Boever, Post, Delberghe, Gustave, Desmet, Hoban. Bodard and Bouquet crash …"

On hearing of the approach of the *peloton*, Pingeon decided to go it alone. His young team-mate Van Der Linde – a first year pro. – had ridden his heart out on his behalf and now had nothing left. Rattling over the *pavé*, slithering along the dirt-tracks, pedalling powerfully on the concrete, the Peugeot man pressed on and must have taken heart ten minutes later when he learnt that he was now three and a half minutes up on the field.

But over Radio-Tour we had heard the reason why: a level-crossing delay had held up the field for nearly two minutes. At Valenciennes, where Pingeon grabbed his *musette* from Gaston Plaud, he heard that his lead was down to two and a half minutes again.

As well as giving the Press information about the race, Radio-Tour also gives us instructions:

"Press cars which are now behind Pingeon should pass him in the next six kilometres. After that the road is very narrow. This is essential because the *peloton* is coming up fast and the road between it and Pingeon must be kept clear of cars."

We obeyed instructions. Buffeted by the wind, red in the face, Pingeon looked beaten, but defiant. He brought off the ride of his life last year in the Tour de France on a stage which started at Roubaix. Today, for a time, it seemed that he was going to end an equally notable ride in the same city.

"Two minutes difference between the *peloton* and Pingeon … one minute … thirty seconds …" the radio tell us. "Now Pingeon punctures, changes wheels quickly, is away, but the *peloton* are on his heels. Pingeon is caught. Pingeon now actually leads the *peloton*…"

And so the first phase of the 66th Paris–Roubaix was over. Forty-five miles still to go, of which 35 at least were cobbled.

During the last half-hour of Pingeon's courageous effort, that big black cloud has come and gone with no more bother than a few big drops to lay the dust. And dust there is in plenty. It is blown there from the hedge-less fields through which the Stablinski route is winding. Most of the "white" stretches on the plan of the course are brief bits of main road, off which we turned by sharp corners on to fresh examples of the kind of "road" that has not changed for 50 years. In the distance are black pyramids of coal slack; on either side of the road heaps of good old-fashioned manure. Both these commodities have played a part in the construction of this unique cycle-racing route: the so-called cycle-paths are largely composed of coal dust; manure straw has been blown from the fields and then trapped in the considerable gaps between the granite stones.

And look at those "paths"! Once upon a time they were doubtless on the same level as the *pavé*, and it would be possible to switch from one to the other without much trouble. But nowadays the rain drains off the *pavé* on to the coal-dust track which becomes a gutter, and so the "path" is on an average six inches below the granite and sometimes as much as a foot! Hard luck on the chap who decides to keep down below for suddenly he will find a recently dug drainage channel across his path. In most races through cobbled country, the cycle-paths are kept clear by the police, but here the crowds are sometimes massed along them as if to warn the riders to keep to the comparative security of the granite blocks.

Such is the setting of the final stage of the 66th Paris–Roubaix, the Flanders plain that saw less sporting battles fifty years ago. Yet being in front on those flat roads is, from the reporting angle, rather like being on the Galibier or the Tourmalet! The road twists and often doubles back on itself so much that it is possible to stop every now and then to look across the fields and clearly see what is going on.

On one such stop we see a rider speeding away from the *peloton*, which is now no more than 30 strong.

"Gimondi attacks", comes the message. Exciting news followed by a sad but inevitable piece of additional information: Pingeon has been dropped as the pace increases to bring back the dangerous Italian. Immediately Gimondi is caught we can see another attack developing, and this time we learn that the runaway is Cooreman, a Belgian of the Mann-Grundig team. Twenty seconds lead … a useful springboard. Across the fields we see a dozen riders sprinting after him in ones and twos, and soon in our notebooks we have their names: Janssens, Merckx, Bocklandt, Brands, Zooltjels, van Springel, Godefroot, Duydam, van Schil, Gimondi, Poulidor. They are soon 40 seconds up with 35 miles to go. This could be it! But the bunch is not beaten yet. We do not know until afterwards that it is largely due to Rudi Altig that the runaways are brought back. Thirty men together again just over 30 miles from the finish. Will they arrive together at Roubaix and confound all predictions of a merciless time-trial through the closing miles of hell?

Now turn, please, to the "plan of the *pavé*" and note particularly the little portion that finishes at 211.8 kms. It is here, on a narrow and very bumpy stretch, flanked with high grass banks, that Eddy Merckx attacks, and it is not by chance that he does so. He knows the stretch is short, and by the time his rivals realise what is happening the World Champion is on the concrete and they still struggling on the granite.

Although Merckx has succeeded in getting rid of most of his rivals he is not yet ready to part company with all of them and is glad when he looks round to find three on their way to join him. First comes Edward Sels. Not so good! Sels is one of the best sprinters in the business and quite capable of beating him on the track at Roubaix. Next is Bocklandt. No real worry here. Willy has for years always been "there" at the end of a tough road-race; he'll work like a horse over this *pavé* and be a useful ally. Lastly there is van Springel. A dangerous enough man – but it could be worse. Altig, for instance. But unknown to Eddy, Altig is at the moment taking an awful hiding and will soon be dropped by the chasers of whom Barry Hoban is among the most active.

So four Belgians are in the lead and are in their element, for if the organisers have to call in experts to find this sort of road in France, they themselves have been brought up on this kind of thing. On the smooth patches they relay each other powerfully like a pursuit team; on the "other" they pick their way expertly over the granite paving blocks, switching on and off the dirt-paths now and then when things promise to be smoother that way.

Four such men – who must be among the strongest to be there at all – with the "road" to themselves, have a great advantage over the two-dozen group behind, which includes many men who either can only just hang on, or are team-mates of the break-away group and therefore causing general obstruction to desperate chasers like Poulidor, Janssen and Gimondi, the latter of whom punctures with the battle at its height.

By now our leading four are on the blackest of all stretches between the 226.7 and 242 kms. points, which in parts is nothing more than a farm track with gaping holes where blocks of *pavé* used to be, strewn with mud dropped from tractor and wagon wheel, or occasionally covered with sand and gravel. On this cyclo-cross country track the four gain steadily and have now nearly a two-minute lead over the main group from which Godefroot has parted in a powerful counter-attack with one man on his wheel: Van Schil, team-mate of Eddy Merckx.

In front Bocklandt is in trouble, and no surprise at that, for last year the Belgian had a bad accident and is only just getting back to form. Soon he sits up, beaten. Now there are three. And, alas, only too soon, only two, for Sels punctures, changes wheels, and then punctures again almost immediately.

Two riders pedalling all out for Roubaix. Merckx in the world-championship jersey pushing a gear some five inches higher than the more supple van Springel who is riding a bicycle with wooden rims which are said to be faster and more comfortable over cobbled roads. All journalists are scribbling furiously in notebooks, radio reporters jabbering into their mikes, and so is Robert Chapatte the TV man who, for the first time, is giving a direct commentary from the back of a motor-bike. There is but one theme: the "comeback" of Merckx. This seems a bit odd. For how long has Merckx been "absent"? The answer is for about a month, and that is an awful long time for a rider of his talent to be out of the picture. The facts are that Merckx took the first stage of the Tour of Sardinia in February by six minutes and easily won overall. Many of his rivals were upset at the way he emphasised his superiority, and vowed to make life difficult for him by pitiless marking – van Looy in particular. The knee, injured in Paris–Nice has been giving him trouble, too.

The Merckx–van Springel tandem forges on, a dense crowd of spectators on either side of them, the TV helicopter zooming overhead. They are the only two in it, and know they have the race in hand. Behind, Godefroot is chasing furiously; with van Schil still on his wheel he has gone right by the distressed Bocklandt and the unlucky Sels and is gaining on the runaways. He is tremendous, this Godefroot who a week earlier won the Tour of Flanders, and he's not just a sprinter. He is riding so strongly that even the non-working Van Schil is eventually dropped.

Now it is time for us to leave the battle area and move quickly to the Roubaix track where we follow the last five miles of the race on the TV screen. The position is clear as we see first the Merckx–van Springel tandem, then the energetic Godefroot, finally the beaten main group.

We watch the leading pair, noting that of the two, Merckx looks the more anxious, turning round every now and then to check that Godefroot is out of harm's way. His anxiety is understandable. Everybody expects him to win. It will be an awful let down if he doesn't.

Now there are roars from the far side of the track. The spectators on the top terraces can see the pair a few hundred yards from the track, and within a few seconds shrill blasts of a whistle herald their entry on to the scene for the lap and a half that finishes every modern Paris–Roubaix.

It is a two-up sprint in every sense of the world, almost like Reg Harris v Arie van Vliet. The pair are three minutes up on the pursuing Godefroot and take their time, van Springel slowly leading the watchful Merckx. But on the last banking the World Champion is in the lead, swoops down with his biggest gear and has a clear length lead over the line. As he throws his arm up in triumph I hear a Belgian radio commentator telling his listeners: "Eddy Merckx, our young cycling god, has ridden through hell to the paradise of victory in the greatest of all cycling classics."

And so, true to tradition, despite the terrors which the organisers scheme out each succeeding year, Paris–Roubaix remains the cycling steeplechase which an outsider never wins. Nor can it be said that the World Champion was lucky to get through without trouble – he punctured twice. Curiously enough, despite the severity of the course, there were no serious crashes. I believe the reason for this is because of the thorough way in which the organisers kept the "battle area" clear of Press cars which, I must confess, have often been responsible for causing accidents.

Victim of a minor fall was Michael Wright who thought he would have finished in the *peloton* without his trouble. Derek Harrison, suffering from a bad cold, was in the sag-wagon before the really bad *pavé* started.

Barry Hoban gave me a lift into Roubaix town before he turned east for Ghent. His 16th place after two punctures was a very fine ride in such an exacting race. I asked him if he had used any special equipment for the extra bad roads.

"No," he replied. "All that stuff about using wired-on tyres, sprung saddles and thick rubber grips on the bars was a lot of newspaper talk. But I did make one mistake by keeping on my usual 53 x 42 chainset, with the 13–17 rear block. The ideal gear for the bad *pavé* was what, at home, we call 84. To get that I had to use 53 x 17, and, of course, the constant bumping made the chain jump on to the 16 and 15. I noticed that Janssen had the right idea. He had 53 x 50, and he was all right with the 50 x 16 with the chain in a nice straight line. You live and learn. I ought to have known that, living in Belgium."

Next day I had lunch with Louis Debruyckere and his family at their home near Lille. I expected the Bic No1 mechanic to be up to his eyes sorting out wrecked material, and to get an expert account of the special technical preparations that had been made for this exceptional Paris–Roubaix. Not a bit of it. Louis was having a day off, all the equipment had gone back to Paris, and he confirmed what Barry had said.

"The only thing M. Louviot, our *Directeur Sportif*, insisted on was that his riders should use 10-ounce tyres instead of 8.5. On Saturday night Sels asked me to change his back to 8.5-ounce – Monsieur Louviot said he could "at his own risk" – in case he was there with a chance in the final sprint. You know what happened. Perhaps Sels lost Paris–Roubaix through not taking advice."

Paris–Roubaix is always an Ifs and Buts race. But if a World Champion wins there can't be much wrong with it.

International Cycle Sport, June 1968

INTERVIEWS

Cycle-racing is about riders as much as it is about races. It is their personalities, not simply the drama of the event, that give the sport its vitality, and it is certainly they who breathe life into any cycling magazine. Interviews with riders, both past and present, figured repeatedly in J. B. Wadley's writing. He sought them out, particularly on his trips abroad, and he seemed remarkably successful at getting them to talk.

We are calling them interviews, yet that is almost too formal a term: it suggests an arranged meeting, and a pre-determined list of questions. Wadley, on the other hand, just seemed to call in, almost on the off chance, and the 'interview' that saw its way on to the pages of *Sporting Cyclist* was simply an account of the conversation that ensued.

Frequently these were quite opportunistic encounters, as in these three instances: on a trip, by bike and train, to report on the Paris–Nice, Wadley had planned to break the journey in Luxembourg to visit Charly Gaul, but Gaul was not available. Undeterred, JBW made full use of the occasion to renew his acquaintance with the Duchy's other great Tour de France hero, Nicolas Frantz.

In similar fashion, finding himself in Antwerp two days after Paris–Roubaix, JBW sought out reigning World Champion, Stan Ockers. Two French journalists had got there first, however, so he walked down the road to Georges Ronsse's café.

As for the legendary Eugène Christophe, Wadley was the first English journalist ever to interview him, and again you have the impression that he just happened to be in Malakoff, on the outskirts of Paris, that fortuitous morning, and that both men had the whole day at their disposal.

You don't read interviews like these nowadays – perhaps editors are not willing to indulge their reporters – but it is precisely that relaxed, but informed, quality of Wadley's encounters with men who had shaped Continental cycling's history that makes reading them a pleasure, even 40 years later.

Rest Day in Luxembourg

Only 300,000 people live in the Duchy of Luxembourg, a quarter of them in the fine capital. While Mr. Harold Wilson had come on a matter not unconnected with Charles de Gaulle, my own plans included a visit to see Charly Gaul. To track my man down the first morning call was to the Syndicat d'Initiatives – a most helpful organisation in most Continental countries – where I got the address of Jan Goldschmit, who I found at his café in the picturesque fishmarket area.

Jan Goldschmit rode several Tours de France finishing five times in the first 20, his best place being eighth. He won two stages, in 1949 and 1950, the second being the 350-kilometre stretch from Paris to Metz. Jan was twice first in his national tour, once second in the Tour of Switzerland in which event he won seven stages over the years. He is well known and respected for this good record, but his name is now usually associated with a Tour de France feat accomplished after his retirement.

In 1958 Jan Goldschmit was director of the Luxembourg–Holland team, one of their number, Charly Gaul, winning in sensational style. The two men have remained close friends, and on hearing my story, Jan was soon on the phone to Charly asking if he could spare time to see an English journalist who had just arrived from Ostend by bicycle. It seemed that I had caught Charly on a busy day – something to do with a brand-new Jaguar he had recently piled up – but I could call round at six o'clock.

In Goldschmit's café is this fine photo of Gino Bartali, autographed for his friend. Bartali is seen here using a Campagnolo gear in which the wheel moves along the rear ends as the sprocket changes, the chain taking up the correct tension at once.

"Don't forget what I told you," said Jan as I left. "It's no good asking where Gaul lives if you pronounce it as they do in France. You must say 'Gowl'."

It so happened that when I went back at six Charly was still not at home, and still not back at ten. But my journey to Luxembourg was by no means wasted, for the tiny Duchy has provided two other Tour de France winners – François Faber (1909) who was killed during the first world war, and Nicolas Frantz, first in 1927 and 1928.

Nicolas Frantz is still with us, and to find him I rode back for five miles along my overnight route to Mamer, where he keeps a cycle shop. He remembered me from the 1955 Tour de France when he directed the Luxembourg mixed team in which Gaul and Russell Mockridge were team-mates.

I found 67-year-old Nic a picture of health, and over an aperitif in his comfortable home at the back of the shop, he recalled some highlights of his great career.

"My first race? It was in this village where I was born. It was on 25 June 1914; I was 14 years of age; a kermesse; I won it using a gear of 48 x 18. I didn't really get going, though, until after the war finished and racing was resumed in France and Belgium. In 1922 I rode the Independent Tour of Belgium. The first stage was from Brussels to Huy and I won in a sprint finish from Verelst and Gérard Debaets, who later became a great six-day and motor-paced rider. The Belgian papers were not impressed: 'Who is this young Frantz, anyhow?' they asked. 'A sprint win can be lucky. We wonder how he will fare in the tougher stages to come.'"

"The second stage finished here in Luxembourg. I won again – this time by 14 minutes. The papers now admitted I wasn't bad after all. But for all the good it did me, I might just as well have saved my energy and won in a sprint again. The race was decided on points, and the 14 minutes didn't mean a thing. I eventually won the five-stage race by 23 points to the 29 of Dewaele."

During his career, Nicolas Frantz was to win many big single-day races, including Paris–Brussels and Paris–Tours. It is, however, as a Tour de France rider that he is most famous. Indeed, his record in six Tours is quite remarkable. With 21 stage wins Frantz stands third* in the list behind Leducq and Darrigade; and on general

*He now lies fifth, the list being headed by Merckx and Hinault.

classification he was twice first, twice second, once third and once fifth.

"I suppose you had your share of adventures," I remarked. "Did you have to do any blacksmith work like poor Christophe in the 1913 Tour?"

"No, the Tour was by then humanised to an extent, but there were still many strange rules. In 1928, for instance, I won the first stage and kept the yellow jersey right through to Paris – only Bottecchia, in 1924, had done this before. With three stages to go, though, I nearly lost it. My frame broke at a level-crossing. The rules said I could take a bike from a spectator provided it was not the same *marque* as my own, or one of its subsidiaries. If I took an Alcyon which I was riding, or a Labor, Armor or Thomann I would be penalised an hour! I had an hour and a half lead on general classification but didn't want to risk that. They found me a Peugeot girl's bike, complete with mudguards and rear lights. I rode that, lost 28 minutes of my lead in 100 kilometres, but still won the Tour by 51 minutes from Leducq.

"Gears? No derailleurs, of course; Desgrange wouldn't accept them for the Aces, although some of the *touristes-routiers* used them. We had 47 or 48 chain-wheels on the front and double-cogged free wheels of 17–18. In mountainous regions we had 43 and 22–24. They used to call me a *coureur complet*. I was pretty good at everything. Bottecchia was a terrific climber, but, strangely for an Italian, he couldn't descend.

"My greatest joy, as a rider, was to win the Tour twice. My greatest disappointment was not to have won a World Championship, although I honestly believe I was first over the line in 1929 at Zürich. In the sprint many spectators saw me first, ahead of Ronsse and Binda – but the judges gave it to Ronsse.

"Now I must leave you. Somebody's just come in the shop to buy his boy a bike. I hope he'll keep cycling all his life, and not pack it up after a year as most youngsters do nowadays."

A few days later I saw Georges Ronsse, gave him Frantz's kind regards, and asked him about that 1929 sprint. "Yes," Georges agreed, "it was close – but I just won."

Sporting Cyclist, May 1967

The Champion who Learned
to Ride at Shepherd's Bush

When wishing to impress on our friends how popular cycle-racing is in Belgium, we often say that every other café is owned by a champion or an ex-champion *coureur*. While this may be an exaggeration in general, it is true of particular areas – of *rouleurs*, in West Flanders, for instance, where there is a whole group of them with names like Hector Martin, Valère Olivier and Maurice Blomme over the doors.

But Antwerp is the city where they do things in a big way. There the champions are not just local champions, or even merely champions of Belgium, they are current or ex-*wereldkampioenen*. Outside the Sportpaleis there is the establishment kept by Karel Kaers, who took the title in 1934 and subsequently became well-known to London track fans through his extraordinary exploits in the Wembley six-day races. And in the middle of the city, within 50 metres of each other, are two cafés whose owners between them have won three world professional road titles.

In the Winter issue of *Coureur* I gave an account of my visit into one of these to talk to Stan Ockers. Two days after Paris-Roubaix I was in Antwerp again, and in the afternoon looked in at Stan's place for a coffee. The distinguished owner was "bagged" by two French journalists to whom he was relating his misadventures in the "Hell of the North" and outlining his future programme. And so, instead of having my coffee *chez* Ockers, I walked about 30 metres up the road and had it in the second of these renowned cafés.

On the wall on the left as I entered was a coloured picture of the owner, Georges Ronsse, wearing the rainbow jersey that he won two years in succession in 1928 and 1929. Below the picture was a life-sized head and shoulders statue of Ronsse in bronze, presented to him from the proceeds of a public subscription on his retirement from racing in 1938. For even if Ronsse had never been World Champion, he would nevertheless still have been one of the greatest roadmen Belgium has produced.

The safest way to interview any well-known cyclist is to start at the beginning. Often the "early days" material would be interesting enough if one were writing the complete life story of the subject in book form, but is relatively unimportant when the aim is to condense the highlights into a short article. Nevertheless, the interviewer is able to keep track of his man and note the various small factors that have had their influence in building him up into a champion.

Right away I found that the "early days" of Georges Ronsse were far from dull. Indeed, my very first question revealed the fact that he had not learned to ride a bicycle around the back street of Antwerp, but in London!

"I was born in Antwerp in 1906," Ronsse said, "but I went to England with my parents as refugees during the 1914–18 war. At first we lived in Basingstoke, but then we moved to No. 1, Askew Crescent, Shepherd's Bush. I went to school in Ealing.

"Of course, I wanted a bike and my father bought me a Rudge-Whitworth with a back-pedalling brake. I was always tearing about the streets, and on Saturdays I used to go with some friends for trips out into the country – I can't remember the names of the places."

The year after the Armistice, the 13-year-old future World Champion returned with his parents to Antwerp where he resumed his schooling. On the Rudge he also resumed his cycling, experiencing for the first few days the obvious difficulties of riding on the right hand side of the road. Clattering over the *pavé*, he soon fell in line with other boys of his age in pretending to be Philippe Thys or Firmin Lambot, then carrying all before them in the resumed Tour de France. (Incidentally, Lambot still lives a few hundred metres up the road from Ronsse and Ockers, but he's not in the café business.)

A customer of his father (who kept a garage) saw the youngster on his Rudge and told Mr. Ronsse that his son had the makings of a good bike-rider, but wanted a more suitable machine. By a coincidence – an astute man, evidently – the customer had just the very bike to sell, and it duly became the property of Georges Ronsse junior.

Thus equipped, the 14-year-old youngster began his racing career and, like so many others who eventually reached the top, he was a failure.

"It was not just a case of not being able to win the races, or to get a place, I couldn't even finish them," Ronsse explained. "Although my father had been giving me a certain amount of encouragement, he was a realist, and eventually told me that if I couldn't make a better show of it than that, I'd better forget all about racing and start earning my own living. That thought did not appeal to me, at all, so during the week, unknown to my father, I went off to race again, determined to be successful."

The fairy-tale denouement of the Ronsse drama would be that Georges swept to victory in that race, with a proud father breaking through the frenzied spectators, to embrace and forgive his disobedient son. In actual fact, the story is much more romantic: once again the boy failed to finish, and was terrified of going home to face his father. Thoughts of running away entered his head, but eventually he plucked up courage. He found his father at dinner, whereupon the following dialogue took place:

"I know you've been racing again; well, what sort of a show did you put up this time? Come on, now. Out with it."

"I finished thirteenth."

"Hmm. That's better. Where's the prize?"

"They only gave twelve prizes."

If George Washington never told a lie, Georges Ronsse had just told a whopper. With an uneasy conscience he lay awake most of the night, dreading the morning when his father would learn the facts from the newspaper.

But, luckily for Ronsse, and for the whole of Belgium come to that, the paper only gave the first twelve finishers, and the young-ster was allowed to continue racing. Had his father known the truth, Georges would never have been allowed to race again. Eventually, in that first year, he managed to land a second prize. The hoodoo broken, the following year's record of performances reads much more like that of a future *wereldkampioen*: ten first places. In 1922 the total was 14, and in '23, by coincidence, the tall, thin 17-year-old youth from Antwerp, crossed the line the winner of no fewer than 23 races.

Conveniently for a reporter, Georges Ronsse today has all his chief successes neatly tabulated on a duplicated sheet. In the short time available for our interview I was therefore able to glance down the list and question him on any point that came to mind.

Of that impressive list of wins and places, the most important, of course, are his two World Championship wins in successive years, in 1928 and 1929.

When I first came into the cycling game in 1929, news of what was happening abroad was very scanty, and not always reliable. But we gathered that long distance Continental road-racing was not unlike sprint-racing on the track: nine-tenths of the actual distance was a crawl, with a big sprint for the line at the end.

This was, of course, largely true – indeed some road-races in Italy are still run off on those lines – and later on in this Ronsse story we shall see that many of our subject's greatest successes were scored in this way. Yet Ronsse, the roadman-sprinter, could ride unpaced when occasion demanded. His first World Championship win in Budapest was secured by the comfortable margin of 19 minutes from the second man, Nebe. That winning margin was, I believe, the greatest in the world professional series.

Next year, in Zürich, Ronsse made it the "double" – this time by one of the narrowest wins on record in the championships. Ronsse outsprinted Nicolas Frantz and Alfredo Binda by five inches.

In 1930, almost on his home ground at Liège, Ronsse was at the top of his form and all set for a "hat trick" of world titles. A great Belgian crowd was there to see him pull it off. Disaster came early: he punctured, but rejoined after a 20-minute chase, and now, once again, found himself away with Binda. Towards the end they were joined by a third man.

Had the newcomer been Frantz again, or a Swiss or a German or a Frenchman, then Ronsse might still have scored that hat trick. But the man who caught them up was Learco Guerra of Italy. In those days of the world title races – the first was not held until 1926 – team work was not officially recognised, but all the same, the Italians understandably ganged up on their Belgian rival. Ronsse told me about it philosophically.

"It was only to be expected, of course. You saw the other day in Paris–Roubaix how Bernard Gauthier paved the way for Louison Bobet by forcing van Steenbergen to chase. In Liège, Guerra attacked again soon after joining us, and obviously if I were to have any chance of winning again, I had to go after him. When it came to the sprint Binda was fresh enough to win, and I could only finish third."

Although riding French machines throughout his road career – he started with Automoto and then moved to La Française – his World Championship wins were scored with the help of a German made Torpedo coaster (back pedalling) two-speed gear, giving the equivalent of 47 x 17 and 47 x 18 gears.

Next on the list of Ronsse successes comes his series of wins in the classics. It was particularly interesting to talk to him about Paris–Roubaix, the race I had seen only two days previously, and about Bordeaux–Paris, the race I hoped to follow in six weeks or so. Ronsse knows all about both these races: he won Paris–Roubaix in 1927 and his record of three wins in four years in the "Derby of the Road" was an epic achievement in the 63-year history of the race.

We talked first of the "Derby" – the race of the changing formula over its near 600 kilometres. How was it run off in Ronsse's day?

"There were 15 riders accepted for the race," he explained. "The start was on the outskirts of Bordeaux at eight o'clock on the Saturday night, and we kept pretty well together in the early stages which was an ordinary mass-start event. We didn't pick up our pace until 200 kilometres later. Pacing in my day was done by other riders on single bicycles.

"Those pacing riders were not, as many people imagine nowadays, placed at intervals along the road to pick the rider up. Each competitor had ten pacers, split into two teams of five. Each team of five 'nursed' their rider for 20 kilometres, riding in front and on either side of him, according to the direction of the wind. Then they were replaced by the other five who had leap-frogged ahead in a motor lorry.

"It was mid-summer, the roads were very dusty, and in the early stretches of the paced section there would therefore be 15 competitors and 75 pacemakers kicking up a dust, not to mention the 15 team lorries that were trying to get ahead to take up the fresh pacing teams. These were the days when you really needed goggles, and did not just carry them around for show!

"We were not allowed to ride Torpedo gears; fixed wheels were compulsory. I used to ride 47 x 17. We were certainly saddle-sore after about 20 hours riding, but we soon got over that.

"With single gears and pacing teams of near enough equal ability, it was difficult for any rider to take substantial margin. In all three "Derby" races that I won, I had four or five other riders with me when we arrived at the old Parc des Princes track, which was much bigger than now.

"On arrival at the gates of the velodrome, the pacemakers had to go straight on and we turned into the tunnel leading on to the track. The regulations laid down that the lap (666 metres) and the extra distance (120 metres) had to be covered on a track machine, and there was a mad scramble off the road bike to grab the other. As you can imagine, after twiddling a 47 x 17 for nearly 20 hours it was a big jump suddenly to find yourself on a 24 x 7.

"Towards the end of the 1927 Bordeaux–Paris I thought I was going to win in a break-away, I felt so strong. Too strong, in fact, because 60 kilometres from the finish I dropped my pace-makers up a hill. Of course, they came back, but still with the 'enemy' near at hand, and it was a sprint finish at the Parc. I beat Benoit by five centimetres.

"My next win, in 1929, was more decisive, but not what you might call a break-away. There were four or five of us together for the final lap at the Parc, and this time I managed to win by five metres from Hector Martin. Nicolas Frantz and Jef Demuysere were placed, I think."

Ronsse's third Bordeaux–Paris win was particularly notable because he was involved in a terrific duel with Francis Pélissier, who himself had already won the "Derby" on two occasions, and was trying hard for a third as he approached the end of his long and notable racing career. Verdict: a win for Ronsse by 50 metres from Pélissier.

In 1931 the formula of Bordeaux–Paris was once again revised. Instead of teams of pacing "singles" taking over early on the Sunday morning, ordinary road motor-cycles were introduced. But although Ronsse started the race, he never survived to pick up the new form of pacing.

After riding for only an hour on the Saturday night, he punctured, and that was the signal for a general attack by the other riders who felt certain that if Ronsse was allowed to come back easily, then more than likely he would win the race for the fourth time.

And so all night long Ronsse chased on his own – at one point being 1 hr. 20 mins. in arrears – until after 220 kilometres of solitary effort, he at last managed to get on, ten kilometres before the paced section started at Orléans. Whereupon he immediately punctured again, and one can understand why the race favourite failed to make contact with his pace-maker.

If Bordeaux–Paris was the race Ronsse won three times by narrow margins, Paris–Roubaix was that which he lost three times by narrow margins. He started the series brilliantly enough, winning in one of his characteristically fast finishing bursts by ten inches from J. Curtel.

But from then on his luck was out in the Easter classic – out, that is to say, when it came to the final sprint because *en route* between Paris and Roubaix he enjoyed a certain measure of luck in successfully surviving the tram-lined, cobbled, dirt cyclepath road to "hell". In 1928 he went down to André Leducq, the popular Frenchman who was later to win the Tour de France on two occasions. A flat tyre hampered his effort, but he was still able to finish second, ahead of 13 others involved in the final scramble.

After breaking away after Arras with Meunier and another rider, Ronsse had every reason to believe he would win, in 1929 – that he would sprint his way to win his second Paris–Roubaix. On the last lap of the cinder circuit surrounding the local football pitch, he fell, smashing his bike. While Meunier pedalled over the line an easy winner, Ronsse ran the final metres cyclo-cross fashion to take second place.

Yet another second in 1932, this time for an unusual reason.

"I was in the lead with a small group including my great rival Romain Gijssels. Then I got news that one of my team-mates, Jean Aerts, was not far behind. Thinking he would be a useful aid to me in the sprint finish, I waited back and then took him up to the front. Near the end I asked Aerts to lead me out in the sprint, but he refused, saying he wanted to try to win himself. That made me mad, because without my help Aerts certainly would never have got up with the leading bunch. So when it came to the sprint I felt bound not only to beat Gijssels, but to stop my own team-mate from winning. I managed one of the jobs – Aerts did not win – but I failed to beat Gijssels, and I was second again.

"As in Bordeaux–Paris, we used a gear of 47 x 17; indeed, that was the gear used for most of the single-day events. The only exception was Paris–Tours, but not for the reason you may think. Nowadays Paris–Tours is the fastest race of the year over comparatively flat roads. In those days, instead of going straight to Tours, there were long detours through the hills, and so we used to use 47 x 18."

Although nobody can accuse Ronsse of living in the past on most matters, he does not think much of the large number of gears to be found on the modern roadman's machine.

"Ten gears on a bike? That's all nonsense, I think. It is one of the reasons for the declining interest in road-racing. Instead of there only being the very strongest riders left at the end of a race, there are nowadays many second-class riders there as well, whose big gears have enabled them to follow the wheels. Three gears if you like, but not ten. A car has only three gears and can climb anything; what does a bike rider want with ten?

"I believe that for economic and sporting reasons there will be a return to single gear racing in the future. In any case, I don't much like the derailleur system of gears. I reckon the hub system, like your B.S.A. and Sturmey, is much better: it doesn't get damaged in an accident and you don't have to bother about the weather."

Similarly, Ronsse does not altogether agree with the extremes to which the "scientific" trainers are going in their efforts to bring out the best in their riders.

"Nowadays the riders are told that eggs are bad for them. Well, they weren't bad for me. I won Bordeaux–Paris three times with eggs as my principal means of nourishment. I ate 68 eggs in one 'Derby'. Raw eggs, of course, cracking them on the handlebars and throwing away the whites. How can eggs have been good for us, and bad for the modern rider?

"Everybody is taking vitamins nowadays, too – concentrated horse's blood and all that kind of thing. Sure, horse's blood is good for you. When I was racing, I used to eat lots of horse meat for preference.

"Having spent four years in England where you have such big breakfasts, I never had any trouble eating a big meal of horse-steak before a raced. I still like my English breakfast of bacon and eggs. During races I used to drink lots of tea, well sugared but without milk."

Ronsse looks back with pleasure on his four years in England, but regrets that he never raced there when at the top of his form. He took part in the 1938 six-day race at Wembley, partnered by Karel Kaers, but voluntarily retired in order that Kaers might make a reformed team with the Australian Joe Buckley, the sole surviving "Britisher" in the race. Incidentally Ronsse was a good friend of Hubert Opperman, with whom he raced on many occasions. One of their first meetings was in a Paris–Brussels event. Ronsse "invited Opperman to lead" as the saying is, but Oppy was unwilling to do so. Ronsse had made the invitation in French, which the Australian did not appear to understand. So Ronsse said in English, "If you don't lead, I'll knock you in the ditch." Opperman thereupon led – probably in no way intimidated by the threat, but because he was so startled to hear a Belgian speaking English. Nowadays, of course, every other Belgian speaks our language, but between the wars very few did so.

Ronsse retired from road-racing in 1933, and took up motor-pace following. While his record was a good one at this kind of racing, he by no means hit the heights as he had done on the road. Behind tandems, however, he was unbeatable in the Antwerp Sportpaleis. In 1935 he beat Karel Kaers by ten laps in a challenge match, and the next year in a special record attempt covered 55.444 kilometres in the hour, which stood as an unofficial world record until Stan Ockers rode 56.001 kilometres.

Today, if you go to any indoor track race in Belgium, you will almost certainly see Ronsse in action in some capacity or another. If there is any kind of paced race on the programme, whether behind big motors, scooters, or Dernys, then Ronsse will be one of the pacemakers.

"I like pacing on the scooters," he said. "It's much easier than the Dernys where you have to pedal. And I don't get much time for training nowadays. But I must get out on the bike a little because I hope to pace De Bruyne in Bordeaux–Paris in June."

You'll see Georges Ronsse at the end of most road races, giving an expert's commentary over the Belgian TV system. You'll see Georges Ronsse, too, if you drop in at his café in Antwerp. But make it an afternoon call, because this friendly and modest ex-champion usually is busy until 4 a.m. in his café, and still likes his eight hours sleep.

Coureur, Summer 1956

Christophe – the Greatest Loser of the Tour

It is many years since I last saw the story of Eugène Christophe printed in English, and a new generation has come into our sport which has never heard of his exploits. To them, perhaps, "Christophe" is just the name of a toe-clip, or they may be vaguely aware that he was an "old-timer" of some sort.

In France, however, the name of Christophe is legendary, and before he is very old, a boy born into a sport-loving household has heard from his father or grandfather, the romantic tale of how the "*Vieux Gaulois*" rode 11 Tours de France, finished in eight, never won the race, yet earned a fame far greater than quite half of those who did.

Christophe rode his first Tour in 1906, finishing ninth on final classification. In 1912 he was second to Defraye and, full of confidence, entered the 1913 fray determined to win.

He rode the early stages from Paris out to Cherbourg and down the flat, west coast with caution, ready for a grand assault in the Pyrenees. At Bayonne, overnight stop before the first mountain stage of 326 kilometres, which included four major *cols*, he was second on general classification, 4 mins. 55 secs. behind Defraye, still at the head of affairs.

On the foothills of the Pyrenees, leader Defraye "cracked" and retired. Inspired by this news, Christophe attacked the 7,000-ft. Tourmalet with such force that he dropped everybody except Philippe Thys, who was a few hundred metres ahead. Thys was well behind on "general" at the time and, although the Tour had not yet reached the half-way mark, Christophe sensed that barring accidents the Tour was his.

Barring accidents … On the descent of the Tourmalet, Christophe suddenly noticed his steering was faulty and, jumping from his bike, found that the stem of his front forks had broken.

In 1959 such an incident would cost a rider only a few minutes. In 1913 the penalty was measured in hours and lost fortunes. There were no following cars with spare material. This was the Tour de France, a test for the machine as much as for the man. If the bicycle gave way, then the man had to put it right.

And so, shouldering the body of the bicycle, and grasping the shattered forks and front wheel in the other hand, Christophe walked and ran down the pass, clambering now and then down a goat track through the rocks to cut off a hairpin bend.

After eight kilometres of this enforced cyclo-cross (at which sport Christophe was also a champion) he came to the outskirts of the village of Sainte-Marie-de-Campan, where a woman directed him to the blacksmith's shop.

By this time all his opponents had swept by, and a race *commissaire* had been dropped off to see that the rules were obeyed. And what cruel rules they seem today! Christophe had to repair the stem himself.

Tired, hungry, already sweating from his eight kilometres on foot, Christophe got to work, watched by the *commissaire* and rival managers, who had also gathered to see what they ironically called "fair play". The blacksmith was eager to help the wretched *coureur*, but he knew the penalty might be Christophe's disqualification from the race.

At one point it was impossible for him to work the hand-bellows as his hands were fully occupied with hammer and broken forks. A seven-year-old boy worked the bellows for him, and the *commissaire* penalised him 10 minutes on the spot (it was later reduced to three minutes). Had a spare fork-stem been available, then the job would have been over much more quickly. But Christophe had to shape a piece of metal and then weld it on to the shattered stem. The job took two hours.

With four hours lost, Christophe took to the road again, to arrive at Luchon in last position for the day. Thys had won, and went on to win the Tour. Christophe continued, too, and finished seventh on general classification of the 25 finishers.

All during the 1914–1918 war, Christophe dreamed that when peace came again the Tour would be revived, and he might still achieve his ambition of winning the great event.

Christophe survived the war and, in 1919, he was back in the thick of his own particular battleground, the Tour. After three stages he became race leader at Les Sables d'Olonne in the west of France. He maintained that lead safely through the Pyrenees – with the inevitable memories of the tragedy of 1913 – right up through the Alps and, with two days to go, was still in the lead with half an hour to spare over Lambot.

Then, on the war-battered roads of northern France, came tragedy anew – both front fork blades snapped! And so it was Sainte-Marie-de-Campan all over again. Except that, this time, he was just outside Valenciennes, and a properly equipped workshop was only half a mile up the road.

Again supervised by officials, Christophe drew out the broken blades, brazed in the new which he had obtained from the local bike shop. Timed by a journalist, he lost 1 hr. 10 mins. He finished the 466-km. stage at Dunkirk in last position for the stage. He had lost another Tour de France, finishing third at the Parc des Princes next day to Firmin Lambot.

This is a summary of the misfortunes in the Tour de France of Eugène Christophe, and I have no doubt that many of my older readers will have known it off by heart for years. It is in all the "Tour books" and is frequently featured in articles on the world's greatest sporting dramas.

For my part, I have known the story for 30 years and, to me, Christophe has long been a legendary figure. But just recently I had the privilege of meeting the *Vieux Gaulois*, now 74 years of age, and in the following pages you will read not of Christophe the Legend, but of Christophe the very-much-alive, in whose company I spent the best part of a wonderful day.

*   *   *

I rang the bell of No. 26 in a street at Malakoff which, although only 20 minutes on the Metro and bus from the centre of Paris, is, officially, a country town. There was no answer. I enquired at the butcher's next door.

"Monsieur Christophe?" said the friendly tradesman. "I don't think he can be far away – but wherever he is, you can be sure he'll be on his bicycle. Even if he goes 200 metres down the street to post a letter, he takes his bike!"

After a stroll round the town – *un petit tour de ville* – I returned to find Monsieur Christophe at home, and expecting me, his neighbour having explained that an English journalist was on his track.

"Ah – an Englishman, that's rare. I get journalists from all over the world, but I think you are the first from England."

The famous old warrior of the Tour de France invited me into the living-room. As well he might be, after 2,000 hours hard labour in the Tour, he is slightly bent, but still quick on his feet, and with a lively and (as I was later to discover) tidy mind.

On the way through the hall we passed his everyday bike, a neat little Camille Foucaux job, the flat 'bars fitted with a pair of handlebar-muffs. I noticed with interest that he was riding a Torpedo coaster hub-brake.

"I used to ridicule them when I was racing," he said, "but during the war, when I often carried big bundles across Paris and needed both hands, I found the back-pedalling brake ideal."

M. Christophe apologised for the living-room table being covered with papers. He was just going to write to Garrigou, he explained – Garrigou his friend who had won the Tour de France and other classic races.

"This year is the 50th anniversary of the first Milan–San Remo race," he went on, "and all the former winners who are still living have been invited to a big celebration at Milan. I won in 1910 and

Garrigou the next year. I am writing to make arrangements for us to travel down together."

Milan–San Remo … I must confess I had completely forgotten that Christophe had won the famous Italian classic. For me, as for thousands of others, whenever we hear his name mentioned, our thoughts immediately go and stay with him in the dramas of the blacksmiths' forges and the two Tours that he might have won.

But, in fact, you could wipe Christophe's eleven Tours de France from his record and still be left with a list of achievements worthy of a high place in the annals of old-time racing. I asked him about that Milan–San Remo.

"Hou-la-la – that was a race. It was bitterly cold from the start, and then as we began to climb the Turchino pass, we ran into snow. I was in the lead, but shaking with cold and unable to control the bike on the terribly rough road. I fell into a ditch. Spectators carried me into a cottage and gave me hot drinks and rubbed me all over. They gave me a pair of long trousers to put over my shorts, and I continued. While I had been inside, others had passed by, but I caught them before long, and kept on my own until the finish."

"On his own" is putting it mildly. The next man, Ganna, finished 20 minutes behind, but was disqualified for hanging on to a car, second place going officially to Cocchi who arrived 1 hr. 10 mins. after Christophe.

Nowadays, the smooth-surfaced Turchino presents no difficulty at all and, since the hey-day of Coppi, lone breaks of any duration in Milan–San Remo have never succeeded. Moreover, the winner of a modern "San Remo" of 180 miles is probably racing the next day on the track.

It was far from the case in Christophe's day. Conditions were always so bad – roads inches deep in mud or dust, single gears, heavy tyres which nevertheless were always puncturing – that a man would not want to race for another month after finishing a Classic. In the case of Christophe in 1910, victory in the arctic, early-April Milan–San Remo cost him not just one month's racing, but a whole year, and the best part of another, too.

On returning to Paris, instead of "coming round" as he usually did after four or five days, he found himself without any strength, feverish and barely able to walk. He spent a month in hospital, and did not race any more that season.

Next year, he was still not right, could only manage second place in the Tour of Belgium, and had to abandon the Tour de France through boils.

"But you were all right in 1912!" I remarked.

"Yes, that was probably my best year in the Tour de France. I finished second to Defraye, and had no regrets at the time, but since then I have thought 'if only'. You see, in 1912, the classification was by points. I won the third, fourth and fifth stages, and actually finished the Tour with a lower total time than Defraye. I think that influenced M. Henri Desgrange, the Tour 'boss' to change the formula next year to the time system, which is still used today."

And then, of course, the following year was the famous 1913, the year of the broken forks in the Pyrenees, the four lost hours – the story of stupendous courage that I have already outlined.

I was proud enough to be in the presence of this great old rider, without asking him to relive for the thousandth time, the incident that made cycling history. Every little detail of the day has long since been wrung out of him by eager journalists. I preferred to use my time finding out something of the lesser-known side of those early Tours and Classics. Those were the days of enormously long Tour stages – some of them more than 300 miles – with racing only on alternate days.

At the end of his career, Christophe rode a Tour with shorter stages and racing every day, and found it much easier than the old system which (in theory) gave the rider two nights sleep after every stage. In point of fact, after 12 to 18 hours in the saddle, the first night was often a restless one, and the second – well, the stages mostly started at about 2 a.m., and sometimes 10 p.m., which meant no second night at all.

"Every second of rest counted, though," M. Christophe told me. "I used to have everything ready in the room, like a fireman, so that the moment I was called in the morning, I didn't waste time looking for my clothes and equipment. Shoes, jersey, goggles, shorts and the rest of it were laid out neatly. Then, round my neck in the race, I carried a piece of string with a pencil, so that I could sign the sheets quickly at the control towns, and get going again. Round my neck, too, was a length of tape carrying a little chamois-leather bag. In it was a 20-franc piece, a 10-franc piece, a chain link, nipple key and the details of the route.

Philippe Thys – the only man other than Bobet to win the Tour three times – used to ride up to me and say, "Hello, you enquiry bureau, how far have we to go?"

He was now talking of the days just prior to the 1914–18 war, by which time he was well-established as a star of the Tour. He also spoke of his very first Tour in 1906, and of his contact with the fabulous René Pottier. So far, the big mountains had not been included in the itinerary and when, that year, the 4,000-ft. Ballon d'Alsace, and other climbs, were introduced, many riders would dismount and change their wheels round from the customary fixed, to free. Christophe preferred to use free the whole time.

"Bah – *touriste*!" exclaimed Pottier to Christophe.

"But what a rider he was – he won four stages in succession, and was first at the top of the Ballon d'Alsace with an hour lead over the next man. But – alas – René was missing from the 1907 Tour. He had committed suicide in the February."

By now we had moved into the front room, where he had "something special" to show me. This was a series of photographic plates of the 1912 Tour on the Galibier which, seen through a stereoscopic viewer, gave an extraordinary impression of the grandeur and loneliness of the Giant of the Alps, and of the strength and the courage of the men who urged their simple bicycles over its savage slopes. One of those pictures shows Christophe nearing the end of the climb of the Galibier, which he topped with a 20-minute lead over the next man.

"I had broken away with Jean Alavoine, but then dropped him and rode the Télégraphe and Galibier cols on my own. After Galibier, it was a descent to Grenoble to the finish of the 336-km. stage. Journalists called out that I was 30 minutes ahead, and advised me to take it easily. I did, so as to avoid an accident. But, on reaching Grenoble, hardly had I received the winner's flowers than Lapize arrived. It turned out those journalists were his pals! It was the last year of the points system, you will remember, so my reduced lead on time made no difference on general classification."

Among the other photographs I was shown was one of Christophe in a cycling battalion of the 1914–18 war. The machine was obviously heavy, but the pedalling action at least enabled him to keep the famous legs in trim, and he safely survived the great conflict, determined to win a Tour de France.

From the opening part of this story you will already know that 1919 provided another *déception*, even more cruel perhaps than in 1913, for the broken forks at Valenciennes came when he was race leader, with only one day to go. Yet the *Vieux Gaulois* looks back on 1919 with pride for another reason: during the tour he became the first rider ever to wear the *maillot jaune* of leadership.

Many readers will recall an interview I had in 1952 with Firmin Lambot, and published in *The Bicycle* that year. I understood from M. Lambot that he had the honour of being the first man-in-the-yellow-jersey.

The truth is that, as winner of the Tour that year, he was the first to wear it into Paris, and that our friend, Christophe, was the first ever. He explained how it happened.

"So soon after the war, the cycle industry was not yet in action again, and the only *marque* supplying material was La Sportive, and there was little difference between any of the jerseys they supplied. One day – it was on the 482-km. stage from Les Sables d'Olonne to Bayonne – M. Baugé, an official, remarked to Henri Desgrange that it was difficult enough even for him to pick out the various riders, and the public must find it impossible. Couldn't the race leader wear a special jersey? M. Desgrange thought it a grand idea. They decided, on the spot, to make it a yellow one, that being the colour of the pages of *L'Auto*, the organising newspaper.

"Desgrange telegraphed that night to Paris for them to be made and rushed to the race. They arrived at Grenoble, ten days later, and as I was leading, I was the first wearer. And I was still wearing it at Valenciennes, when the forks broke … That year, only 11 of the 67 starters finished the Tour."

Never two without three, they say, and this indeed proved the case in the sad chapter of Christophe and the broken forks. In 1922, he held the *maillot jaune* for four days, "blew up" in the Pyrenees, and then on the descent of the Galibier in the Alps – bang went the forks again. The rules had now been changed, and he was able to borrow the only bike in sight, a lady's model belonging to the local priest. He changed that to something lighter at St. Michel-de-Maurienne, but was so far behind he quit the race.

In 1925 he rode his last Tour, at 40 years of age, and finished 18th. That was the year Émile Masson, Snr. asked Christophe to punch him in the face so he would not go to sleep!

But let us turn from the Tours de France that he lost, and consider the important one-day Classic races that Christophe won. One was Paris–Tours of 1920, then 340 kms. by a round-about route. The time of 13 hrs. 22 mins. 30 secs. does not sound impressive today, but it was ridden on a 48 x 16 fixed gear with 18-oz. tyres; he won by 15 minutes from Barthélemy after a lone break-away of 106 miles.

But, perhaps, of all his exploits, Christophe is proudest of his two Bordeaux–Paris wins. Certainly the "Derby of the Road" kept cropping up in our conversation, even at a time when I was trying to confine the interview to other topics.

He made contact with the "Derby" very early in his career, acting as one of the team of bicycle-pacers, strung out in twos every 30 kilometres after the half-way mark (the first half being unpaced).

Then, after the war, he entered the scene not as a humble "extra", but as a star of the annual drama that began in 1891 with the victory of Englishman, G. P. Mills. His win in 1920 was a typical Christophe effort, with hours of rain, making conditions ideal for a man who had, in his time, served so many weeks hard labour in the mobile punishment camps of Desgrange's Tour de France.

The race should have finished at the old Parc des Princes track but, with the rain still falling in torrents, *l'arrivée* was switched to the Vélodrome d'Hiver, where Christophe arrived 21 hrs. 33 mins. and 15 secs. after leaving Bordeaux, 572 kilometres away.

That victory proved, more than ever, how right the journalist Victor Breyer had been in calling Christophe "The Man of the Mud". Moreover this same writer had written, "When suffering is called for, Christophe is always there!" The legend of his toughness in the cold, and rain and snow was so firmly impressed on the minds of the sports-loving public, that they could not imagine Christophe shining in the opposite conditions.

The following year, in Bordeaux–Paris, the day was a scorcher, as well the thousands knew who sweltered at the Parc waiting for the road derby to finish. With no electrical announcement system yet in operation, the public were kept informed from time to time by two men walking round the ground and holding up a newsflash chalked on a blackboard. The telegraphed news was scanty, and when several bulletins announced that Christophe was in the lead, well, the crowd thought it was the same old message coming round again, and referring to an earlier part of the race. How could Christophe, the man-of-the-mud, be leading on one of the hottest days of the century? Yet, leading he was. But not until he arrived at the track did the public really believe it, and stand to applaud his splendid win.

"I was dropped early on, after picking up the pace-makers," he explained, "and I was not hopeful of repeating my win. Then, as the day got hotter, and hotter, I refused to drink much water, while my opponents, apparently, were taking bottle after bottle. In normal conditions I would have taken drinks of champagne for the last three, or four hours, but in such heat, I cut that out, too. Again, most of the others took too much of it, became dizzy in the heat, and many, including Henri Pélissier and Mottiat, retired. I did not touch my champagne until the last 30 kms., but stuck to my staple diet – water, bread and sugar."

Christophe finished that remarkable year of 1921 with a very famous second, in the 1,200-km. Paris–Brest–Paris, the world's longest single-stage race.

As we talked, and moved from room to room in M. Christophe's home, the hours passed by. We adjourned to a neighbouring restaurant for lunch. Every British racing man will now take him to their heart when I report that during the inevitable discussion on food, he revealed that he used to start most of his Tour stages with two eggs boiled for five minutes.

"I used to eat lightly at night, and not too much before the stage, then take food regularly every two hours in the race. It paid off. François Faber was a giant of a man and needed a lot of food, but he didn't need six steaks and two eggs and a bottle of red wine which he used to have at night. In my early days in the Tour, he used to dominate me because he had more class. By living carefully, I was able to dominate him, after a few years. Faber was an enormous man with a big, kind heart."

Back at No. 26, we returned to the front room to look at some of the old prizes and trophies. I noticed for the first time an illuminated address, presented to him in 1923 by the U.V.F. (French governing body) for his services "in the encouragement of cyclo-cross-*pédèstre*". Yes, our old friend was one of the pioneers of racing on the footpaths and fields, and a "man of the mud" long before gaining wider fame in the classics and Tours de France.

Christophe was unbeaten in French cyclo-cross championships from 1909 to 1914, and took his seventh title in 1921 as part of his training for the great road-season already described. Needless to say, he recommends all roadmen to "have a go", now and then, to keep their breathing in trim.

Time was getting on. What else did I want to see, or ask?

"Those forks," I said. "Where are they now?"

"The 1913 forks were taken by Peugeot to be examined, and I never saw them again. But I still have the ones I repaired at Valenciennes. Come down to the cellar."

And in the workshop were the forks – the original stem and crown, and the cheap, stamped-out blades he had brazed into them in the forge at Raismes; Christophe the blacksmith, whose apron was a *maillot jaune*.

Once again, the theme quickly switched to Bordeaux–Paris, for lying on a bench, was a curious saddle, a home-made looking job. And that indeed was what it was.

"I used that in Bordeaux–Paris in 1920," the winner told me. "The roads were so bumpy that I wanted something sprung. So I got a Brooks B17 top and fitted it on a three-spring frame which I made myself. I have a B70 on my tandem upstairs, and I think they got the idea from my home-made job."

From this, and other evidence (apart from the incidents of the forges), I could see that Christophe was, and still is, more than useful with his hands. He did not merely "sell his name" to the manufacturer of toe-clips, but made his own in 1912, and then gradually modified them, year by year, until at last, in 1922, he had them manufactured and put on the market.

Christophe invented something else of extreme importance. I quote from my Lambot interview of 1952:

"In the 1911 Tour we were still using ordinary nuts on our hub spindles and brakes which operated on the front tyres," said Lambot. "Then next year came two very important improvements: cable brakes and wing nuts. Wheel removal was still difficult, however, with ordinary fork-ends and chain adjusters. In the middle of the 1912 Tour, Christophe had an inspiration: there was rapid work in the Peugeot factory, and at Perpignan every bike in their stable was fitted with forward opening drop-outs. For a time it was almost a pleasure to puncture!"

I said, earlier, that M. Christophe still has a "tidy" mind. That is why his workshop is tidy, with every tool clean, and in its place. His home is equally in order. I had merely to mention some subject and he would go to a drawer, take out an envelope or a file, marked "Tour 1912" or "Paris–Roubaix 1920" or "Cyclo-cross-*pédèstre*". Every photograph had a neatly written caption on the back.

As I collected together my notebooks and camera, and photographs which he had taken from the files, and prepared to leave, he said, not for the first time during my visit, that he was not a rich man in the monetary sense, but had a wealth of happy memories and good health to show from his riding exertions.

He still rides a lot, and is at most of the touring rallies in the Parisian area, but likes to take it easily. "I have suffered enough on a vélo," he said (but last year he did 115 miles in eight and a half hours, with 12 lb. of luggage, stopping 10 minutes every two hours to eat biscuits, pears and grapes and drink a glass of Vichy water).

"Tell your young readers there are no secret recipes for racing success," were his last words to me. "If there were, then all the champions would be the sons of doctors and chemists."

Sporting Cyclist, May 1959

THE VELODROME

In an editorial celebrating ten years of *Sporting Cyclist,* J. B. Wadley felt able to claim that if the journal had had one significant 'educational' achievement it had been in 'introducing thousands to the pleasures of indoor track racing'. This was not an immodest boast: there had, after all, been a regular flow of articles which not only conveyed his own unabashed enthusiasm for this branch of cycle sport, but also taught us about the intricacies of those tight, steeply-banked arenas and the mechanics of the six-day formula, as well as introducing many of its star exponents.

For JBW himself, the indoor track was not so much a pleasure as a passion – one that he acquired early and which never deserted him. It was, in fact, love at first sight – that first sight of the Olympia boards on which the London six-day was being ridden in June 1934. And yet, as he explains in 'Six Appeal', when he got back to his native Colchester the following morning there was seemingly only one other Rover who could understand how he had managed to become so smitten. He was an older member who had also ridden up to Olympia to watch the race, back in 1923. 'I know,' he said. 'You must see it to believe it.'

Perhaps Wadley remembered those words because, in 1962, *Sporting Cyclist* arranged for 115 readers to go to the Antwerp six-day race. The trip was a success, and many similar visits to various Continental vélodromes were to follow.

For JBW they had been a regular feature from his first reporting days with *The Bicycle.* 'I have almost set up camp at all the major six-day races,' he once remarked and, for him, the delight was to be had not just in the racing, but in the whole atmosphere of the vélodrome. 'First Visit to Ghent' evokes this, on a night when there was virtually no racing to be seen.

'Sprinters…Stayers…Américaines' is, like many of J. B. Wadley's articles, the product of opportunism. Invited, along with a party of journalists, on a winter visit to the Peugeot cycle factory in Eastern France, he simply couldn't resist the chance to drop in to Basle and Zürich, and catch three days of indoor track racing.

First Visit to Ghent

My first visit to Ghent just before the war lasted about half an hour. It came about this way.

During one of the six-day races at Wembley I got to know a French mechanic who invited me to call to see him at his home in Lille if ever I were that way. I eventually accepted the invitation, arriving at about 5 o'clock on a murky November afternoon, and found my friend and two other fellows preparing for a trip in his ancient motor van.

"We're just off to Ghent to see the 100-kilometre *a l'Américaine*," he said. "Want to come? We'll be back by mid-night."

What a chance! For two years when on the staff of *The Bicycle* I had been milking the Belgian and French Press, and radio for results and stories about racing on the Ghent indoor track without ever having been there, or even to Belgium for that matter.

So, after booking an hotel room, I joined the party and we were soon rattling – in every sense of the word – towards the frontier at Mouscron, a few kilometres to the north of Roubaix. The whole trip from Lille to Ghent was little over 40 miles and my friend said we would be there in ample time to get a good seat to see the racing.

But, by the time we got to the customs post, the racing had already started. First, trouble with the plugs. Then a back wheel puncture which had to be mended (in the dark), the spare being useless. Finally, and disastrously, fog. We crawled through Courtrai, where my friend decided to call the whole thing off. But a sudden – and, as it happened, temporary – clearance encouraged him to press on, only to find it thicker than ever at Harelbeke where the River Lys runs close and parallel to the road.

When at last we got to Ghent, a few were already leaving the vélodrome in the same way that spectators do towards the end of a football match, to catch a train, to avoid the crush, or because the result is no longer in doubt. With only 20 minutes to go there was but one official on duty at the gate. He told us the fog had not hit Ghent until just before the meeting started, the vélodrome was packed, but we could go down into the *Middenplein* – or the track centre – if we liked.

We had to negotiate a 1-in-5 descent under the track, then climb immediately at the same rate to get into the centre. I was astonished later to learn that the leaders of a road race had on occasions somehow scrambled through this dangerous tunnel and on to the track for the final sprint.

Astonished I was, too, at the atmosphere inside. A good bit of fog had crept into the building and merged with the smoke of several thousand cigars. It was hardly possible to see the riders on the far end of the track, which was 150 metres and made up of two wide sweeping bends and virtually no straight. In fact, it was very difficult to see any riders at all! The track centre surface was mainly earth, with a high point in the middle formed by a concrete oblong on which the wise early arrivals among the spectators had taken up their positions. The only spot we could find was in a sunken patch of earth affording perhaps 30% visibility at the best of times, and only 20% in that smog.

Not that there was much action to see. The battle of the 100 kms. was over; the leading pairs were on the defence. I think Karel Kaers was one of the winning team.

International Cycle Sport, January 1971

Sprinters…Stayers…Americaines

The Basle vélodrome is housed in the Sporthalle, a long narrow building which determines the layout of the 166-metre, 10 laps to the miles track, for whereas the late burned-out "saucer" at Ghent was virtually without straights in order to squeeze it into the Floral Hall, that at Basle is all straight and very little banking. It looked very similar to the first indoor track I ever saw, at Olympia, where in 1934, Piet Van Kempen and Sid Cozens won the London "Six".

There is a general happy air of improvisation about the place: a tight spiral staircase takes some customers up to seats high above one banking and to get into the Press box I had to climb a vertical ladder. All the seats were plain wooden benches on tubular scaffolding. There must be 50 halls as big as this in Britain where a track and spectator accommodation could be built.

I climbed that ladder behind Mr. Walter Jacobs of *Sport–Zürich*, an old friend of the Tour de France. He told me that until two or three years ago the track had a bad reputation, and many riders would just not accept contracts there on the grounds that it was dangerous. "But now the bankings have been altered a bit and it is perfectly safe. There is rarely a crash," he said.

All the same, the track requires special ability and some sprinters, notably Gaiardoni and Maspes are uneasy on it. At any rate, the World Champion and his predecessor had originally been down to ride the international *sprinterrennen*, but had withdrawn with two days to go.

Down in the track centre I chatted with Oscar Plattner, looking half his 42 years. He deplored the absence of the Italians. "Of course it is easier for us when they are not here. But they rarely race on the foreign winter tracks, and promoters are unwilling to put on sprint races without the World Champion whom the public want to see. That is why the sprint game is in a bad way. The trouble is that Gaiardoni and Maspes are both so well paid by their sponsors that they don't need the contract money and are able to concentrate on building up for the World Championships."

Oscar and his fellow professionals were sitting in a small enclosure at the foot of one banking. Along at the other was a busier scene, for here were 30 or more amateurs, local youngsters and members of the "inter-city" match Basle–Zürich–Amsterdam.

If this had been an entirely amateur meeting, it would have been well worth while making the journey to Basle. The youngsters rode the popular omnium – over scratch, points and devil-take-hindmost – in energetic style, tearing up the straights into the step bankings with the utmost confidence, and out of them in no time at all.

The orange jerseys of the Dutchmen dominated the inter-cities match. Indeed, in the "Devil", contested by the twelve riders, they all but "orange-washed" the Swiss teams, by taking the first three and the fifth places (on such a small track the devil takes his victim every other lap). They swept the track, too, in the three-kilometre team pursuit. Three teams of four on a ten-laps-to-the-miler!

The four fine lads in orange jerseys rode their lap of honour to the strains of "Tulips from Amsterdam" and then all stopped in the home straight to hand their bouquets to a lady who already had one on her lap, a very special bouquet which marked an historic occasion. It was the last one that would ever be presented to her husband, Jan Derksen, who had just ridden his last race. It was a lap of honour in the truest sense of the word, too, for Jan has brought honour to himself and his country for more than 25 years, and spectators, riders, officials, journalists – everybody in the building, in fact – stood to applaud the final lap of a great sport and gentleman.

Derksen did not win the professional sprint, little Gaignard of France taking the *Grosser Preis der Nationen* from Plattner and Potzernheim – all of whom were anxious for news of Reg Harris.

I asked if this tiny track demanded any big alterations in positions; I learned that apart from lowering the saddles half an inch, and using slightly lower gears (23 x 7, or 88) they rode their normal bikes. They told me, too, that the long straight did not mean that a sprinter could win from behind unless he had real class, the tight bankings giving a great advantage to the lower man.

The big attraction of the meeting was the *Winter-Welt-Championat der Steher*, the winter World Championship for stayers. The event had no official recognition, but one could not argue that the best men in the business had kept away, as in the case of the sprinters. The list of riders was headed by World Champion Leo Proost and the men who occupied that position immediately before him – Timoner (Spain), Marsell (Germany) and De Paepe (Belgium). In addition there were 17 – yes *seventeen* – other motor-pace followers on the bill, by far the biggest list engaged on any track in the world.

The 20 stayers contested four heats of 80 laps (eight miles) each on the Friday night, and I awaited the first of these with impatience. I always enjoy a motor-paced race on a properly banked track, and I could hardly wait to see five of them on the track at once – a track a third of the size of Herne Hill or Fallowfield!

By the end of the evening I had seen the four heats and I had not been disappointed. The spectacle of those 20 riders all giving of their best behind the normal-shaped pacing machines (though with a German moped engine) rushing and buzzing round the tiny track was magnificent. In reading the results of such events at Basle I had always imagined that there would be little passing, and that a race might well end in the order of starting. On my first night there I could not keep count of the number of successful attacks: often two riders engaged in a side-by-side battle would be forced into attacking a third just ahead, and there would then be three of them momentarily side-by-side on that 55-degree banking. Behind, of course, there would be a fourth opportunist hovering, his wily pacemaker winding up the pace, ready to pounce and pass the three of them in one terrific sprint when he sensed his rivals were suffering from their efforts.

An *entraineur*, or pacemaker, is always an important man, and nowhere more than on the Basle track where his skill provides a splendid spectacle for the public, and a safe passage for his follower.

The four heat winners were world champion Leo Proost, Fritz Gallati, Paul De Paepe and Guillermo Timoner. Each race had been thrilling and fast, a fast rider lapping in under 10 seconds. Yet the average speed of each winner was only just over 34 m.p.h., which I knew to be no faster than events behind Dernys on the same track, with the cyclists riding normal forks. Later I talked about this with Paul De Paepe.

"Yes," Paul agreed. "The times show that the riders behind Dernys go as fast as we do. But you must remember that the Derny follower can keep right down on the line, and he rides little over the distance of 166 metres each lap. But the 'stayer' has to ride higher, and perhaps rides an extra 10 metres a lap."

From the look of their chainwheels it seemed that there was a wide difference in the gears used by the pace followers. This was not so. The size of gears is strictly controlled so as to keep the pace down, otherwise there would be a danger of riders going over the top, as happened so frequently in Germany in the early days of pace-following before restrictions were imposed. The combinations actually permitted are: 27 x 8 or 54 x 16, and 64 x 19. This works out at 91 inches, and when I heard this I marvelled more than ever at their suppleness. De Paepe told me that riders sit a little further back than on normal tracks to keep their back wheels down.

The following night, Saturday, the crowd was bigger, about 4,000 being there, some 2,500 below capacity. The programme was roughly the same as Friday – local amateurs, inter-city amateurs (with Amsterdam again winning), pro sprinters – and the stayers. When I arrived, one of the Dutchmen had fallen in a team time trial (the only fall I saw in eight hours' racing) and there was a ten-minute delay when the pedal-damaged lath on the banking was repaired. Some riders lent a hand with the carpentry, while others sandpapered other rough edges in the way that cricketers might smooth a pitch during a pause in play.

After thrilling qualifying races, *six* men lined up for the the motor-paced final over 120 laps. Again there was action all the way and when Timoner took over the lead after six miles or so (about half-way) it seemed that he would stay there. But Proost is a stayer worthy of his world championship jersey. For 20 laps he attacked Timoner, without success, but had the courage and reserve to resist the opportunist attacks of De Paepe and Gallati from behind. Then in the very last lap a supreme effort got him by, to the roared applause from the crowd, who also showed their disapproval of Marsell, who finished last, seven laps behind.

It was 11 p.m. when the Saturday meeting was over, and I had now but little time to make a final decision on a matter of conscience. Many months ago I had accepted an invitation to attend the Yorkshire Cycling Federation lunch at York. Although I had already phoned Roy Green to take my place and sent a telegram of apology, it was still possible to fly back from Basle to London and then north to arrive in time for the Yorkshire pud.

I stayed in Switzerland – and I think even a Yorkshireman in my place would have done the same! Fifty miles away, on the Hallenstadion track in Zürich on Sunday afternoon, was the European 100-km. Madison championship.

Going from the improvised track at Basle, to the tailor-made Hallenstadion is like moving from a prefab into a palace, from a do-it-yourself collection of board and scaffolding to an architect-designed theatre of sport. The track is as wide as a street, the great smooth bankings turning gracefully and merging without fuss or bother into the straights. This is the indoor Vigorelli, the fastest indoor track in the world, that on which our own Reg Harris broke the world standing start kilometre record in 1957 with 1 min. 8 secs.

And yet, after Basle, this 250 m. perfection seemed enormous, and the riders warming up as I arrived seemed to be creeping, which they most certainly were not. But if Basle favours the spectacular rider, Zürich allows the best man to win. As Plattner had already told me: "Nobody can ever blame the Zürich track if he does not win." Our friends in the orange jerseys were there again, this time eight of them representing Holland in a match against Switzerland. There was a tandem match, too, and the sprints (which the Dutch pair won) were fast, safe and regular. The tit-bit of the match was a splendid team-pursuit in which the Dutch quartet covered the 4,000 metres in 4 mins. 35.9 secs.

While in the track centre I met Robin Buchan, the Norwood Paragon star, who is now working in Lucerne. Robin had brought along an Indian colleague to see his first cycle-race meeting. He returned to his seat outside the track to explain the complications of an *américaine* (madison) to his friend.

On a smaller track the task would have been a difficult one, but on Zürich's 250 m. it was not so bad. On the 150 m. and 160 m. tracks laps are won and lost in bewildering fashion; on those of 250 metres the job takes longer.

Fifteen teams were engaged to ride the 100-km. *Americaine-Europa-Kriterium*, including last year's winners, van Steenbergen–Lykke, "Rik" having won it the four years previous to that with Severyns. Would the great van Steenbergen win for the sixth time? Within a quarter of an hour we knew he would not. Young Lykke, soon to be his son-in-law, was riding brilliantly, but old Rik was having an off-day. Peter Post and Pfenninger were the dictators, bursting the field with frequent powerful attacks. The only team that could go with them were the Germans, Bugdahl and Renz, and for the greater part of the race these two pairs were sharing the lead, usually one lap ahead of the rest.

The issue, clearly, would be between Post–Pfenninger and Bugdahl–Renz. Post launched a dozen attacks, but the team lost ground to the chasing Germans every time Pfenninger took over. One got the impression that the crowd would have been sorry if their local hero and his Dutch team-mate had succeeded, for then they would have been denied the tit-bit of the day: if Post–Pfenninger were a lap up, there would be no need to contest the sprints (the only ones in the race) every lap from 70 laps to the finish.

So with 70 laps to go, both teams had to sprint it out to decide the destiny of the 1963–4 honours – and what a tremendous spectacle it was as in the maelstrom of 30 pairs of whirring wheels, hand-slings and "sower" changes, Post sent his Swiss team-mate into spectacular last-lap sprints. And neither were they the only teams involved in the seriousness of the occasion, for all the teams at one lap had to be separated, too, and the mix-up was terrific.

Apart from Pfenninger's domination of his German rivals, the feature of the last 70 laps was the splendid sprinting of Lull Gillen, the popular Luxembourger who remains one of the best men in the business, despite the fact that he has ridden in every World Championship since 1946 – sprints, pursuit and on the road.

It had not been a great championship (watched by only 5,000 spectators; the stadium holds 13,000), chiefly owing to the absence of stars like van Looy and Altig and Reg Arnold who twice took the title. The winning time of 2 hrs. 1 min. 2.4 secs. tells the tale of long, quiet periods; in a go-all-the-way 100-km. team race in the Hallenstadion they get down to 1–55.

Result:

1. Pfenningen–Post	28 pts
2. Bugdahl–Renz	5
At one lap	
3. Tiefenthalter–Gillen	23
4. May–Roggendorf	14
5. Eugen–Gallati	10
6. Scraeyen–Aerenhouts	0
7. van Steenbergen–Lykke	0

Sporting Cyclist, March 1964

Six Appeal

The first six-day race in Britain for 15 years will be run during the Cycle and Motor-cycle Show.

"Where's Wadley, today?" they would ask of a Saturday night at Ted Hawkins' cycle shop in Colchester in the early 30s.

"He's riding up to London."

"I wonder what he'll bring back this time!"

For some time I had been noted for those Saturday rides in search of something newly advertised but not yet seen on a Rovers' club run. The very first "prize" I brought back was a suede zip jacket; the second a Continental sweater.

On another later expedition I might have been seen pedalling out in the morning through Marks Tey on a 69 fixed, and twelve hours later coming back on one of three gears. This had been a difficult mission. Firstly to persuade Constrictors at Forest Gate to sell me, retail, one of their freshly imported "Super Champion" Oscar Egg gears; secondly to get F. J. Sanders of Leytonstone to fit it on a busy Saturday afternoon.

In June 1934 I was missing again from the usual Saturday night rendezvous.

"Where's Wadley?"

"He and Albert have ridden to London to see the six-day race."

"Well, they can't bring *that* back!"

But we did, you know. We brought back an enthusiasm for six-day racing. I haven't seen Albert since 1952, at the last Wembley "six", but I'll bet we'll meet again at Earls Court and will talk of that famous ride to London 33 years ago.

We left our bicycles at Romford, Albert and I, and somehow found our way to Olympia by train and bus. We paid 1s. 6d. at the turnstiles, hurried to our places high up in the back straight, looked down and just gaped.

Not that we were complete peasants, even though grass-track handicap riders. We had even been to Herne Hill!

We gaped, though the riders were then ambling round at a walking pace. It was the track, a white squashed "O" with bath-tub bankings at each end that left us open-mouthed. Herne Hill, we knew, was seven laps to two miles; this Olympiadrome was ten-to-one.

Four hours later we stood and cheered wildly as Piet van Kempen and Sid Cozens rode their lap of honour. We roared even louder when the American promoter Willy Spencer asked over the mike if we wanted another six-day race. Albert and I, and most of the crowd, I think, would have emptied our pockets there and then if Willy had come round with the hat to raise the wind for his next promotion.

We rode back through the night from Romford on the A12, which now, with Ingatestone, Chelmsford, Witham and Kelvedon bypassed has become the fast E8 course. We continued beyond Colchester on to the Clacton road just in time to see the first man off in the Rovers' open "25". Riders, officials, lookers-on thought the lack of sleep had driven us crazy. What on earth were we babbling about – jams, primes, Kilian, Vopel, Cozens, van Kempen gaining laps, and Charly Winter snatching a woman's hat and somebody else an umbrella? How could a six-day race be exciting? It must be as dull as ditch-water. Why didn't we have a nap in the meadow for an hour? We could still see the first man finish, they said.

But an older member, one of the Kettle brothers, came to our rescue.

"I know how excited you are," said Alf. "I rode up with some of the boys to see the 1923 race at Olympia. I tried to tell them back here how thrilling it was, but it was no use. You must see it to believe it."

Two years later a score of my doubting colleagues saw and believed. They went to the first of the Wembley sixes, and went back home to Colchester just as crazy about it all as Albert and I had been. They were there again in 1937, '38 and '39 … and some of them in '51 and '52. Now, I'm told, two of them are about to be taken to Earls Court by their sons who haven't yet seen a six-day race in Britain, but have been to many a *Six Jours, Zesdaagse* or *Sechs Tagen* on the continent. Inevitably, there will be family arguments about the merits of Peter Post and Piet van Kempen … and also about the formula of the 1967 Skol International which will be different from those Olympia and Wembley promotions.

When, in 1936, I joined the staff of the newly launched weekly, *The Bicycle*, and saw a lot of indoor track racing on the Continent, I found the Belgians and French quite satisfied with the classic mixtures of "Sprints, Jams and Primes". The idea of the whole thing was to find the team which rode the farthest in 144 hours, and the emphasis was on *La Chasse*, or the Jam as we were calling it at Wembley.

In 1937, however, at Wembley, two helpings of spicy stuff were added to the traditional mixture: we had individual time trials over one lap and one mile (ten laps) and these proved very popular with the big proportion of club folk among the spectators. One of the greatest things I have ever seen in cycle sport was Karel Kaers's flying mile during the 1938 event.

Ten years later I found Kaers, two or three stones heavier, in his café outside the Antwerp Sportspaleis. Inside the great building I watched the new Kaers, Rik van Steenbergen, paired with Marcel Kint, mixing it with Schulte–Boyen and Bruneel–Debruycker in chases that sometimes lasted three hours. I hardly left the trackside from two in the afternoon until two in the morning.

Shortly afterwards I saw practically every racing hour of the 1947 Paris and Ghent sixes, and it was the same story: the Chase was all important. A chase still went on even though the official "sprint time" had arrived; there were a few freak sprint results when an obscure rider somehow, in the maelstrom, happened to be an inch or two ahead of the unbeatable Bruneel over the line. What did it matter? Points were not worth much.

When eventually Antwerp and Brussels introduced Derny-paced racing into the closing hours, it was not to relieve the monotony of the proceedings, but to break up the influence of the "Blue Train".

(This was the coterie of big teams controlling the race, who helped themselves to the big primes, which they shared afterwards, and generally had the thing sewn up.) Antwerp also adopted the three-man team formula, finding work for the extra rider in daily sprint and devil competitions, and half-hour Derny-paced sessions. Slickly presented, the formula apparently satisfied the discerning public who still packed the Sportpaleis for most of the week.

It is evidently the belief of the organisers of the Skol International "Six" at Earls Court that a wide variety in the racing will also please the general British public, most of whom will be seeing cycle-racing for the first time. I hope they are right. For my part, I have taken similarly "ignorant" aunts, uncles, girlfriends and business acquaintances to Wembley sixes and they sat fascinated with the old formula of Sprints, Jams and Primes with a few time trials thrown in. My guests didn't quite know what was going on at first, but were thrilled to bits. After an hour or two, though, they knew the idea of the Jam, could identify the teams and individuals, and even tell when a pair had gained a lap.

At Earls Court the newcomer to the sport will find his Jam ration reduced considerably to make way for pursuits, individual and team time trials, "devils" and motor-paced races. He will have to learn, too, that these extra events have absolutely no bearing on the eventual result of the six – that a rider can lose ten laps in a motor-paced session and yet not drop a single lap in the overall contest.

The formula of the Earls Court event is not so much that of a six-day race, as of six days of racing, strung together by a short madison in each of the three daily sessions. In the earliest two-man six-day races, there were no points competitions at all; if two teams were equal on laps at the end of the six days, the result of the very last lap sprint determined the placings. A few daily sprints were later added to separate equal-distance teams (a kind of goal-average system). The classic six-day formula was for hours of chasing and a few min-utes sprinting for points. The new idea seems to be for hours of every conceivable kind of racing in order to get points to separate teams which are still equal after short madison sessions.

If the end result of the six were all that mattered, then those with aspiration for overall honours would not need to bother themselves too much with these events for points, and merely exert themselves in the all-important madisons. Fortunately they will do no such thing, first because they realise the public is there to be entertained, and secondly because the races will add pounds to their pockets as well as points.

In the seven London six-day races I have seen there were many brave attempts to inject a British flavour into the starting-list. Some, like Sid Cozens and Harry Grant who had ridden the Continental vélodromes, came out very well indeed, but others came out … in a few hours. They had been thrown in at the deep end without ever having seen an indoor track, let alone ridden one.

Our "novices" at the Skol six at Earls Court have been carefully prepared for the test by race director Charles Ruys. Selected by their performances in a series of madison events, they will have had the chance of getting used to the Earls Court track weeks before the flag drops.

The 1967 formula is in their favour, too. Instead of the old system of riders snatching an hour's sleep in a track-side cabin at odd times during the day or night, and then taking over from their team-mates the wearying business of poodling around the track at a snail's pace on sorbo-saddled bikes with upturned bars – instead of all that, the men will be able to get a good night's sleep. Moreover, there will be an hour off-duty between each of the three daily sessions, as well as the frequent breaks caused by the wide variety of events on the programme.

1928. An early morning "potter" by the Paris "Six" field at the old Vél d'Hiver. The race was won by the French pair Wambst–Lacquehay.

Sporting Cyclist, October 1967

France, the land of contrasts. Above, the field swishes down a wide mountain road. Below, passing Thionville on the Moselle in the rich industrial area south of Luxembourg. Two scenes from the 1964 Tour.

TOUR DE FRANCE

J. B. Wadley always remembered the first time he heard that mystical phrase – Tour de France. It was one night in March 1929, and he, not yet 15, was out on the Colchester Rovers' mid-week club run. In darkness, barely pierced by their acetylene lamps, they veered off course and braked to a halt on a narrow, sloping farm track. 'Cor,' exclaimed one of the older riders. 'Just like the Tour de France.'

It was another 26 years before JBW got his first opportunity to follow the race from start to finish, and, then, in 1955, he was the only British journalist on the Tour. But he was lucky, René de Latour used to say, because he got there just in time, when journalists were still having to use their eyes and not rely simply on what they heard broadcast over Radio-Tour. In fact, Wadley never stopped using his eyes. He developed the habit of jumping out of the Press car at the critical moment of a stage, closely watching the entire *peloton* pass, and then, by prior arrangement, getting picked up by one of the following cars.

In those early days he did his Tours the hard way, organising his own accommodation on the spot. Nothing was booked in advance; he would seek out lodgings in the stage town at the end of the day's racing. What he liked was the kind of cheap *auberge paysanne* where you could go into the kitchen and refill your own glass of wine or cognac from the barrel. He was a fully-fledged Francophile, as well as being in love with the Tour.

For his second Tour Wadley asked Brian Robinson to keep a diary, and in the week after their arrival in Paris (where Robinson finished fourteenth overall) they polished his personal, day-by-day account which then formed the basis of the fourth edition of his *Coureur*. It was an instant sell-out, and it established a pattern. From then on, every September's issue of *Sporting Cyclist* was devoted to the Tour.

It would be impossible to do justice to J. B. Wadley's work without including one of these reports in its entirety. In 1959 he was able to describe a particularly interesting Tour, for here was Bahamontes with more serious ambition than ever before, not content simply to secure the climbers' prize, and aided in his intent by some remarkable intrigue within the French national team. And from the British viewpoint it was a good year – Vic Sutton transforming himself in the mountains to become the revelation of the Tour, and, of course, there was Brian Robinson. Not only did he win his second stage by a massive 19-minute margin, he was the animator of a scorching stage through the Massif Central. It was surely one of Robinson's best rides, and JBW's description and analysis of it is masterly.

Two years earlier, Wadley had only been able to follow a part of the Tour, and a rather dull race it had been. One particular day in the Alps was fascinating, however, and his report of it is included here. It was not so much that it paved the way for Anquetil's first Tour victory, but that it was a throw-back to the pre-War days, and offered a true glimpse of what had come to be known as 'the Heroic Era', when riders performed on roads that were no better than the farmyard track on to which the young JBW had skidded all those years before.

The final piece in this section, 'Time-Trial Without Bracke', shows a different side to J. B. Wadley's Tour. He chafed at being confined to the Press car throughout the three weeks, and, whenever possible, begged, borrowed or hired a bike. In 1964, the rest day in Andorra gave him that opportunity.

Carpentras 1970. Receiving La Medaille de la Reconnaissance du Tour de France from Jacques Goddet (left) and Félix Lévitan. (photo: Neville Chanin)

Bahamontes Wins from the Front

In previous years, Federico Bahamontes' only interest in the Tour de France was to prove himself the best climber. He really believed he was not good enough on the flatter stages to win the race itself.

This year he was given some good advice by his new trade-team "boss" Fausto Coppi. "Don't lose time on the flat stages and you must win the Tour," the *campionissimo* said.

Bahamontes obeyed orders. Strong in the Pyrenees, and brilliant in the Massif Central, he was already wearing the yellow jersey of leadership at Genoble. And, like a sprinter who jumps in the back straight and is then never seriously challenged, Bahamontes controlled the home straight of the Alps, and finished at Paris the great winner of a modest Tour.

The story of the Tour is told by the Editor in three parts.

Part One: Mulhouse to Bayonne

There is a world of difference between the modern, streamlined Tour with its wheel-changes in 20 seconds and the Tours of Christophe's day. But one thing hasn't altered: the town of Bayonne remains a strategic point in the great sporting battle. If Bayonne is on the route at the end of the mountain stages, then the wearer of the *maillot jaune* has a good chance of reaching Paris with it still on his shoulders. If – as this year – Bayonne comes immediately before the Pyrenees, the forces are massed within its walls ready for the first big attack by the "winged climbers", as René de Latour calls them. The sporting citizens of Bayonne can tell dozens of great Tour dramas that have been enacted to the immediate north and east of their lovely old town, and to them now has been added that of Robert Cazala – a story which will always touch deeply. Cazala is almost a *Bayonnais* himself, a native of Orthez, some 30 kms. away in the Pyrenees.

Cazala was the last member of the French national team to be selected by director Marcel Bidot, getting his place through the recommendation of his distinguished Mercier stable-mate Louison Bobet. Louison had been impressed with Cazala's class in early season races, and when he won the Tour of Champagne and then finished second in the Boucles de la Seine within 48 hours of that tough little stage-race, Bobet was confident he would make an ideal tourman.

The job of 25-year-old Cazala was clearly that of a team-man, and principally to Bobet himself. The two were immediately booked as room-mates for the Tour, and the youngster from the Pyrenees sat around in quiet respect when at the start at Mulhouse and then, at Metz and Namur after the first two stages, the photographers, journalists, and radio reporters invaded their room to get pictures and stories from Louison Bobet, the only man ever to have won the Tour the France three years in succession – the man who had worn the *maillot jaune* on 36 days of his 10 Tours de France.

And then at Roubaix it happened. Into the Grand Hotel in the City of Cotton streamed six times as many pen, word and picture reporters; over the telephone buzzed a succession of messages of congratulation from all parts of France. At the same time, on the outward wires from Roubaix, the journalists' stories were being passed to their offices, where the make-up men took one look at the advance flashes and prepared their headlines:

CAZALA MAILLOT JAUNE!
Louison Bobet lounged back on his bed, rejoicing in the success of his young friend, and remembering that wonderful day way back in 1948 when he had first worn the magic tunic of leadership.

How came young Cazala to achieve that honour on the third day of his first Tour de France? Truth to tell, it was an accident, the by-product of obeying the orders of manager Bidot. Cazala was, as I have said, in the Tour as a team-mate, principally to Bobet, but overall to the whole of the French nationals, with Anquetil and Rivière at the head. The Tour started perfectly for the Bidot boys. André Darrigade won the first stage at Metz – the fourth year in succession he had performed this feat – and successfully defended his *maillot jaune* on the second day. France led the international team race.

The third day, from Namur to Roubaix, was through a version of the notorious "hell of the north", with its cobbles, level-crossings, tramlines and dirt cycle-paths, which are just as bad either side of the Belgian–French frontier. It was obviously going to be a day on which the French nationals would have to watch the Belgians. And so when, just before Charleroi, massed by miners who had abandoned their pits for an hour, a break developed which included Belgians Desmet and Pauwels, the faithful Cazala slipped in with it, accompanied by his fellow *domestique* Jean Stablinski.

With orders not to lead, but to defend Darrigade's *maillot jaune*, the two sat in. Also in the 10-strong group was fighting Bernard Gauthier, strong time-trial rider Vermeulin, and the North–France Regional J-C. Annaert. On such a devilish course as this, with the constant switching from *pavé* to cycle-path and back again and the need for constant vigilance on the treacherous tram-lines – it was raining heavily to add to the troubles – a group of 10, even with a couple of non-workers in their midst, had the advantage of the big bunch of nearly a hundred.

The 10 drew away; two minutes, four, six, eight, and approaching Roubaix it was nearly 11. Darrigade had clearly lost his *maillot jaune*, but to whom? Two names were already marked down on our list as the contestants for the honour: Gauthier and Cazala.

It was Cazala who won a tight sprint and a minute bonus on the Roubaix track from Annaert, and he was already posing in his yellow jersey, bewildered by this astonishing turn of events, when the enormous *peloton* swept on with Darrigade coming in just behind Dejouhannet and van Geneugden in the spectacular fight for the bunch sprint.

Whereupon Darrigade took off the yellow jersey he had just lost to Cazala, and put on the green jersey as leader in the points classification, and together the two team-mates rode their lap of honour. Then up to his room at the Grand Hotel at Roubaix went the new *maillot jaune* to face the cameras, the notebooks, the microphones of an army of reporters.

And Louison Bobet sat back, content with the success of his protégé, but thinking philosophically ahead to the day when he must surely lose it.

The Tour went on. Rouen, Rennes, Nantes, La Rochelle were left behind: Cazala was still *maillot jaune*. The boy had hung grimly on to his lead, thanks to his own courage, the circumstances of the race and a little help from his team-mates. For, truth to tell, it was not the intention of Bidot to defend his leadership at all costs – the price might prove disastrous in the long run.

All the same, when Cazala reached Bordeaux still in the *maillot jaune*, it was generally believed that his team-mates would see him through to Bayonne, virtually his home town, and where thousands of local fans would be waiting to give him a hero's welcome.

When the great day came, not only his friends were waiting, but the mayor of Orthez, too, with an official address of congratulation. And in the front row of the stand, sheltered from the burning sun which flooded the rest of the velodrome, sat Cazala's wife and their three-year-old daughter Isabelle, a sweet little child dressed in yellow, although she could not understand why.

At the beginning of the track meeting the news was good. The first two hours of the 207-km. stage had been terrific, with a series of brutal attacks following quickly in succession. Then, within two hours of the finish everything was quiet: over the loudspeakers it was announced the riders were "promenading" under the burning sun through the forest of Landes. It looked like being a traditional dawdle to the finish, with a massive sprint on the track deciding the day's stage – and a roar of welcome greeting the yellow-jerseyed hero in the middle of the bunch.

That was a dream.

In reality, events took a surprising turn in the last 40 miles. The Belgians attacked; Anquetil, Bobet, Rivière sensed the danger – if those Belgians got away they would wrest the team leadership from the French who had held it since Metz. In the torrid heat Cazala was in trouble, and was unable to go with his still more famous team-mates. What were they to do – let the Belgians go and save Cazala? As team captain, Bobet was in a spot; he wanted to save his young friend, realising the tragedy for Cazala, his family and friends if the issue were lost at the last moment; at the same time he wanted to save the team leadership, knowing in his heart that this was a more vital issue than the individual jersey, which the tiring Cazala would be bound to lose in any case within a stage or two.

Still Bobet hesitated, then, running his eyes over the others who had joined in the pursuit of the Belgians, he noticed that while the three chief enemies, Gaul, Baldini and Bahamontes, were all there, two men were missing – Favero, second to Gaul last year, and Suarez, 1959 Tour de Spain winner. It was this which finally decided Bobet to shout to Anquetil and Rivière to "ride" and get up with the Belgians, for a few minutes gained by Anquetil and Rivière on Favero and Suarez might be of vital importance later in the race.

And so, when this news came through, a metaphorical shadow

fell over the whole of the Bayonne velodrome, despite the ultimate stage victory of another local, Queheille, who sneaked away near the end.

It is true Cazala got his roar of welcome, but it had not the loud-pedal of triumph about it but the dimmer tone of disappointment. For, already, four minutes earlier, the Belgian–Bobet–Baldini–Gaul group of 24 had arrived, among their number being 24-year-old Eddy Pauwels of Antwerp (a member of Cazala's winning break to Roubaix), and it was he who became the new overall race leader.

Cazala took his disappointment bravely, the mayor crumpled up his address of welcome and improvised a few words of consolation and encouragement, and Pauwels quietly went up to Cazala's wife and gave her his own bouquet, taking out a flower for the little girl in the yellow dress.

The French lost their team leadership, after all, to the Belgians. On the financial side, though, the Bidot boys had no worries. They had won five stages out of nine, and the team so far had won just on £4,000!

Strategically, the French had earned some severe criticism. It had been in their interests to attack Gaul all the way from Mulhouse to Bayonne, in the hope of softening him up before the mountains.* But, in the words of one journalist, "Gaul has ridden from Mulhouse to Bayonne in an armchair."

That is not quite true. Nearer the mark is the fact that Gaul is now such a strong all-rounder that he was become increasingly difficult to attack. Proof of his strength was in the 45.330-km. time-trial stage to Nantes, when Gaul only lost 1 min. 36 secs. to Roger Rivière (who was on 54 x 14 most of the way) and 1 min. 15 secs. to Baldini (on 56 x 14!). Rivière's time for the undulating trip, with a favourable wind, was 56 mins. 46 secs. – almost 30 m.p.h.

Rivière is strong, there is no doubt about it. But will he be able to keep his slight lead over Gaul on the Tourmalet, whose majestic outline I can just see from my window as I write this opening summary? Tomorrow, the opening day of the second side of the Tour, will tell.

*   *   *

---

* Charly Gaul, who had won the Tour the previous year, was considered the main danger to the French team.

And what of the Internationals? I am writing this at six o'clock in the evening of the rest day. A few minutes ago two cyclists waved good-bye as they "went out for a potter". They were Brian Robinson and Shay Elliott, by far the strongest element of the "foreign legion" as they are known in Tour circles. In a neighbouring room of this hotel is Vic Sutton, keeping in bed in a desperate effort to clear up the sinus trouble that has been affecting him since the opening days of the race, with their hours of drenching rain.

Not surprising, in his first Tour, Sutton is lying right at the tail of the table. A crash on the first day gave him a bad start. Even in perfect health he would not have expected to be near the top, but I'll warrant he would not have been content to hang about at the back of the bunch all day. Until now, most of his riding has been done with the French Independents and amateurs in the provinces, and he says the difference in riding standard between those races and the Tour de France is enormous. Sutton has proved a good team rider, and has worked heroically for fellow unfortunates in his *équipe*.

That team is now reduced to eight. We have lost the two Danes, Jonsson and Retvig, and on the third and seventh stages John Andrews and Tony Hewson had to quit.

Like Sutton, Andrews and Hewson were not really well at the start and the rain did not help matters. They were both victims, too, of their devotion to the team. When each could have done with a nice, steady ride in the bunch, they did not hesitate to drop back to give a hand to their mates. Ironically, just as he was beginning to get back to form, Hewson stopped to help Retvig, only to find the Dane had already retired. In an understandable attack of depression, Hewson climbed into the sag wagon, too!

Brightest note among the Internationals is the good form of Brian Robinson. Whereas most years Brian is all keyed up at the start for "his" Tour, this time he was more relaxed, though not entirely hopeful that his stomach trouble would allow him even to finish. On the second stage he made a remarkable climb of the Namur Citadel to take sixth place. That was a good sign.

Best sign of all, though, was at Nantes when he murmured to me on the starting-line: "Today we attack."

He kept his word, and at the stage end at La Rochelle he was in the leading break of twelve which arrived five minutes up on the pursuers, finishing a creditable eighth.

Brian's general classification position is sound, although he lost four needless minutes in yesterday's awful heat. He kept with the unfortunate Cazala's group when perfectly capable of joining in the Belgian–French battle (he proved this by dropping Cazala by two minutes in the last 10 kms.).

But Robinson's chief aim in this opening side of the Tour has been to get Shay Elliott away to that stage win which still eludes him. Elliott nearly brought it off at Namur; away on the climb he was caught only 500 metres from the line, and it took the combined efforts of Gaul and Bahamontes to get him.

Then at Bordeaux, before a great crowd on the splendid vélodrome, Elliott sprinted in third of his party of nine which had formed largely through his effort. He had no complaints at being beaten by Dejouhannet, whom he regards as being even faster than Darrigade.

Part Two: Bayonne to St Etienne
Already the Old Firm on the Pyrenees

The general classification position as it stood at Saint Étienne showed young Pauwels still leading on time by half a dozen seconds. But he hadn't spent the week from Bayonne defending his *maillot jaune*; he had, in effect, lost it within a few hours of the resumption of racing, and only snatched it back in the closing minutes of this second "section" of the Tour.

It was a characteristic move on the part of Belgian director Jean Aerts. "The yellow jersey? It's nice if a Belgian wears it, but I don't think one of my men can win the Tour. But we can win the international team race, and to do that I don't mind throwing away the yellow jersey now and again." That was Aerts's attitude.

And so, on the first day in the Pyrenees, the Belgians went into action on the gradual climb through the verdant foothills of the mountain chain. It was a brilliant, sunny Sunday, a day out for the sporting thousands along the route, ready to raise their berets or straw hats to the Tourmen about to attack the distant 6,500-foot Tourmalet.

Of course, from over the border the Spaniards had come with shouts of encouragement for Bahamontes; and in the village of Bardos a group of Rivière supporters held high a sign: *Rivière lachera Gaul* – Rivière will drop Gaul…

On this Tourmalet stage, there is always a "morning special", an early break-away excursion which reaches the foot of the pass with a few minutes in hand, only to be absorbed in whole or part by the mountain expresses. True to tradition, it happened again – but with a difference; the *échappé* reached such proportions that at the foot of the Tourmalet the lead was 17 minutes over the *peloton* which contained all the race favourites and the *maillot jaune* Pauwels.

But if Pauwels was imprisoned, three of his team-mates were at liberty with the group of ten. Pauwels was certain to lose his jersey, but two of his compatriots, Desmet and Hoevenaers, had every chance of taking it over. Each of them fell on the descent, without much hurt, but losing just enough time to allow the young Frenchman Vermeulin to take over the leadership.

The Belgians were not worried. Pauwels had dropped to eighth, but behind Vermeulin in second, third and fourth positions on "general" they had Desmet, Hoevenaers and Janssens (the last-named winning the stage)! Aerts had lost a yellow jersey, but the yellow caps of team leadership were now firmly placed on his men's heads! Behind the leaders, some eleven minutes down, there arrived together the two super-climbers, Gaul and Bahamontes, who had romped away on the Tourmalet, with Rivière on their wheel. But far from dropping Gaul, as announced by the placard bearers, it was the hour-record man who was *laché* by Fred and Charly.

As I expected , Brian Robinson climbed steadily in company with Bobet, Anquetil, Baldini and Co., finishing with them 13 minutes down on the Janssens group. What I did not expect was to find over-geared Vic Sutton sitting happily with the heads, a strong and stylish climber. Only steamed-up goggles on the descent prevented his finishing with the Bobet party.

At dinner that night Sauveur Ducazeaux, the team's experienced manager, was still talking of the way Sutton dropped such well-known names as Bergaud, Brankart and Adriaenssens on the Tourmalet. And Jean Bobet, who is now a full-time journalist and saw all the climb from a pillion seat, said he was convinced that Sutton could have dropped his brother, Louison Bobet, if he had wanted.

As for Brian Robinson, happily surprised at the good mountain form of his fellow Yorkshireman, he had this to say: "Vic even started talking about the race, the heat and other riders on the Tourmalet. I told him to shut up!"

Shay Elliott was unable to join in the general high spirits. He was all set to do a ride on the Tourmalet (in which he first made his

Continental name in the 1954 Route de France) but broke his chain at the foot of the pass. Only after a long delay did he get going again, to finish 24 minutes down.

*   *   *

At the end of the next day Shay looked just as sad – five minutes back in 83rd position, after the second Pyrenean stage, Bagnère–Saint Gaudens, with its two *cols* coming in quick succession. But this time I sensed the Irish boy was simply taking things easily in view of tomorrow's flat stage. There was a twinkle in his eye when he denied that anything of the sort was afoot…

Brian Robinson came in strongly in 12th position of the 25 leaders, which contained all the heads, except Favero who retired with sickness (leaving Baldini as sole Italian leader). Although preceded by Dotto on the Aspin and Peyresourde, again Bahamontes and Gaul had shown themselves to be the strongest climbers in the race. Sutton arrived nicely three and a half minutes down on the leaders, one of whom was Vermeulin and, therefore, still race leader.

*   *   *

Next morning at the start, Shay did his best to look glum, but he was really fit and howling with health. I knew he was going to have a go today however he might look or say he felt. You see, I had seen the mechanics fitting a pair of very light tyres to his bike overnight!

St. Gaudens–Albi is near enough flat. There was a two-man break during the day which was wiped out near the end, and within ten kilometres of the finish an enormous group of 90 were preparing themselves for the sprint. Near the head of that group was Elliott, poised ready for one of his now-celebrated power-punch attacks which means the *peloton* behind him will be fighting for second place.

Then, from the bunch shot the Swiss rider Graf, followed immediately by a second rider – Vermeulin. Shay's immediate reaction was a natural one: "They won't let the *maillot jaune* escape on his own", and got ready to make a counter-attack immediately the junction was made.

But "they" didn't react, and Graf and Vermeulin got clear away, finishing 46 seconds up on the Darrigade-dominated *peloton*. Darrigade, however, was only fourth, for on his own in third place,

125

ten seconds ahead of the 86-up sprint, Seamus Elliott finished with a remarkable effort that would have given him victory if only he had gone with Graf–Vermeulin.

Not one person could criticise Elliott for his hesitation. Never in the history of the Tour had a *maillot jaune* brought off so audacious a move – and with his 30-seconds time bonus for second place Vermeulin increased his lead.

Shay wasn't worried.

"It was an easy third, for about five minutes hard work. At Bordeaux I had worked for five hours for third. I am not nearly as disappointed as at Namur when I thought I'd won with only a kilometre to go."

*   *   *

And now we come to Albi–Aurillac, a day that will be talked about for years, a day out in savage hills of the Massif Central that I shall never forget. A day for various reasons that none of the riders will forget, although some – presided over by Charly Gaul – will wish they could.

Charly Gaul was, in effect, a marked man from the start. The French nationals were still being criticised for not attacking the Luxembourg star. He had gone from Mulhouse to Bayonne in an armchair, they had said. Over the Pyrenees he had got up from his armchair and gone for a stroll. In less than a week they would be in the Alps, where all Monsieur Charly would have to do would be to get up from the armchair again and stamp the whole of the field beneath his talented feet.

"This is our last chance, today and tomorrow," Jean Bobet confided to me (by "our", of course, journalist Jean meant the French nationals). "If Gaul is not attacked, then he will win the Tour in the Alps, perhaps in one day, perhaps even in one hour, as he did the Giro d'Italia. Today is a terribly tough day; those hills on the profile map look small, but they are hard. Géminiani knows the roads well and says a 45 x 24 is needed for them."

Why should the super-climber Gaul be vulnerable on hard hills. Was it not likely that the biters would be bitten? There was always that chance, of course, but what everybody had in mind was this: that Gaul hates really hot weather – and today, already at the 10.30 start, the sun was blazing away from a pure blue sky.

It was soon clear that the French meant business, for in the early attacks (which Gaul and his team-mates neutralised), Roger Rivière was involved. And so was Brian Robinson. For nearly an hour last night Brian had been in close conversation with manager Ducazeaux, a map of the course spread out between them. It had been Shay's day yesterday, no doubt it would be Brian's today!

The pace was fast, despite the need to climb gradually from the start. Bruni and Suarez were dropped. Then Brian's efforts were rewarded, and he found himself away in the admirable company of Darrigade, Adriaenssens, Privat, Busto, Dotto and Mahé.

By the time they reached the feeding station at Rodez, they were two and a half minutes up on the next bunch. I waited there to see the leaders through (the field was split by now into several sections), and then for their immediate followers. In the latter group I saw Baldini snatch his *musette* from Alfredo Binda who yelled an order to the World Champion. What Binda yelled I don't know, but Baldini did; he stuffed food quickly into his pockets and went hard into action. With him went his team-mate Falaschi, the two "A's" Anquetil and Anglade, the two "B's" Bergaud and Bahamontes, and Schellemberg. The seven chased the Robinson group of seven ahead, eventually catching them, after a hectic descent, in the valley at Villecomtal. The 15, therefore, all began the ascent of the Polisal third-category hill together, but after a while Schellemberg and Falaschi got tailed off as little Dotto forced the pace in search of mountain points, with Bahamontes and Robinson close behind.

Have you noticed something? The *maillot jaune* was not around, and neither was Gaul.

Four years ago I, as a race follower, would have had to wait by the roadside for the arrival of any delayed rider and taken a time-check, or rely on the shouted news of a fellow journalist who had been busy with a watch and his eyesight a few kilometres down the road. Nowadays that is not absolutely necessary; each Press car has a short-wave radio receiver, getting news of distant *pelotons* direct from a mobile transmitter following the riders concerned.

The news that came over as we made a crazy descent of the Polisal was red-hot: Gaul was in the group three minutes on the road behind us accompanied by one team-mate, De Jongh, by race leader Vermeulin, French nationals Louison Bobet and Rivière, the inevitable Belgian squadron, today comprising Brankart, Planckaert, Pauwels and Hoevenaers, plus the dropped Schellemberg and

Falaschi from the Robinson–Baldini vanguard.

Usually on those mountain descents I take my mind off the constant danger of the car shooting over the edge into space, by pretending to sort out my notes. Today it wasn't necessary; I looked back and above for signs of the Gaul expedition, and away and down to where a tiny blur of white indicated the position of the team cars following the leaders.

At last, above, we saw not a group of riders, but one shooting down like an arrow towards a hairpin bend, hovering for a few seconds, then swishing away to the next dead turn. With the sun in our eyes we could not identify the rider. Then again the Radio-Tour came to our aid: "Louison Bobet has broken away from the Gaul group on the descent!"

Bobet was clearly out to try his favourite dodge, to break away on a descent, build up a lead on the following flat, and then catch up with the leaders on the next climb.

We in the car roared along that flat – actually it was a switchback along a river valley, in and out of a tiny village, hot and dusty and burning with Tour-fever – until a local *gendarme* frantically signalled us to slow ready for a vicious turn off our comparatively main road on to a narrow lane, freshly tarred and shooting up through a cluster of houses to perilous heights above.

In no time at all we saw two riders tailed off from the leading Robinson group – Privat and Darrigade, both French nationals. Here, thought I, was another part of the Bobet-plan: Privat and Darrigade both dropping off voluntarily from the front ready to help Bobet when he joined them.

How wrong I was! Darrigade and Privat had both been dropped: just plain dropped; it was written all over them. We waited in a lay-by for a few minutes half-way up the awful climb, as steep as a Devon lane and long as the Snaefell rise from Ramsey, and along came Bobet – and he, too, was in a state. So much so that less than 100 metres behind came the Gaul group that Bobet at one time had preceded by two minutes.

Charly-boy, the mountain-prince, was sweating but riding strongly, Rivière looking quite cool, the Belgians labouring hard, Vermeulin game but looking ready to crack. Then only 50 metres above us, Gaul punctured, but manager Goldschmidt had changed the wheel and was pushing him off before I could run into camera range.

For five glorious minutes on the remains of that Montsalvy climb we saw Gaul the Great, pedalling his 45 x 24 at such a pace, sitting still and looking straight ahead, and catching and dropping in rapid succession four notable victims: Bobet, Privat, Darrigade and Vermeulin, whose yellow jersey had also now dropped out of the Rivière group.

Yes, in five minutes Gaul was up again with Rivière just at the official top of the pass. Before the descent there followed a further slight rise, of no more than 1 in 20, I should say. On this Gaul went to the front, forcing the pace, no doubt with the intention of preventing Bobet and Co. getting up with them. Then, along the final "straight" of that rise, Gaul dropped to the back, with Rivière at the front. Unaccountably, Gaul tailed off a few metres – at first we thought it's just a joke – but then the interval went up to 50 metres. It was then the manager Bidot raced up alongside Rivière in his car and shouted to the hour-record man something which, obviously, we did not know at the time, but learned in the evening of this remarkable day: "Ride, Roger, as hard as you can!"

"But the Belgians, they won't work," Rivière gasped. "If I ride they'll have an armchair ride for the team race."

"Never mind; I say, if you want to win the Tour de France, now is the moment above all to ride and get rid of Gaul."

This was Rivière's first Tour, Bidot's 20th as rider or manager. Rivière "rode".

And he therefore began to "ride" on the steep descent of Montsalvy, and Gaul, who is never happy on a descent at any time, began to lose ground rapidly.

We were close on his tail on that swish-swush descent through the woods, and again we were looking back for Bobet, who in due course swept by us with Privat close at hand. What would happen, I wondered, when they caught Gaul; what would be their tactics?

We never were able to see, because at the foot of the descent in the village of Junhac, a crowd was surging over the square to the fountain where bicycle No.1 of the Tour de France was in view with its owner, Charly Gaul, dipping his head in and out of the water while Goldschmidt filled his *bidons*.

From Jean Bobet we learned later that Louison and Privat actually saw him stopping, and Louison called to his team-mates: "We may be cooked, René, but Gaul is beaten!"

I am sorry to say that for a few minutes I then saw the "cooked"

Louison Bobet, with the biggest "packet" of his life, the result of what he later declared to be an absolutely suicidal bid to get up with Robinson, Anquetil and Co. Yet, at the same time, I am glad I saw him in such a state, for his courage was superb.

But let us away from the dropped riders, even if their names are Gaul and Bobet, away even from the astonishing Rivière and his escort of Belgians, and jump several minutes ahead to the leaders, of whom Bahamontes, Baldini, Anquetil and Robinson were doing most work at the front. We were still in a country of narrow lanes; the official climbs for the day were over, but coming as they did after such an opening session, the last 80 kilometres of short, tough hills were killing.

On them, Bergaud was dropped, poor little Dotto fell on a gravelled bend: suddenly I saw the International team-car pull up sharply ahead. Had Brian fallen, too, or punctured, or broken his frame? No – the team-car had conked out in the heat and hills and was being revived by mechanics and manager with *bidons* of water! For a moment it seemed funny, then disastrous. If Brian punctured with no car directly behind him, he would never get back with the leaders.

After five minutes – which seemed like five hours – the team-car sped by us back into position behind the little bunch, manager Ducazeaux giving me a thumbs-up sign as he passed.

At last they were out of the narrow lanes and on to the main road. Only 20 kms. to go. At 10 to go, with Brian still safely there, we went by to the finish, just as the Radio Tour announced Gaul was 15 minutes behind and *maillot jaune* Vermeulin 17.

I waited in the middle of the 550-metre Aurillac track (bigger, even than Herne Hill). "The riders are 5 kms. from the finish," it was announced. Then "At two kilometres, the group is all together." Finally: "One kilometre from the track Bahamontes is leading with Robinson slightly ahead of the rest."

But all were together on running on to the track, Brian still on Baha's wheel. They slowly circled the cement oval until, in the back straight Robinson attacked from the front, rode strongly into the final banking, but up the long, long, oh-so-long home-straight, Anglade, Anquetil and Bahamontes all went by.

Robinson's had been a perfect finishing sprint for a 350-metre track, and would have won against Darrigade himself – but it was too early on the wide spaces of Aurillac. A Robinson win would

130

have been a fitting reward for one of his greatest performances, which shot him up nine places on general classification, now being ninth, 12 minutes behind new leader Hoevanaers.

Gaul, escorted by Privat and Bobet and Planckaert, finished 20 minutes behind Robinson (but still in 17th position!), while Elliott and Sutton were tired but undistressed in the main *peloton* of 60 which finished a further 12 minutes in arrears. Fifteen riders retired or were eliminated on this extraordinary day when Gaul had been given a ride in an electric chair.

Albi–Aurillac, the finish of a dramatic stage. Bahamontes leads on to the big track, with Robinson, Anglade and Anquetil in his wake. Below, it is all over, and track stars Forlini and Varnajo are saying, "If you had left your effort for another 50 metres, you would have won!" But even at fourth, Robinson has just finished the finest ride of his career.

Just 24 hours after sharing in Robinson's triumph, we were commiserating with him on a disaster. Within a few minutes of the start of the Aurillac–Clermont-Ferrand stage, Brian was calling for the Tour doctor. During the night he had had a recurrence of the stomach trouble which caused his retirement last year. Although the stage was hard, topographically, the pace was only moderate after yesterday's hard labour. Yet it was far too fast for Robinson, with whom Elliott dropped back.

Shay stayed six hours by Brian's side, or rather for most of the time in front of him giving pace, sheltering him from the wind, splashing water in his face and encouraging him to stick it out. Being in the car of French journalists who naturally wanted to see the front of the race, I could do nothing to help them. But once again Jean Bobet was around on his pillion, and he told me that rarely had he seen such a display of devotion as that shown by Elliott for his friend Robinson.

Meanwhile Sutton had been riding comfortably with the "grands", even finishing ahead of Baldini and Bobet on the two big climbs. But as Vic said, the "big uns" weren't worried, and that was true. They were not worried about a group of a dozen or so who were away most of the day. One of the group was Géminiani, out to do a ride into his home town of Clermont-Ferrand; another was Pauwels, who crept up to within six seconds of team-mate Hoevenaers on general classification.

Elliott and Robinson limped in 47 minutes later, and were declared to be outside the time-limit and eliminated. But an ancient rule was remembered which safeguards a rider in the first ten on general classification from elimination, and Ducazeaux was able to get Brian reinstated. But not Elliott, whose sacrifice had allowed Robinson to finish.

Robinson was terribly upset at this, but Shay wasn't worried: "I came in this Tour to help Brian," he said. "There are mountain stages ahead in which he can still do well. Good luck to him."

And so Brian started first man off in the Puy de Dôme mountain climb. When the starting list was compiled he was officially out of the race, and was not reprieved until later – hence his number one starting position.

Sutton – revelation of the Puy de Dôme

Most popular spot for British clubmen "doing" the Tour on their holidays was the Puy de Dôme hill-climb – a punishing test of twelve kilometres, rising 3,300 feet. They saw a storming Bahamontes win the climb to get within four seconds of the *maillot jaune*. Our clubmen expected something of that sort!

What they hardly expected was the great climb of Vic Sutton, who, one of the earliest starters (being then near the end on general classification), put up a remarkable ride which remained fastest until 40 riders had finished, and the "heads" began to arrive. Indeed, one of the check shows him to have been in fourth position at 8.4 kms.

Many of our clubmen visitors called at the Clermont-Ferrand hotel during the evening to congratulate him on his ride. During their visit manager Ducazeaux told Sutton the good news that he had been awarded the 100,000 francs for being the most combative rider of the day.

* * *

Last day of this "section" was Clermont-Ferrand to Saint Étienne. Hot, tired and in need of a rest day, the riders took things easily for 200 of the 210 kms. Then in Saint Étienne itself three riders got away, Buni, Graf and Pauwels. They finished in that order, just far enough ahead of the 67-up sprint for Pauwels to get back his *maillot jaune* with six seconds to spare!

Part Three: St. Étienne to Paris
"Baha" and Sutton Ahead of Schedule

Saint Étienne is not the ideal rest-day town for a Tour de France. It is big, hot and noisy. And so manager Ducazeaux organised a small party to spend an hour or so fishing in the surrounding mountains. Robinson and Sutton were the only two riders to go on the trip.

That night, after dinner, and the riders had gone to bed, M. Ducazeaux and I sat talking.

"Young Sutton is the freshest rider left in the Tour de France," he said, "but do you know what he told me today up there in the mountains? That his only ambition in this race is to be the fourth

Englishman to finish the Tour de France. I have tried to tell him, and so has Brian, that it is absolutely essential that he tries something in the Alps. Will you have a go at him too?"

I did, next morning. Vic merely grinned.

His reply was not to try something in the Alps, but before the Alps – a day ahead of schedule.

And it was a day ahead of schedule that Federico Bahamontes, too, went into action to take over the *maillot jaune*. He was expected to launch his big-scale attack in the great Alpine passes. Instead, he chose the less glamorous but terribly tough *cols* on the second half of the Saint Étienne–Grenoble stage.

As far as I know, no race starting from Saint Étienne misses the 15-km. Col du Grand Bois, or Col de la République (it goes by both names), which begins its climb on the outskirts of the city. In this Tour de France, the *col* dealt with the riders in its usual fashion – it strung them out on the summit, prior to the inevitable rapid descent and regroupment in the valley of the Rhône.

That strung-out field, however, gave an indication of the state of the parties: Bahamontes first, with Gaul and Huot three seconds behind, and three main groups at 30 seconds, 1 min. 30 secs. (Sutton was in this) and 2 min. 30 secs. (Robinson in that). Then four minutes down, dropped, sweating and generally distressed was … Louison Bobet. It was a hard sight to bear, the once-so-great Louison in such trouble.

An oasis in the burning desert of the Tour. Vic Sutton (right) joins Queheille for a quick drink and fill-up from the garden hose. A typical village scene somewhere in the second part of the Tour.

Bobet's little group eventually made contact in the valley. That was not a difficult feat, for already the pace had dropped to a crawl. The heat was terrific. Riders were jumping off to raid village fountains and cafés, and even pinching peaches, all ripe and juicy, from the plantations.

The roads were excellent, and if, after making contact with the pleasant valley of the Isère the route had made straight for Grenoble, the day would undoubtedly have continued with such pleasantries, and concluded with a full-field sprint.

Instead, the hard *route nationale* was left in favour of a "D" road, which, after many tough and tortuous climbs and drops through difficult country, led at last to the Col Romeyre which many experienced followers had been telling us for days was a real tough 'un. How right they were! The *col* got down to business right away, with an abrupt turn on to a narrow road with sand and gravel on its verges and a sticky mass of tar in the middle.

Robinson, obviously still not the real Brian, had an early setback with a puncture. Sutton waited back with him and then the Yorkshire "tandem" began threading its way back through the strung-out field, when the effort was again halted, this time by a solid block of cars built up behind a fallen rider.

Yet, despite this handicap, Sutton attacked the middle-slopes of the Romeyre with an effort that not only earned an underlined entry into my note-book , but in those of every other journalist with the race as well. Just think of it: from being near the tail of the field, Vic worked his way steadily to the front, up along the narrow track that in places was like a balcony hanging slenderly to mighty rocks, with only the tiniest of walls on the "open" side to prevent actors and audience tumbling into the deep pit of the Isère Valley.

Just think of it, and share my pride when, after Vic had drawn away from our car (we were blocked behind a small group on the narrow pass) and vanished into one of the many tunnels, we eventually heard this announcement over Radio-Tour: "Here are the positions at the summit of Romeyre: First , Bahamontes. Second, at one minute seven seconds, Gaul. Third, at one minute forty-five seconds, Sutton. Then, at two minutes forty-five seconds, Huot, Saint and Bergaud, followed closely by a *peloton* including the *maillot jaune*, Pauwels, Baldini, Rivière, Anquetil and Anglade."

Sutton had replied to M. Ducazeaux by not only trying something, but doing something – something that put the name of

"Soo-tun" on everybody's lips.

But let us keep our sense of proportion. Although Sutton's was a magnificent ride, it was not the most important of the day. That distinction went to Bahamontes, who on the savage slopes of Romeyre virtually won the Tour de France.

This was not the first time that Bahamontes had topped the Romeyre alone in the lead. He did the same in 1954 when he was still something of a "clown". With pretensions only at being King of the Mountains, he stopped at the summit and ate an ice-cream while mechanics dealt with an alleged fault in his machine. He finished the stage in the bunch.

The Bahamontes who topped Romeyre on July 13th, 1959, was in a much more serious frame of mind. He continued his effort on the breakneck descent, but not so fast that Gaul could not join forces with him after 10 kilometres. Together the two great mountain specialists did a sensational bit-and-bit to Grenoble, where Gaul won the sprint for first place. That did not worry "Baha". He had taken over the *maillot jaune*, and now instead of having to attack in the Alps, he could – if he so wished – merely defend his lead.

It was, then, the Spaniard's day. Yet Sutton must not be dismissed without a further paragraph of praise. For he, too, continued his effort on and after the first descent, and made a mighty effort to get up with Gaul. He was within 100 metres of success, but could not quite close the gap. Had he succeeded, then the cheering thousands on the sensational run-in to Grenoble – which for nearly an hour we could see like a toy-town far below – would have seen Victor Sutton, the humble, unknown Independent from Thorne, Yorkshire, sharing the glory with the Mountain Kings.

As it was, Sutton was sandwiched out there in no-man's land, between Gaul–Bahamontes and the bunch of chasing heads, now thoroughly alarmed at Bahamontes' flight. It was hopeless, as Sutton eventually realised. He sat up, was caught by the bunch of 36, in which Robinson was rapidly becoming restored to health.

Brian finished 9th of the big sprint, Sutton 13th. They were both happy – much happier than the "heads" who saw Bahamontes don his yellow jersey and heard that the Spaniard now had 4 min. 2 secs. over the second man, Hoevenaers.

*   *   *

136

And so came July 14, the French national holiday. Today there would surely be a race to be remembered – part of the great Galibier to be climbed, the Iséran (the highest road in Europe), and finally the Little Saint Bernard Pass! But it turned out to be far from a great day's racing so far as the overall positions were concerned. Bahamontes was race leader; he had no need to attack the mountains now, all he had to do was to defend his lead. It was a negative policy, but in a way understandable. So many times in the past Bahamontes has put up astounding rides in the mountains, then cracked up on a comparatively easy stage. With the Tour within his grasp, the "reformed" Spaniard was obviously playing safe.

Not that the stage was completely dull for the followers!

How could it be dull when it began, in a cold rain, at Lautaret, half-way up the Galibier (the start was therefore 50 miles from Grenoble)?

How could it be dull when Gaul took to his wings to win the 200,000 francs for the Henri Desgrange souvenir prime at the top of Galibier? How could any descent from the Giant of the Alps to Saint Michel de Maurienne be dull, with the tail of the stretched-out *peloton* dropping incautiously in their efforts to join up with the leaders?

How could it be dull when, along the valley of the Arc, with long stretches of the road little better than gravel tracks, a weary Louison Bobet finally made contact with the main group after having been once again dropped, this time on the Galibier, theatre of so many of his greatest exploits?

No, to the follower it was not dull. But to the millions following the Tour from distant radio-sets, it was disappointing. After all, what was happening? Gismondi and Christian away on the approach to l'Iséran with a lead of five minutes and both of them over an hour behind "Baha" on general? That was, after all, nothing!

There was far more drama in the news that on the summit of l'Iséran, 8,750 feet above sea-level, and the highest road in Europe, up there among the snows, a *coureur* rode the final metres of his final Tour de France. Louison Bobet had retired.

The descent from l'Iséran, then the climb of Little Saint Bernard, the scene of Gaul's triumph in the Tour of Italy. Would he "try something" today? No. The field tackled the Little Giant all together, still undismayed at Gismondi and Christian being nearly five minutes ahead.

It was on the descent that things happened. The summit of the *col* marks the French–Italian frontier, and within a kilometre the road was bad, then as it dropped alarmingly into the unknown, it became atrocious – loose stones, rocks, dust, pot-holes, the lot. Inevitably, punctures galore were suffered. Poor Gismondi collected five! The Italian's misfortune undoubtedly prevented him and Christian from staying away until the end.

Just two kilometres from the Aosta track the pair were caught by four men – Gaul, Saint, Anglade and Baldini. And on the Aosta cinder track dominated by the distant, mighty Matterhorn, Baldini sent the fans crazy with joy by winning the sprint.

Forty-seven seconds later another eight arrived, and the winner of this little group proved to be Brian Robinson, with as neat a little slip-through-on-the-inside of Anquetil as you ever saw. But Brian was angry: "My back tyre rolled off on the descent – there's mechanics for you! If not I would have been with the Baldini group."

He didn't say so, but I believe Brian was confident he could have beaten Baldini in the sprint.

Sutton arrived six minutes later. He had had no trouble, of a mechanical nature. He had just been scared stiff of the awful descent from the summit of Little Saint Bernard which he had topped in company with Baldini & Co. I am not surprised. It was the kind of ordeal that he had not previously met in his young career. And when manager Ducazeaux had to abandon him to his lot in order to follow the fearless Robinson, and handed an extra tyre from the team car, Vic dared not even take a hand from the bars.

In the evening M. Ducazeaux was still deploring the fact that Sutton lost six minutes on the descent: "He descends worse than Dotto – and that's saying something."

I replied that on a good road Sutton is as fearless a descender as any, but this was something new to him. By happy chance I was struck be a parallel which helped calm down the team manager. I remarked that Reg Harris was terrified on first being confronted by a steeply banked wooden track, and that no doubt Sutton would overcome his fear as completely as did Harris.

"But it has cost a lot to learn," M. Ducazeaux said. "If Sutton had stayed with Robinson the team would have won the 200,000-francs daily team prize."

Bahamontes had had his scare, too. He was with the Robinson group at 47 seconds from Baldini's advance party, which include Anglade, now his nearest rival (Hoevenaers had fallen back). But, ironically, it was Bahamontes' other two arch-enemies, Rivière and Anquetil, who saved the day for him. They were frantic lest Anglade (not a member of the national French team) should take over the *maillot jaune*, and (together with Robinson) worked heroically to help Bahamontes save it!

*   *   *

The mixture as the day before. "Local" thrills for the followers on the stage from Saint Vincent (20 miles from Aosta) in Italy, to Annecy (France) by way of Martigny (Switzerland). But for seven of the eight and a half hours' racing, there was nothing of importance so far as the Tour "general" was concerned. In fact, the stage was similar to yesterday's in that two riders, Graf and Saint, were away for a long time. Their long *échappé* was more interesting than the Gismondi–Christian break, though, because Saint was 11th on general classification, and Graf, the Swiss star, was on his home ground.

Moreover, after breaking away on the first Forclaz climb (there was another *col* of the same name at the end of the stage) the pair shared primes worth £400 in the towns at the foot of Mont Blanc, before Graf surprisingly dropped Saint on the second Forclaz and won the stage.

If the public has already forgotten the St. Vincent–Annecy stage, I haven't, and neither will the riders for many a long day, or night: many will surely suffer from a Grand Saint Bernard nightmare. It was not the ascent of the great pass dividing Italy and Switzerland, although this was bad enough, the excellent cement road giving way to a muddy track for the final kilometres. It was the descent – a descent which, on a fine day, would be every bit as bad as that which upset Sutton so much on the previous stage. Today, to add to the perils, the summit of the *col* was literally in the clouds. The road was, therefore, not just dusty and rough, but treacherous mud. Visibility was, on the first five kilometres of the descent, about five yards – and that was the stretch on which the road snaked and dropped, with little or no protection on either side. It was a frightening experience in a car, even though (for once) the drivers were careful. You can imagine the plight of the riders, tired from the climb, numbed by the icy rain, blinded by the cloud, slithering down the muddy mountain lane.

Yet, there were no serious crashes. The leading riders were all together when the road finally dropped from out of the clouds, and, as I have said, Graf and Saint "went" on the subsequent Forclaz climb.

Not until the last hour, on the second Forclaz, did the final battle start. Again, Bahamontes and Gaul did a "tandem" to reach the lovely lakeside town of Annecy five minutes after Graf. Sutton finished 18th, another four minutes later, very tired after another remarkable day.

"I was second to Charly Gaul on two of the *cols*," he managed to say (he didn't know that Graf and Saint were ahead on the road).

Then, oh so proudly:

"On one *col* Charly rode alongside me and said in English, 'You are a good boy!'"

And Brian? He finished 27 minutes after Sutton. I spent some time with them in their room that night. Brian looked and sounded good. He drifted out of the conversation from time to time to examine carefully the profile of the next stage. He just winked when I asked him why.

Down below in the cellar mechanics worked for a long time on Robinson's pale blue Géminiani bike. They fitted a pair of very light wheels collected in Italy, shod with sleek, fast tyres.

"But they are Brian's time-trial wheels," I exclaimed. "The time trial is not until tomorrow. What's the idea?"

The mechanics just winked.

*   *   *

Much of what I have written already about this Tour de France will, I expect, be completely fresh to you. But the next headline will be old and wonderful news: "Brian Robinson wins at Châlon with a 20-minutes lead!" I cannot add a great deal to it, for the reason there is not a lot to tell. Brian broke away; he built up a lead over an indifferent *peloton*; the lead mounted up – and he won.

It would be criminal to pretend that this was an important stage of the Tour. It would not be unkind to Brian to say that it was, perhaps, the least important of all. The Alps were over; many riders were tired; it was the day before the time trial, for which the heads were reserving their strength.

But a thousand cheers for Brian for his intelligence in picking such a day for his great effort. For (as he admitted afterwards) taking it easy yesterday and giving his rivals the impression that he was "done"; for his perspicacity in remembering from a previous racing engagement in the Bellegarde Criterium, that a sharp-angled bend in the town followed by a steep climb was the ideal break-away ground for his flight on the ensuing Échallon climb.

A thousand cheers for Brian in making a reckless descent from the summit in order to build up the vital first-minute lead (he would have welcomed the company of Dotto, ahead of him by 10 seconds at the summit, but the little climber had not the nerve to follow Brian in his break-neck enterprise).

A thousand cheers, too, for the way in which Brian accepted the enormous task ahead – 90 miles on his own, often against a wind, with open, difficult wild-west type of hilly country to be overcome before the flat run-in to Châlon. Nine out of every ten roadmen would have chucked the idea and waited for the bunch. Not Brian. Hadn't he ridden an occasional "12" in England? Hadn't he once stayed away on his own for 200 kilometres in winning a stage of the Tour of Europe? And hadn't *she* (and he was thinking of his wife, Shirley!) ridden an out-and-home 100 in 4–45?

All the followers acknowledged that the *peloton* behind was indifferent, but not one denied that only a rider of the greatest class could have won by 20 minutes, even from a sleeping bunch.

With Sutton and Christian safely in that bunch, the winning of the daily 200,000 francs team prize was automatic, and, not surprisingly, Brian took the 100,000 francs for being the most aggressive rider of the day. We were all happy at Châlon that night, you may be sure. But when I said goodnight to Brian in his room I confessed:

"Brian, your name has gone round the world as winner of a stage of the Tour de France. But for me, your first today is still not as important as your fourth at Aurillac in the most vital stage of the Tour, when every man-jack of the field was doing his nut."

Brian agreed, but wisely observed: "The public are not interested in a man who has finished fourth in a stage, however hard it was. But they will pay to see a stage-winner, and that's how I earn my living."

*   *   *

Having ridden his time-trial a day ahead, and over twice the distance of the official event, Brian was "dead" over the 69 kms. to Dijon next day. He finished well down the list, with Sutton even lower. It was into the wind all the way, and proved a battle of prestige between Rivière and Anquetil, with the honours going to Rivière. He beat Bahamontes by over six minutes, thus proving that a similar effort in the mountains might have upset the Spaniard after all.

* * *

Dijon to Paris, the longest (331 kms.) and dreariest of the lot. No attacks, even though Bahamontes had only a four-minute lead over Anglade, with Anquetil and Rivière another minute behind. Why didn't they attack? That is a question which I will leave friend René de Latour to answer.*

For myself I will be happy to finish my three-sided story of the Tour with this memory of the Parc des Princes: sitting on a bench at the famous track awaiting their lap of honour were Brian Robinson [who finished 19th] and Vic Sutton [37th]. A lounge-suited gentleman shook hands with Brian, congratulating him, in French, on his stage win. "And is that 'Soo-tun' with you?" he asked.

Brian said it was.

"My congratulations Monsieur Sutton," said the visitor, shaking his hand. "You have ridden well. You are the revelation of the Tour."

Suttons's happiness was complete. Charly Gaul had told him he was a good boy, and now Fausto Coppi had heard of him, too.

---

*René de Latour's footnote included this explanation:

This year Bahamontes was far from being the scatterbrain of previous years; he was riding strongly, seriously and thoughtfully.

"If they expect me to crack, they are crazy," Federico said. "At last I know how to win the Tour, and win it I will."

Bahamontes kept his word, and the press gave him due credit for it. He is a rider of great class, and nobody can question his right to join the long line of great names to win the Tour. On the other hand, the journalists were very severe with Anquetil and Rivière, many of them putting into print the attitude expressed by the whistlers and boo-ers at the Parc des Princes track.

"They spoiled the Tour," said some headlines. "They were like scared rabbits, lacking courage and initiative."

That is not my opinion. They did not lack courage or any of the accepted qualities of bike racing. *They just did not want Anglade to win.* And that is what might have happened if Bahamontes had been severely attacked. If they had to be beaten, then they preferred the Spanish boy to do it. This may seem puzzling to you, but it is really easy to explain.

Actually Anglade was climbing higher and higher on the ladder of popularity. If he won the Tour, then he would immediately be put on the same level as Anquetil, Rivière and Bobet, the three best-paid French riders, if not (with Baldini) the best paid in the world.

Sporting Cyclist, October 1959

INTO THE ALPS
The Day Anquetil Won the *Maillot Jaune*

"What, are you back again?" asked a Belgian journalist at the start of the tenth stage of the Tour de France at Thonon-les-Bains, on the French shore of Lake Geneva. He knew that following the fifth-day retirement of Brian Robinson on the Belgian border, I had gone back to London. To him, that was the natural thing to do. With no Englishman now in the race, what possible interest could I have in following it?

I explained to my friend that although for British cyclists much of the interest in the 1957 race had gone now that Brian was out, there was still a great deal left, and I had come back for three days in order to write my impressions of the Alpine stages for the sake of those thousands of readers who would dearly have liked to be there themselves.

"Why," I told the Belgian journalist, "on the way to the airport I met an enthusiast who said that so far as he was concerned I could devote an entire issue to the mountain section of the race!"

That was four days ago. I am now at Marseille about to pack my bags and say good-bye to the Tour again. Was the trip worth the rush and expense?

Well, quite frankly, so far as the actual racing and its influence on the competition as a whole was concerned, the three Alpine stages were quite disappointing. With the known climbing experts, Gaul and Bahamontes, already out of the race, no new stars of the mountain came into view, and the climbing honours went to men who "got to the top" on all-round riding ability.

Instead of the big bunch being split into many small sections by the explosive jumps of men who somehow have the ability to sprint in the mountain, it was generally a question of a steady plug into the gradients, with the weaker elements being burned off the back. And yet, in another respect, the journey really was worth it after all, because in the course of the two days in the Alps I had a glimpse into the past – a glimpse of what is known in Tour de France circles as "the Heroic Era".

The Heroic Era was, roughly, the twenties; the era of Opperman, Frantz, Dewaele, when the riders had reached a tremendously high standard of ability and yet still had to perform on roads that – especially in the mountains – were often no better than farm-yard tracks. "You will never see the likes of these men again," we have often been told, "and you will never really be able to imagine the conditions under which their exploits were achieved."

Well, part of their argument will never be settled – whether Anquetil is as good a *rouleur* as was Faber in 1910; or if Charly Gaul could have held the wheel of René Pottier, the man who topped the Ballon d'Alsace climb in the Vosges with an hour lead over the next man.

But through a freak of nature, I had a small peep into the past and the kind of conditions those old-time Giants of the Road had to endure. A month or so before the Tour the worst storms in living memory, plus the exceptional thawing of the mountain snows, had transformed trickling streams into raging torrents tearing everything away in their path. And among the items washed away were long stretches of macadam road surface. All that was left was the gravel bed on which it had been laid … the kind of road the Tourmen faced thirty years ago.

The riders were being warned of these treacherous road conditions as I arrived at the assembly point at Thonon. "In certain sections it might be necessary to dismount", the microphone man was saying. They didn't seem too upset at this announcement, and busied themselves with their preparations for the long day ahead. With the sun beating down strongly, priority in pockets was given to *bidons*, rather than to solid food.

Much more anxious were the team mechanics! Louis Debruyckere (*mécano* for the N.E. Centre team) told me that most of his colleagues were averaging three hours sleep a night, and were now wondering if there would be any at all following those rough-road sections. Anxious, too, were the team directors. Would the rough roads allow them to keep behind their leading men and go to the immediate rescue in the case of mishap? Happiest of the lot seemed to be the photographers with the prospect of taking old-time pictures with modern equipment.

The field were called into action, reluctantly leaving their shady corners and once again facing the scorching sun.

The first miles gave no indication of the hard work to come, the road winding pleasantly through a green and fertile region. But soon the real character of the region was unfolded: a long, straight road heading for the mountain mass ahead.

Two years ago along this same road I saw Charly Gaul take to flight, accompanied on the early miles by Jan Nolten whom he used as an occasional pacemaker until the real hard work of the day began. Then Gaul dropped the Dutchman as effortlessly as the Dutchman would have dropped me.

Alpine Giant

There seemed little likelihood, considering the heat, of anybody "trying a Gaul" today, although his team-mate Barbosa (from Portugal) did open a gap of 100 yards or so, thought better of it and went back to the security of the steady club-run-like pace of the main bunch.

They looked a colourful bunch, those bright-jerseyed *coureurs* of seven nations and five regional French teams, snaking their way round the corners and curves of the undulating approach to the mountains, cheered on by a no less colourful Sunday crowd of bronzed enthusiasts.

This stage was, of course, to be dominated by the 8,500-feet Galibier, the Giant of the Alps, and yet there as well, at the beginning of the profile map of the course, was a succession of nasty little *cols* that any road-race promoter would be glad to include in his itinerary. In single-day races these hills would be tough enough to cause the breaking up of any bunch, but here in the Tour, with the Galibier Giant ahead, such dislocations of the *peloton* as there might be would inevitably be followed by a regroupment on the descent.

Typical of these early little difficulties was the Col de Tamie, where Bergaud and a few others became detached at the front with a 25-second lead over the bunch. But, as we anticipated, it was soon all one long line of riders cork-screwing down the other side towards the valley of the Isère. Then, just as the descent was about to finish and the field form one compact bunch again, there was a sudden burst of activity, with the Belgians and Italians to the fore. Jacques Anquetil had punctured!

Until two years ago, a puncture in the Tour was quite a serious matter for a top-line rider. The rules did not allow a wheel, fitted with a pumped-up tyre, to be taken from the following team car. The wheel and deflated tyre had to be separate, and the mechanic was not allowed to start slipping it on to the rim until his feet were on the ground. However quickly he worked there was always a fair gap left for the puncture victim and team-mates (who had waited back for him) to bridge. The mechanics were therefore ever alert and peering up into the bunch for signs of any trouble to their men. Last year, however, two moves were made which have considerably lessened the disadvantage of puncturing. In the first place, complete wheels and inflated tyres were allowed to be fitted, and secondly, a system was introduced into the race known as "Radio-Tour".

Radio-Tour was primarily intended for the use of the journalists covering the race. There are so many of them nowadays that it is impossible with one's own eyes to keep abreast of the various moves of the race, and so the race director's car is fitted with a transmitter working in conjunction with a second radio-car. All the Press cars are tuned into this station and are able to pick up details of any move made by the riders.

Also tuned into Radio-Tour are the team cars. And instead of the rider wanting attention having to hang back at the back of the bunch in order to attract his team car – which might be 100 yards back in the queue of vehicles – all that is necessary is for him to signal to the race director's car, from whence an S.O.S. is sent out.

And that was what happened when Anquetil punctured. The announcement came over: "Marcel Bidot: you are wanted in the *peloton*. Jacques Anquetil has punctured."

The system is, of course, an advantage in many respects, although many regret its introduction on the grounds that the initiative has now been taken out of team directorship.

Another disadvantage is that formerly it was possible to keep a puncture secret. A team-mate of the victim (provided, of course, the trouble was only a "slow" and not a completely flattened tyre) would drop back and signal to his car that help was wanted. Nowadays a puncture is immediately public knowledge in all the cars and if, say, an Italian Press car is passing the bunch at the moment of an announcement that a dangerous French opponent has punctured, who can blame them if they pass on the news to their compatriots racing in the bunch?

When Anquetil punctured on this tenth stage, however, the news got around in the bunch without radio. But, as I have said, a puncture when the field is compact and early in the race, while not a laughing matter, is not disastrous. Nevertheless, Anquetil had a few worried moments wondering if he would get back on before the mountain climbs. His worries were soon over for, with the help of one or two team-mates, he was quickly back in the bunch along the fine, wide road, gradually climbing alongside the River Isère to the little town of Saint Jean de Maurienne, the gateway to the Alps.

At least, the road is usually a wide one, but suddenly the riders had a taste of what was in store for them later on: the Isère, still high and swift flowing, had burst its banks a month ago and washed part of the road completely away, leaving nothing but a narrow, gravel path.

Was this the section the riders had been warned it might be necessary to walk? We thought so at first, but the almost complete absence of photographers indicated that it was not. With few exceptions the field clattered over the stones and were complete, though strung out into a long line, on taking aboard their food supplies at Saint Jean de Maurienne.

And then it came, that sudden glimpse of the Heroic Era of the old-time Tours. For stretches of 200 yards at a time the macadam road-surface had somehow been torn away by the surging floods, and all that was left was a pebbly beach. A few of the field tried to ride, but this was no place for 280-gram tyres, and soon the Tour de France took on the aspect of a sea-side cyclo-cross, with bikes-on-the-shoulders *coureurs* charging at the mass of photographers who voted this the best thing that had happened in the Tour since Wim van Est fell over the ravine in the Pyrenees.

This, then, was the punishment that the riders suffered before starting the real work of the day, the ascent of the Col du Télégraphe, which is, in effect, merely the half-way stage of the 34-km. climb to the top of the Galibier.

By comparison, the lower slopes of the Télégraphe were smooth going – and yet, by normal standards, absolutely shocking. One minute the riders would be throwing up clouds of dust, the next they were ploughing through miniature water-splashes caused by the swollen mountain streams.

Burned off

The "captain" of the Press car in which I was travelling, M. Raymond Huttier (on his 30th Tour), decided to see the climb from behind. That is to say, we would keep behind the field for a bit and then gradually work our way to the front as the road mounted upwards. Among the first to be burned off the back were two men who had won stages only a few days previously. The almost unknown Trochut of the French S.E. team, and the colourful Roger Hassenforder who, for once, had no time for pleasantries as he toiled up the mountain path.

"Hassen", despite that win into his home town of Colmar, had been having a rough time since, and nobody was really surprised to see him off the back so early. But an unexpected member of the rearguard turned out to be last year's winner, Roger Walkowiak. For the first few stages of the Tour "Walko" had confounded the critics who dismissed his 1956 success as a freak win, and had been well to the fore – but the cruel mountain was now revealing his true form, too.

The uphill dirt-track race continued. Past the toiling, sweating riders we went, frequently having to ease down until the dust dispersed. We marvelled that less than half the riders were using goggles. There was so much to occupy our attention on the "road" that only occasionally did we glance down at the widening valley, or up to the snow-topped giants ahead.

I will not confuse you by listing the names of all the riders we passed on our way towards the "front" of the race, but outstanding in one little group was the *maillot jaune* Jean Forestier, with no other French rider in support. This meant that Jacques Anquetil was ahead of him on the road!

And, sure enough, there in the next group of ten riders was the phenomenal Jacques, the time-trialist who they said could not sprint – and had yet already managed to win two Tour stages in bunch finishes; Anquetil, the *rouleur*, who the critics said would never make a mountain-climber – and yet was there not only surviving a classic test in a defensive capacity but attacking the job as well.

Still further ahead were the actual leaders of the stage, the winner of the Tour of Italy, Nencini, the French national Bauvin, and the Belgian surprise, Janssens. The three of them ran the gauntlet through a cheering mass of fans, sprinting like mad for the points counting in the Best Climber's prize. It was Nencini first, with Bauvin three seconds back and the Belgian another two seconds in arrears.

"So this is the Tour de France ..." Riders cyclo-cross one of the storm-ravaged passages near Saint Jean de Maurienne.

Towards the Snow

Their lead was obviously something like two minutes over the Anquetil group, and it now seemed likely that these three would also be involved in the sprint for the Galibier prime as well. But this proved not to be ... Bauvin had made his effort on a softening tyre, and immediately the top was reached looked back for help.

But help was not there. I have already explained the Radio-Tour system which summons aid to the rider in need, but this only operates to perfection when the field is *en peloton*. In the fantastic, dusty free-for-all in the mountains, the initiative of the team director once more comes into its own.

A team has two cars at its disposal. On the climb of the Télégraphe, the French boss, Marcel Bidot, was himself following the *maillot jaune* Forestier with the smaller car way back in reserve in case "Walko" or Stablinski ran into trouble. This meant that Bauvin was three minutes ahead of Bidot on the road, and by the time the car arrived Bauvin had changed his own tyre and was flashing down the crazy, pot-holed, winding ribbon of a road towards the sign which pronounced the final and biggest suffering of the day: "The Galibier summit – 16 kms."

By this time Nencini and Janssens were well ahead of him, and steadily moving up towards the snow line. The surface of the Galibier itself was good – a real road, in fact – and for the greater part of it, no more than a steady climb up an average gradient. "But there," said M. Huttier, pointing ahead, "is the real Galibier; that's where it begins to hurt." Seven kilometres in all and much of it a punishing 1-in-7."

It was easy to pick out the path of the road on the bare mountain side by the zig-zag of humanity lined out on either side.

Poor Bauvin was not now in the best of shape. Ahead of him the Belgian and Italian forged onwards; behind, the Anquetil group became split up and it was not Jacques who did the splitting, but another new French sensation, Marcel Rohrbach, who came into prominence last year by finishing second to Rivière in the amateur Tour of Europe, and this year gained selection to the N.E. Central team after a splendid win in the Midi-Libre classic.

Although Janssens won the sprint to the top from Nencini, the pair were being overhauled at a terrific rate by Rohrbach, who stormed up the last kilometre of the Galibier between two enthusiastic walls of spectators only 50 seconds down. In actual fact, he made the fastest time of the day for the 34-kilometre climb, at an average speed of 19.078 k.p.h. Ignoring the short, intermediate descent, his climb lasted 1 hr. 46 mins. 36 secs.

Rohrbach descended only moderately, yet managed to keep his

third place to the finish at Briançon, the picturesque town that is not only the highest in Europe, but the most independent so far as the Tour de France is concerned. In the Alpine stages it is virtually impossible to miss Briançon as an overnight stop, and as a consequence the Tour organisers are unable to command any payment for the privilege of taking the Tour into the town.

Thirty-nine seconds behind Rohrbach came in Anquetil and Schellemberg, the Franco–Swiss pair having put in a red-hot descent from the top.

A long gap followed during which there was much looking at watches and consultation of the general classification sheets to check by how much race leader Forestier had been leading Anquetil at the start of the stage. Then the news came over officially: "Anquetil *maillot jaune.*"

Great cheering greeted the announcement, and the new race leader Anquetil was riding his parade of honour in a bright new yellow jersey as Forestier – in a yellow jersey, too, but stained with the mud and sweat of a brave day spent in its defence – limped in to the finish.

Up at the top of the Galibier there is the monument to the memory of Henri Desgrange, the founder of the Tour. Perhaps, the spirit of "Papa" was there with the bike-crazy crowd as the riders began their plunge down towards Briançon. Compared with the Galibier battles of his day, and those Bartali–Coppi–Bobet–Kubler–Koblet exploits since the resumption of the series in 1947, this was but a moderate show. But from the sporting point of view, the struggle at the front was full of interest.

Nencini had been accused of winning the Tour of Italy only because enthusiastic spectators had pushed him up the hills – but he had shown on the Galibier that he is a decent climber without such help.

When the Belgian team had been selected, the most criticised name had been that of Janssens. "What will *he* do?" many journalists asked. "He'll be back in Antwerp within a week." Yet he had won the fourth stage into Roubaix, and now was proving himself a useful man uphill as well.

And Anquetil and Rohrbach had proved the old adage that a rider with "class" will always put up a good show in the mountains, if not a brilliant one.

That then was the end of the first day in the Alps, and so far as the denouement of the race was concerned, it was the only day. The eleventh stage, starting at Briançon and ending in Cannes, was scheduled to include two tough passes, the Vars and Allos, both over 6,000 feet, as well as one or two other choice little obstacles thrown in near the coast. But Vars was not ridden. The mountain floods had torn the road to shreds and it was impossible to ride. "No, not even the riders of the *Époque Héroique* could have ridden it," an official told me.

Instead, a great loop was made, increasing the distance to nearly 200 miles but over a decent, flattish road. The Allos climb failed to produce any real decision, owing entirely to Anquetil's resolute defence of his leadership, and neither did the end-of-stage *cols*, although some of the riders were only just hanging on to the Anquetil-controlled bunch. Jean Bobet, who was dropped twice but rejoined bravely, told me next day that if the Vars *had* been ridden, he reckoned that 30 riders would have failed to beat the time limit, which had been increased to 15 per cent.

Three riders (Privat, Lauredi, Wim van Est) finished at Cannes comfortably ahead of the field, all their lead having been achieved in the last 30 miles.

Next day it was Cannes–Marseille and "no decision" again. As a reward for all the good *domestique* work he had been doing for the French national team since the start at Nantes, Jean Stablinski was given a free hand. He took it, breaking away soon after the start with Anglade, whom he later dropped, and won the stage with 14 minutes to spare.

Then it was Marseille–Perpignan for the riders, and Marseille–London for me. I had seen no great mountain climbing as I had hoped, but that glimpse of the conditions those of the "Heroic Era" endured was well worth the trip. But the biggest marvel of all, to me, was the way the slender modern bicycle, gears and tyres stood up to the test, and the mechanics managed to get some sleep, after all.

Sporting Cyclist, September 1957

TIME-TRIAL BIKE WITHOUT BRACKE

Rest day at Andorra. I first heard about that last winter before this racing come-back idea entered my head. I thought how pleasant it will be looking round the "Pocket state" on foot, with maybe a trip into Spain in the car. Then, on re-examining the situation as an active cyclist, I realised that if I could borrow a bike, then, whichever way I rode, it would not just be uphill, but up-mountain. The road running through the little independent republic is only 20 miles in length and this led to and from Spain or France, and there was one route off at right angles to the north which ended abruptly after ten miles at the foot of the great Pic de Seguer.

The Tourmen approached Andorra from the French side, branching off the well-worn Route des Pyrénées after the descent of Puymorens and immediately beginning the climb of the 7,900-foot Col de l'Envalira. Surprisingly this *col* had figured little in international competition and fearful tales were told about its severity. When dirt-surfaced it must indeed have been a tough one; now it is a fine wide boulevard.

We saw Jiménez reach the top well clear of the main group, then swooped down past him into the narrow main street of Les Escaldes at the eastern end of Andorra-la-Vieille, the smallest capital in the world with a population of 600. On the way down I decided that so far as my rest day riding was concerned, my choice was now down to two roads. I didn't fancy toiling up that bit of *col* on my day off! That night, in a restaurant, our table was next to that of Raphaël Géminiani and Raymond Louviot; and by the end of the meal the two tables had become one. I had, too, their permission to borrow one of the Gitane bikes ridden by the Saint Raphaël team. "Call in at our hotel at Les Escaldes in the morning and see my son, or Louis Debruyckere," said Louviot.

To visit a team's hotel often means that the place turns out to be miles away on the other side of the town. In Andorra it was easy. All 12 teams were in a group of hotels at Les Escaldes with 50 yards covering the lot. It was while walking towards the Hotel Europa, where the Saint Raphaël team was staying, that I came across a Peugeot team driver writing cards on the *terrasse* of his hotel. He told me that Tom Simpson had just gone over the road to the field where the team's cars and vans were parked.

"Going for a ride?" Tom asked. He was strapping a spare tyre on the saddle.

"Yes; later on. I have to go to see Louis or Louviot junior to get one of their bikes."

"You don't have to do that," said Tom. "Have one of ours. You want a fairly big frame. Bracke's should suit you O.K. He won't need it, anyway; he was eliminated yesterday. Why not come out now with me?"

An invitation not to be missed. *Directeur sportif* Gaston Plaud approved the loan, and Tom rode with me down to my hotel. While I was changing, my *Paris–Normandie* car-mates came to talk to *le sympathique Tom*, who always finds an interesting paragraph for Pressmen.

"Did you know that I ride the Tour on my wife's handbag?" he was asking as I rejoined the party. " It's true. I am using a plastic saddle, but it is covered with a bit of one of Helen's old leather handbags. It is perfectly comfortable even in the hottest weather."

Then came the choice of which road to take. This way or that? "This," the direction in which our wheels were pointing, was towards Spain. "That" was back towards France, whence Tom had come on Saturday and whither he was due to return on Monday. He would hardly want to go that way on his Sunday off. But he did.

"Do you mind if we go back up the Envalira?" he asked. "I have some Belgian friends camping up there on the pass. They live in Ghent, and I would like to call and see them."

So the bikes were turned round, and back through the town we went, just as you see us in the picture. That was taken by friend Honoré Willems of Brussels whose more vigorous photographs of Tom and others have so often been admired in our pages. If he had not been around, however, this article would not have lacked for photographs. All the Press cars seemed to be heading towards the Envalira, which seemed strange until I remembered that there was a reception up at Radio Andorra. Colleagues photographed us at least half a dozen times.

As for the members of the public who saw us passing by, even in that area where cycling stars are seldom seen and television has not yet reached, Tom Simpson was immediately recognised. But who was the other rider? Even those with newspapers were unable to check the number, since that had been removed on Bracke's retirement.

(photo: H. Willems)

It was tough being an unidentified Tour object, for, from the first stroke of the Stronglight we were beginning to climb. Although Tom took it very gently on my account, it was tough enough. After a few kilometres round the ever-mounting loops we came to the Radio Andorra station on our right, the forecourt packed with Press and official cars.

Upwards we pressed – or rather I pressed, for Tom's pedals seemed to want no pressing at all – until, after seven kilometres, we came to our destination, the "first camping on the left" (appropriately the village is called Encamp) where Tom's friends were staying. The young couple and small son were in a fine tent and the lady of the canvas house soon had coffee ready for us as we relaxed in deck chairs. We spent a pleasant hour in their company before rousing ourselves to tackle the seven kilometres back to base.

On the way up I had not much time to spend considering the bicycle I was riding. I had been on the smallest and the biggest (reading from front to back of the bicycle) with hands on top the whole time. On the descent it would have been possible to switch over to the biggest and the smallest, but there was no point in that since 60 kms. per could have been achieved with no gears at all.

My "discovery" on the way down, when it was necessary to be down on the bars the whole time in order to apply the brakes, was the very forward reach on this Peugeot of Ferdinand Bracke. At the time, of course, he was unknown as a pursuit rider, but with a big reputation as a road time-trialist. Chatting with the Belgian before setting out on this ride, I noticed that he was about 5 ft. 11 ins., or just below my height. I was stretched right out when holding the business-ends of the bars – a bit too stretched for my comfort. Bracke probably has a longer back and arms and looks very comfortable and streamlined in action.

No doubt because of this long extension and forward gripping position and steepish head, the bike's downhill behaviour was quite remarkable; it seemed to be on a descender's beam operated by some past-master of the art like Leducq or Magni, and all I had to do was sit and be dropped down into the town with no more to do than occasionally apply the brakes.

On the way down I noticed the precincts of Radio Andorra were now choked with cars. In there, enjoying the local hospitality, were scores of officials, Pressmen, sporting directors – and one rider, Anquetil. Jacques had scorned the usual rest-day ride, and colleagues who were at the reception say that he sampled all there was to eat and drink without a thought for the morrow. Twenty-four hours later, when passing Radio Andorra at the start of the stage to Toulouse, Jacques was already beginning to suffer, and further up the *col* he nearly retired.

Having promised the mechanics to have the bike returned to the hotel by five o'clock and with work to do in the afternoon, it seemed that 16 kms. or so was to be the extent of my rest day ride. On the way back with the bike just before five I met the mechanic in the street. He had changed his plans – and I could have an extension until 7 p.m., at which time he wanted to lock up the equipment for the night. So, back to my hotel, back into shorts, back on to the bike. Of the two roads left, I rejected that towards the Spanish frontier as I heard it was busy with motor traffic. It was the Ordino road, climbing steeply northwards out of Andorra, through the Gorges of Sant Antoni, that I took.

Whereas the lower Envalira road we had ridden in the morning had the freedom of a wide valley in which to find its upward way by the gentlest possible route, here the path had been hewn out of the towering rocks. Three dark, damp tunnels came near the top of the climb, which revealed a rock-topped bowl of sunlit enchantment which tapered off in the distant Valira del Nord. How I wished that there were time to go right to the end of that inviting road!

My "turn", alas, had to be Ordino, a pretty village where the locals noted my arrival with friendly but puzzled applause. They seemed to recognise a real Tour bike all right, but couldn't quite see the slim grey-head as a rival of Bahamontes or Anquetil (with their country being tucked in between France and Spain, Andorrans are inevitably a little bit of each in many respects; from my brief visit I got the impression that they are much more Spanish than French).

Back towards the tiny capital, up towards the tunnels, through them with care for the surface was wet and slippery, then swish down through the gorge on the shooting-Bracke-bicycle into the town. I returned the bike in good time, and walked back to my hotel, the tops of the legs aching slightly with every stride. That Peugeot may have known its way down the mountains, but it left things to me on the way up.

*   *   *

Just over three months later I saw Ferdinand Bracke again. He had qualified easily for the quarter-final of the World Professional Pursuit Championship, the final of which he was destined to win in splendid style. In common with many riders he used to warm up on the Parc des Princes on a road bike. It was a Peugeot, of course, and it pleased me no end when he told me that it was the same machine I had borrowed in Andorra, the day I rode my slow but enjoyable ride against the mechanic's watch.

Sporting Cyclist, January 1965

J. B. Wadley introducing René de Latour to British clubmen.
Caen, July 1967
(photo: Neville Chanin)

GASTON NENCINI

Sporting Cyclist – the journal for which J. B. Wadley is best remembered. After four issues as a quarterly, called Coureur, Sporting Cyclist appeared each month from May 1956 to April 1968. Its front-cover, designed by Art Editor Glenn Steward, was invariably clean and uncluttered.

Glen Steward's portrait of Louison Bobet which
featured on the cover of the first issue of Coureur.
(Richard Allchin collection)

One of the great Tour de France images. This photograph of Bernard Thévenet on the Col de l'Izoard on Bastille Day during the 1975 Tour was selected by JBW to illustrate John Pierce's work in his article 'Tour Fever' which appeared in Amateur Photographer.
(Photosport International/J. Pierce)

Dr. J. Moore showing J. B. Wadley and his wife, Mary, the velocipede on which his father (James) won the world's first cycle race at the Parc St. Cloud, Paris, on 31st May, 1868.

CYCLOTOURISME

For years J. B. Wadley used to advise cyclists that the best holiday they could have would be to take their bikes to France in July, and to follow as much as they could of the Tour de France. And for years, from his seat in a Press car – 'his prison without handlebars', as he called it – he envied all those he met along the route who had accepted his advice. In 1973, a fortnight before the start of the Tour, his regular contract with the *Daily Telegraph* to provide them with a half-column on each day's stage was cancelled. For the first time in years he had the opportunity to abide by his own recommendation.

This was the point of departure of *My 19th Tour de France*, a book which JBW published the following year. Straightforwardly, it is the story of a cycling journey of some 1,750 miles which took in the official Tour at various points along its circular route, but it goes beyond that: the narrative of the physical journey also involves a journey of the mind – a set of reminiscences back through 60 years of Tour de France history – and contains eulogies to two dead friends – Tom Simpson and Shay Elliott. It also includes as vivid an account of cyclotouring at its toughest as you will ever find.

Bidding a last farewell to the Tour outside Brive, JBW continued eastwards, for he had a rendezvous with the cyclotourists of Grenoble, organisers of the bi-annual *Brevet de Randonneur des Alpes*.

It had been only a few years earlier that Wadley had got to know this aspect of French cycling, an acquaintance which soon had him taking part in the 1971 Paris–Brest–Paris. On that occasion he had planned to ride in his home colours of the Colchester Rovers C.C., but he found himself recruited into the ranks of the somewhat more *sportif* Parisian-based, Union Sportive de Creteil.

At the beginning of 1973, JBW made plans to ride another of the cyclotouring classics, the *Flèche Velocio*, which traditionally took place during Easter week; his intention was to tackle the 40-hour version, and ride it at his own pace. Once again he was dragooned by the U.S. Creteil squad into forming part of their 4-up squad for the 24-hour version of the randonnée. He was to meet up with these zealous hard-riders once more that year, on the slopes of the Col du Galibier during the *27th Brevet de Randonneur des Alpes*. The account of that ride constitutes the final chapter of *My 19th Tour de France*.

27th BREVET DE RANDONNEUR DES ALPES

After paying 20 francs and seeing my name put on the list of over-40s I went out to the forecourt to find my three "Flèchard" friends had been joined by other members of our US Creteil. A club-mate, remembering how I had stopped for a good feed at all 15 Intermediate Controls of the Paris–Brest–Paris, invited me to his "restaurant" on this BRA. "My wife will be with the car at St. Michel de Maurienne. Steak, omelette, anything you like. Stoke up well ready for the Galibier."

I looked round the parked bicycles. Although there were a few stripped machines, by far the greater part were the *Randonneur* type with medium-weight tubular tyres, or light wired-ons, mudguards, handlebar bags and support – the correct dress for most *cyclotouriste* trials. Lighting varied from the sublime – slim, dainty dynamos and elegant white and red lamps – to the ridiculous torches lashed to extensions of front forks, and thimble-sized red buttons stuck in odd places on the back end of the bicycle.

Every other *Randonneur* machine had triple chain rings. I checked gears and found only a few with a "higher low" than my own 36. The 28 x 28 combination was quite common and a nice easy one to work out by the British method: 27 x 28 ÷ 28 = 27…

"It's 5 o'clock – time for the Englishman to have his cup of tea," announced Beaumann, and soon half a dozen of us had a little pot each in a corner of the hot, crowded bar.* Beaumann was on a cycling holiday, something like my own in that he was fitting in a few *Randonneur* events at week-ends and riding pretty hard in between.

Our tea-party broke up with "see you at two o'clock" or "see you at three" according to when our age group started. I added "See you at seven," to Beaumann & Co. who, I reckoned, would catch me after I had been on the road five hours.

Back to the hotel just in time to miss a downpour which in minutes has the city streets awash. Stretch out on the bed in a half-sleep muttering curses about noisy hotels near main-line stations and flickering advertising signs right outside the window. Coming-to with the realisation that trains and neon lights aren't to blame.

---

* Roger Beaumann – President, Union Sportive de Creteil.

It's an out-size thunderstorm. Picking up now the undertones of the Wagnerian spectacular, the dull plonk of rain pouring on to canvas awnings, the swish of car tyres on streaming roads. Black sky gives premature birth to the night, but no need to switch on bedside lamp to see the time. Enough lightning to read a map. Eight o'clock. Down to the hotel restaurant to eat. A simple bourgeois restaurant where surprisingly there are lit candles on the tables. That usually means a franc or two extra on the bill. Not here. Before I've ordered, out go the electric lights, the waitresses carry on by candle-power without so much as a giggle. Just one of those things you expect in these parts during a thunderstorm. Cooking by gas, says my *serveuse*. Bright lights go on briefly during *crudités*, then off for keeps before the steak arrives. Problems for waitress separating Well Done, Medium and Rare in the gloom. Cheese, fruit compôte, no coffee and back upstairs for a shave and another attempt to sleep. Second act of Wagner a bit quieter. Two hours oblivion ended by alarm clock. Lights working, still raining hard, lightning less frequent, thunder grumbling far away. Five minutes past midnight, Sunday 22nd July. Start talking to myself. "Happy Birthday JBW." Born a fortnight before the start of the 1914 war.

The Croix de Fer
Enveloped in the yellow cape I rode through the still busy, wet streets of Grenoble towards the Anneau de Vitesse. The outsize plastic tent had been ideal shelter while waiting in the rain on the Tourmalet, and draped nicely over the handlebar bag on the descent.* When I climbed out of the saddle, however, it rubbed grittily on the front tyre, and I would be doing plenty of that today. In the bag, and in a plastic roll on the rear carrier, there was a change of clothing just in case I had to pack up in some outlandish spot, soaked through. The front lamp was on the right fork bracket (the wrong side for France) and the rear Pifco which had clattered on to the *pavé* 2,000 kms. ago in Flanders, taped solidly below the seat cluster.

Although it was only midnight-30 when I arrived at the launching base, the long veranda outside the building was packed with bikes, and others were stacked piled-arms fashion outside with waterproofs protecting saddles from the steady rain. Pressure was

---

* JBW had watched the Tour on the Tourmalet in pouring rain.

low over Grenoble. Inside the crowded bar, however, the pressure was high and spirits, too. The over-40s were in command, about a hundred strong, and mostly in great form, particularly the smiling fellow who squeezed up to make room for me at his table. While I tackled a pot of tea and bread and jam he extolled on the ideal weather for such a trip.

"Ideal? But it's raining like mad. Have you had a forecast of something good on the way?"

"No. On the contrary, the rain will last for several hours and obviously get heavier the higher we climb."

"So we shall see nothing on the Croix de Fer ..."

"Agreed that we shall not be admiring vast panoramas of the picture postcard type. But the mountain is wonderful at close quarters in the heavy rain. We shall see, we shall hear, the streams, rivers, cascades, falls, torrents, bursting with energy whereas after a drought they are little more than trickles. Very impressive. I'm looking forward to it very much."

Before this cheerful philosopher left to check his bike I learned that he was 63, that this was his fourth BRA and that he hoped to get in another two or three before taking cycling more sedately. This good apostle of the mountain who lifted my morale was soon replaced by the voice of the tempter.

"Just listened to the forecast. Terrible. They reckon it will be murder on the Croix de Fer. You know that descent? Dangerous even in dry weather. Shouldn't be surprised if there were some nasty accidents today. I'm not starting. Going back to the hotel for another few hours' kip. You're not going to *ride* are you? What's your age? Fifty-nine today? Blowed if I would spend my birthday getting soaked through, all for a 50-centimes badge. You should be more careful at your age, you know."

Well now. Something in what the devil was saying. That descent. I knew it well from Tour-following; I was terrified even with an experienced chauffeur at the wheel. It would be dreadful on the bike in the rain. That bit about age, too. I'd manage the Croix all right, but the mighty Galibier ...

To ride or not to ride. I looked round the bar. Scores of cheerful characters, ankle-socked, race-jerseyed, peak-capped, drinking coffee, filling flasks, munching *croissants*, cracking jokes. Some nearly 70. Yes, I'd ride. Then along came the club-mate whose wife was going to feed me at the foot of the Galibier.

"You here, Wadley? Didn't think you would bother to leave your hotel in such weather. I only came to pick up some stuff I'd left in the changing-room. Ride? You must be joking! I've got a wife and family. I cycle for pleasure, not for punishment. Downright danger-ous setting off to climb a 2,000-metre mountain in the middle of the night. Anybody starting wants his head examined."

"So your 'restaurant' won't be open at St. Michel after all?"

"Too true it won't! We're going to drive straight home."

To ride or not to ride, that was still the question. Here now was a trim girl of 17 nearly as far from home as I was, Brigette Decours of Dieppe who many British tourists have met at the Cider Meet at St. Lo and other rallies in the Normandy–Picardy area. She was a bit scared, she said, but meant to start with her father and other members of the Cyclo-Club Dieppois.

"Starting?" Another acquaintance who spoke good English and knew a proverb or two. "Better to be safe than sorry. Discretion is the better part of valour."

And, in more prosaic terms: "Take bloody care!"

At 01h 45 somebody was shouting from the main entrance to the bar. "It is still raining, but we must proceed with the formal-ities. There are Control tables set up outside alphabetically. Go to the one corresponding to your surname and collect your Route Card. Then get out on to the road. You will be free to start anytime after two o'clock."

On the way out I asked an official the grand total of entries. One thousand two hundred was the answer and he reckoned 1,100 would be starting. I found the "W" table where by torchlight a helper went down the damp list to my name, ticking it off and handing me a card marked in squares to take official and secret Control stamps on the way. I slipped it in a pocket protected by a plastic bag.

To cape or not to cape? To climb for four hours without one and get soaked from above, or to pedal in a tent and ditto from conden-sation? No cape, I decided. Lining up, my companions of the road sported a motley collection of short waterproofs and a few, like me, had decided to ride in uncovered tracksuits. And, of course, there was the super-hardy character in shoes, shorts, shirt and nothing else at two o'clock in the morning. "I'll be able to swim through the floods," he was saying.

Beaumann and the other three o'clock starters of US Creteil had arrived to wish me luck, but a couple of defaulting club-mates who should have been on the line with me kept in the background. A photographer's flash bounced off the shiny wet road and with a few cheers and waves we were off on the Circuit des Grands Cols which I had seen described in a brochure as "A wonderful experience for automobilists. Splendid panoramas. Some very difficult roads demanding careful driving. Allow a long day." Our party of cyclists was beginning their own long day. Just two o'clock, and we had until ten at night to enjoy that wonderful experience.

So here we are on the BRA, no connection with the BAR which demands that we ride alone and unassisted against the watch. Here we can have as much back wheel as we like. That wheel in front I don't like. One of the no-mudguard brigade. I drop back a place or two to trail an altruist who has a nice long fat celluloid extension growing from his back Bluemels. Still get wet, though. Rain and drippings from the laden trees. We are on the service road, which is compulsory for the first five miles, at a nice gentle pace, with a police car moving alongside on the central highway. Driver seems to have a pal in the *peloton* and friendly insults pass to and fro. My neighbour is talking politely:

"Well, we shall be all right if we are back here in 19 hours. We shall qualify with half an hour to spare. I only scraped in by five minutes last time …"

Nineteen and a half hours? My target is five hours faster, so I must get a move on. A nice racey feeling, pedalling briskly under the street lamps towards a dull cluster of red lights 200 metres ahead. The junction made (as race reports say), I settle in with what turns out to be the second group on the road, a score or so having sprinted off in front from the start. Crazy guys! But that is probably what my nineteen-and-a-half-hour friend is calling me. Nearly 20 hours, 15 hours, 10 hours, it doesn't matter, and that's the beauty of these *Randonneur* trials because we'll all get the same rewards

At Pont de Claix we leave the restricted N75 and turn left from street lighting into the darkness of the night, capes flapping, the odd dynamo wetly humming. After a few miles a village shows a lamp or two. "Vizille," says my neighbour. "It was here quite recently that the Belgian holiday coach ran out of control down the Col du Laffrey and crashed over a bridge into the Romanche River. Most of the passengers were drowned."

Our road climbs east gently, and with 35 lbs. of luggage left at the hotel I feel as though I am riding downhill. I am in the middle of the bunch of 20, at the head of which a steady pair are doing a good job pathfinding as well as pacemaking. Not so ridiculous, perhaps, those torches driving long wedges of white into the night. Black as ink in other directions. We are in the Gorges de la Romanche. A glance up to the roof of the corridor finds a pinpoint of light. A star! Weather forecast wrong! False hopes. It's a lamp on top of a cliff. A fine rain is falling through the roof of our prison, cool and welcome now the road is rising steadily. Suddenly we are surrounded by light and noise. Thunder? Yes, but this electric storm is made by man. A generating station harnessing the rushing waters of the Romanche whose industrial corridor we are now entering.

During the next 15 miles we pass more factories powered by roaring turbines churning the river into a down rush of foam and fury. One turbulent channel is just over the fence from our road and is terrifying to behold. My little rain-loving friend who had boosted my morale back at HQ is right. Impressive the mountain after it has taken a soaking.

"Attension Rye!"

That's what it sounds like, that shrill cry of warning from two women holding umbrellas and pointing torches on to the road. Three o'clock in the morning it is, and I'm not at my brightest. Then it registers.

"Attention - Rails! Two of the first bunch came a cropper here. Careful. *Bonjour Chéri – ça va?*"

A useful service from French equivalent of the wives and girl-friends who serve and wait on our own road circuits and time-trial courses. Five minutes later they toot by in a car with more cries to their *chéris*, but soon are on the job again warning us against a new hazard. This time it's a crop of *nids de poules* – chickens' nests, or pot-holes.

"This is Rochetaillée coming up," announces a member of the party. "We turn off the main road here."

Time 04hrs. 15. We have covered 26 miles in 2 hours 15 minutes and climbed 1,800 feet. Just a little leg-loosener during which I have not changed to a gear lower than 63. As we swing left off the Route Nationale our lights pick up a sign. *COL DE LA CROIX DE FER 30 kms.* That name on a map or Tour itinerary; in a race report; brought up in conversation by *coureur* or *cyclotouriste*: "Pass of the Iron Cross" always gives me a thrill. This glimpse of it from a bicycle, in the rain, during the early hours of my birthday when taking part in one of the most famous of all *Randonneur* trials – *COL DE LA CROIX DE FER 30 kms.* is the fingerpost to high adventure.

From close-up views of *coureurs* climbing mountains in the Tour de France I know that following a wheel a little bit too fast for you is asking for trouble. All the same I don't mean to drop off from this gang for a mile or two yet. They're obviously old hands at the business and know the way. Once out of the tricky bit round Allemont there will be no chance of going off-course. Surprise! When we're through that village and I am down to the 32 chainwheel for the first time, some red lights are coming backwards to meet me.

"La Grande Montagne n'accepte pas la petite forme," says one fellow sadly as I pass, which being interpreted means that it's no good having little form in big mountains. I am now soaked by the steady rain which no doubt is getting colder as we climb, but with bodies warming with the effort it is no bad arrangement. Glad I am not to be encumbered with that cape brushing on the front tyre every time I take a stretch out of the saddle. Some are tough, though the 32 x 24 is still unused. I think of my US Creteil club-mate who waxed lyrical on hearing that I proposed riding the BRA on my 59th birthday. "What more wonderful way for a cyclist to celebrate his birthday," he enthused, "than to pedal into the sunrise on the Col de la Croix de Fer. The cool, crisp morning air, the burbling streams, the matchless greenery of mountain grass spattered with sweet-scented brightly coloured flowers, the vast panorama of the Alps. To see all this on the Croix de Fer with the first red rays of the sun kissing the snow-capped peaks – that is a birthday gift which no money can buy, a memory that time will never erase."

No good looking for the proposer of this stirring toast. He is one of the defaulters and probably fast asleep in bed. No good looking round for the view, although it is now 5 o'clock and time for the birthday gift to be opened. Just a rainy lane climbing in a tunnel of trees and fog. I might be on a club run in Essex (Col de Fer Rovers?) except for all those front handlebar bags and triple chainwheels and loud water noises. Although the Romanche hasn't been with us since we turned off the main road at Rochetaillée, there is no shortage of water, and that must be the Eau d'Olle roaring down below to our right. It can't be seen, of course, but I know from sessions with a map that the long Chaine de Belledonne rises sharply on our left, riven by a dozen precipitous streams which then pass underneath our road. Today there's not room in the subway and water is spilling over the top. A brief gap in the fog lets us see where it is going, far below to the white ribbon of the Eau d'Olle rushing headlong over the rocks.

Day is coming reluctantly and in the half-light we are able to pick a path through the pot-holed and gravel-rashed road whose skin is constantly being attacked by frost and running water. Just when I think I am going pretty well for an old-un I am left standing by a nicely shaped girl in a red cape, a kind of bathing hat and shorts which appear to have shrunk to next to nothing in the rain. She swerves from one side of the road to the other and half-way back again as if seeking the right trail, then plunges through a two-inch flood of muddy water running diagonally down the hill. A perky grey-head is pushing his bike through. "Nice place to puncture!" he calls as I splash by slowly. "That's the second since Grenoble, and with wired-on tyres, too. Still, no trouble finding the hole with all this water around. I'll finish this BRA like a cyclo-cross man!" And thinking it not a bad idea at that, he lifts the bike on to his shoulder. Splashing like a boy in a puddle, he trots beside me until the road lifts out of the flood.

Round the corner I catch the Queen of the Mountain, but only because she has joined a general meeting taking place across the road and into a lay-by levelled from the rock. A score of riders and bikes, two cars. In the lee of an old building a long trestle table represents official Headquarters. At one end, the office; at the other, the kitchen. We get a watery stamp on our carefully packed Control Cards and a cardboard beaker of hot tea, and biscuits. Strange. I thought the Croix de Fer control was at the summit and not half-way up? And why tea and not Ovalmaltine? Contravention of the *cyclotouriste* Trade Description Act! Between sips and bites I raise the matter with the Minister of Food in this high parliament of pedallers – a lady who speaks even quicker and thicker than the lad I met on the Tourmalet. I only understand the last two words of her reply; *l'autre côte* ... the other side.

The girl-Gaul has already left. Why are these other fellows still hanging around? Reet starved they look, as they say in Yorkshire of anybody shivering with cold. Reet fed up, too, and three are beginning to ride *down* the hill. Packers! Deserters! Chuckers! (as they said in Penny Farthing Days). Suddenly the steady rain becomes a downpour. A fork of lightning flash-lights the chasm, an overhead crack of thunder is answered by a mountain echo dying sadly in a distant combe. Dangerous around these parts: too many trees. Safer to climb above the timberline. I take another quick cup of char and am off, at the same time as two others who had followed me into the Control. The group of packers continues its meeting.

"How far to the summit?" I ask one of the pair.

"A good 10 kilometres – if we ever get there," he replies, sprinting ahead to join his mate.

In fact the next stone says Croix de Fer 16 kms. Ten miles. Mud and rocks the size of footballs, loosened from the embankment by the rain, are now a further hazard. I pass a struggling mixed-tandem pair as lightning flashes and thunder peels, and ripple through another sheet of flood. For hours now the background voice of water has been climbing with us. Gaps in trees and mist have lately given glimpses of the varied list of speakers, from murmuring becks to roaring rapids and long white streaks spilling from the gutters of the mountain.

Now comes a new sound shaking the road like the deep note of a great organ, swelling as I edge forward. Round the corner is the player, a sheet of foaming water wider than the road and thrice as tall pouring from a ledge on the wall of rock. The rain has swollen a torrent many times its normal size and instead of the water soberly passing into the valley by a sunken pipe, it is fighting drunk and spewing all over the road. Besides its overdose of drink the mountain is throwing up – or rather down – rocks and stones crashing on to the base to rip away the metal surface and loose foundations.

I push the bike slowly forward, hardly realising I am ankle-deep in muddy water, and squeeze into a row of a dozen riders standing on the bank of the cross-road rapid. Like them I am fascinated by the torrent on the left, the eyes-front flood, and most of all by the unprotected drop to the right over which the water is falling.

How deep is the barrier? Too deep, my neighbour says with a last look at the flood before starting to ride back down the hill. Now the mystery of the Control meeting is explained, and indeed why the Control is there instead of the summit. The cars couldn't get through upwards with the rubber stamps, nor the van downwards with the Ovalmaltine drinks.

How strong the current? Very, according to another bystander. What's wanted, he says, is about 20 yards of rope to make a handrail and perhaps a car will come along with that very thing in the boot.

Anybody got across? Yes, several. Beyond the channel, through the gloom, I can see two. One stands pushing both hands forwards inside a sleeveless cape to form a tent. His photographer pal squats underneath keeping the rain from his lens. Hope it's a fast film. Should be his picture of the year.

Another is now taking the plunge, bike over shoulder, starting near the middle of the road and going straight as a die until nearing mid-stream where the water is up to his knees. Then the current grabs him by the ankles to draw him several degrees off course. He is learning the hard way the laws of Hydrostatic Pressure and of Hydrodynamic Force. He arrives safely the other side, shakes himself like a dog, and has a celebration drink from a *bidon*.

I boggle (a nice word and appropriate. *I start with fright, shy, hesitate* {Concise Oxford Dictionary}). Think I'll pack up, too. Nobody at home will know. Or will they? They read French newspapers at the Cyclists' Touring Club headquarters in Godalming, Surrey. They'd give me a paragraph in the Touring Miscellany feature in *Cycle Touring* magazine.

> C.T.C. MEMBER J. B. Wadley was among the 1,040 starters in the bi-annual Brevet de *Randonneur* des Alpes tourist trial held in July. Heavy rain caused flooding on the *Col* de la Croix de Fer where the road was cut by a transient stream. The more adventurous participants waded through, but the Englishman – who is President of the Colchester Rovers C.C. – was among those who preferred returning to headquarters at Grenoble. Twelve women completed the course.

No. Can't have that. I will start at the same place as the last fellow, head more to the left and fight the current instead of getting carried away as he was. I make a good start. Complacency sets in. Half-way across and the feet dragging, a side-ways stumble sends the bike slipping off my right shoulder into the water. I manage to hang on to the bars and top tube. The bike is pulled almost horizontal and me with it. The torrent roars in triumph. Journalist to the last a telex message races through my mind.

GRENOBLE FRANCE SUNDAY 22 JOHN WADLEY JOURNALIST KEW SURREY SWEPT OVER MOUNTAIN PRECIPICE WITH BICYCLE WHEN COMPETING 150

MILES CYCLE-TOURING TRIAL FRENCH ALPS
ATTEMPTING CROSS SECTION OF FLOODED CROIX DE
FER PASS WADLEY BELIEVED 59 TODAY MORE
FOLLOWS.

Cancel message. I regain balance, shorten right-hand grip to just above bracket and lift bike clear of water, turn left and stagger ashore. Soggy cold below shaking knees; hot, sweaty, very relieved above. Wring sodden track bottoms, tip water out of shoes, stamp feet. Watch others cross. Three march straight over, one does a J. B. Wobbly and gets 3 out of 10. I am about to check position on map when another successful cross-channel tripper saves me the bother.

"We are in the Défilé de Maupas, and that is the Torrent des Sept Laux. It drains seven lakes high up there in the mountains, like the overflow pipe of a water cistern. It is always busy after heavy rain but I have never seen it as angry as this."

Hopeless, I know, but it's worth trying to get a picture. Hopeless because I'm using a small automatic camera with no device for long exposures, and slow colour film. Colour! Black and grey it is, an oblong of dirty white for the torrent and needles of slanting rain. Half-past five. Time to get moving. A last look back and now forward for the next item on the programme. *Two hundred yards uphill, veterans, pushing bicycle.* Feet and legs now warmer. Next event: *second round of the cyclo-Croix.* Same distance as at Torrent, but with stones instead of water. Here the road is a narrow ledge on a cliff, dropping down on the right to the Eau d'Olle River. On the left a high embankment of loose rock as steep as the bend of an indoor track. You've seen it dozens of times on Westerns, the baddy planting his stick of dynamite, lighting blue touch paper and retiring immediately. Here in the Alps the mountain hold-up man scrambles his landslides by a different recipe. *Soak earth in rain for 12 hours. Rock cakes in rich mud sauce roll down chute over road.*

The first fence of the cyclo-cross is low, but round the bend is a real avalanche as if clawed on to the road by the hand of a crazy giant. A television car has managed to get through the flood and its crew, driver, reporter, cameraman are all in the same union, man-handling boulders over the ravine to clear a path. A bit slippery clambering over, bike on shoulder, and I am pedalling again before realising how much more dangerous falling rock can be than a water-fall. Luckily there are no major slides, just a few rocks and stones which are easy to avoid at my small pace. One round stone is actually rolling lazily on to the road as I pass and ends up in a pot-hole like a well-aimed ball on a pin-table. Instant road repairing. Glassy panes of flood water cross the road briskly *en route* for the valley, patches of mud loiter with intent, giving the back wheel a touch of the home-trainers, spinning fast and getting nowhere.

Visibility downwards, improving, showing a small detail of the mountain picture which, owing to circumstances beyond our control is not fully available today for public viewing. A water-colour of course, and all we can see is the thick white line of the rushing Eau d'Olle and thin transverse feeding streams foaming down each side of its valley. Looks like a long fish bone on a green plate.

Visibility upwards: bad. A water no-colour scene. A shapeless grey blur broken only by the dull upstroke of a road bending to the right and fading away. I have been here before, twice during the Tour de France on sunny days and a hundred times when poring over the map. That bend is Glandon Corner, the 6,100 ft. mark of the Croix de Fer, and a *Col* in its own right when approached by a steep road from the north. Although by the time I get there a dirty curtain of cloud has been drawn over the high cross-roads, the bright message *CROIX DE FER 2.5* shines through the gloom. The home-straight is steep and I prepare for ten minutes out of the saddle on the 32 x 24. A pleasant surprise drops from the clouds. That massive rock wall which has been splashing water and throwing stones for the last two hours has been acting as a wind-break, too. Glandon Corner is a windy gap in the mountains and I am pushed up the hill into the thickest cloud, by a snow-chilled westerly.

Voices. Tyres crunching on the gritty pass, the grumbling of a derailing chain. Three young fellows, stripped bikes, dressed like real *coureurs*, no capes, no *musettes*, pedal smoothly by with a *Bonjour Monsieur* and a continuation of their chat. The first of the under-40s dispatched an hour after us at 03hrs. 00.

Calculation in head. If 3 riders gain one hour in first 44 miles ending in summit of 6,500-feet *col*, how many do they gain in last 109 miles beginning with descent of that *col*, and followed by ascent and descent of 8,400-feet *col*? Answer: two and a half plus 30 minutes for luck = three hours. Record for BRA in this direction is about 10 hours, which is hardly likely to be beaten in these conditions. Say fastest do 11 hours, I do 15 hours, which is 5 hours inside Vet.'s qualifying time.

The summit. *COL DE LA CROIX DE FER. Altitude 2,087 metres.* Population on Tour de France day 5,000. At this moment it is about 30, a dozen of whom are groping round in the fog, occupied in various ways. Some are putting on extra clothing ready for the long descent, others munching sandwiches; one dejected character, shivering with cold, is changing a tyre. By smell rather than by sight I find the balance of the party huddled in the austere comfort of the *col*-top café that has opened early for the occasion. Hot soup ladled out at the far end of the table is not on sale to the BRA public. A wife has somehow got through flood and avalanche to feed her man *d'honneur*.

On being told that there is no Control here, I get out of the café immediately. I have been munching odds and ends on the way up and drinking, too. Sitting around unnecessarily in saturated clothing will only delay the agony of the descent. On the way out I meet half a dozen newcomers, among them my Flèche Velocio team-mate Duvivier, who has taken an hour out of me already. Young Jean-Pierre is good, but that's a bit too fast a start and I reckon he'll gain no more than another hour during the next 108 miles.

"Where's Beaumann? You haven't dropped him have you? That's no way to treat your President!"

"No – there were so many entries they sent us off at three o'clock and Roger and Jean-Pierre Gagneur were starting half an hour later."

In the lee of a dripping rock I leap and prance and stamp the feet and flap the arms for three or four minutes in a hopeful storage-heating exercise. Chew a couple of glucose tablets, struggle to pull cape over head in *col*-top wind. Face what I suppose is the East where, according to club-mate's birthday greetings, the hour-old sun should now be yawning above the peaks. Another satisfied user of Mirk the landscape-tainter, as effective in the Alps as on the Tourmalet.

Although I have spoken of corners and bends on the upward journey, the road is on the whole an uncomplicated one through a glacier-carved valley now occupied by the Eau d'Olle stream. As *cols* go it is, as the French say, as straight as the letter I. In contrast, the northern side I am about to take is a series of battered UVZMWS scattered haphazardly down the mountain side. Unfasten toe-straps please, our descent on St. Jean de Maurienne is about to begin. Much turbulence is expected.

Brakes full on, trying to keep the back of the cape under crutch and off the front wheel. Down we go faster than I want but the blocks don't hold that well. Swishing through water, slipping on the mud, dodging the bricks, bumping through pot-holes, swaying alarmingly over to the side of the road which drops 50 feet, and where does it drop to but on to the same road after it has done the first of its Us. Sliding a foot on the road as an extra brake on the hairpin bends, feeling a rattle in the rear wheel area but not daring to look down. Cape blowing up from behind and when I wriggle to slip it back between legs the release of hand from brake lever shoots speed up too high for next hairpin, which mercifully is banked the right way. Front of cape scraping front wheel but can't be bothered about that, all hands to the brakes, except in those tunnels which are as black as pitch and not much better when I release a hand to switch on the near-spent front lamp. Good job, perhaps, I can't see 'cos I know how treacherous and slimy those tunnel roads can be, but how I miss hitting the walls I do not know especially in that one 600 yards long, perhaps the Lejeune is fitted with Sonar and keeps me off the walls like a bat's echo-mechanism. Dropping now from the cloud top, and so are a dozen other riders passing me like crazy with hands on the tops and one of them taking a long drink from his *bidon* and isn't that the well-built girl who has even less shorts on view than when she passed me on the way up, she must have been in the *col*-top *cayf*, but *Ou là, là*, the more haste the less speed, one of the fellows who lately slalomed by is now picking himself up and brushing grit from a gashed arm and his front wheel smashed and he must do a Christophe down to the forge at St. Jean to repair the damage. Here's another tunnel, so better switch on the back light to warn off other demon descenders. One does indeed speed past, a real *Randonneur* with long torch and dynamo flooding the hole through the rock with light and like I say the floor is a mire and pocked with pot-holes which I proceed to bump into whereas in the dark I manage to ride between them with the help of the bat-echo system. Getting used to the descent now and a bit cocky, taking hands off brakes on the straights and shoving them on before the bends like a real Tour riders, but of course the rims pick up water and the blocks don't work right away and I'm nearly over the edge again. Not that hands are much good for holding on brakes, numb they are with continual squeezing on the levers and dead is everything else with the cold, legs and head especially and serves me right for not wearing a hat. Down, down, down, 3,000 feet since the summit, now past a hamlet where flood water gushes across our path, rain stopped and visibility improving though no time for sight-seeing. Roar of water, frenzied streams white and foaming, others black and dirty-frothing, mild and Guinness pouring down the mountain sink. Hands off the brakes again because all feeling has gone from them, likewise all other parts of the body, think I'll make one almighty heave on brakes on next short straight and get off for a foot stamp and arm flap. No need 'cos descent is broken by a little climb which should get me warm, fumble with gear controls trying to find something like 56. Face frozen like fresh from dental injection, try talking to myself to prove jaws still working but only a squeak comes out and very little response from the legs up that hill. Funny, I know it's always hard taking up the drive after a long free-wheel but not as bad as this. Am I moving? I wonder, yes the wheels are going round, am I in the right gear? Cape is in way so can't look down at the chainwheels or sprockets and hands too numb to do it by feeling the controls. Hill isn't steep and can take one hand off the 'bars and smack it down on rising thigh, repeat other hand two dozen times till warm, face ache going and legs coming round by top of slope when descent of *col* proper recommences and I go to shift right-hand gear lever full forward which is 86. Ha Ha, big joke, it's already there, shows what a state I'm in, thought I was climbing that little rise on 56 when all the time was 86 and legs didn't know and neither did hands too numb to feel levers. Second part of descent through trees another UVZMWS although maybe slightly smaller capitals but very steep through wild lower Gorges of Arvan, which is name of river this road has been trying to follow most of way from summit. Arvan flows in wide curve like Eau d'Olle on other side, but road hasn't a hope of keeping near it because blocked by mountain of rock where tunnels are impossible, or at least not worth cost of construction, hence all those UVZMWS bends which are very spectacular to be sure. Well below top cloud now and starting to drop through next layer which of course soaks me again just as I am beginning to dry out. Pass one rider trotting with bike downhill. NO BRAKES he yells, another Christophe but not so far to go as chap with broken wheel can't help because I don't carry spare cable or blocks. More huge troughs of foaming Guinness my goodness how evil that black whirlpool looks, some of it spilled over road inches deep, like riding through tar though this does not stick. Now it's like flying in on straight home beam after stooging round on a circular stack waiting for permission to land, mist swirling by and can't see a thing then suddenly it's clear and below in distance is our destination St. Jean de Maurienne at finish of descent and about time too my hands are numb with holding brakes and next big mountain ride I do I'll fit those coupled toggle lever things under tops of 'bars which give better purchase and of course you can use ordinary levers too, and what-do-you-know the sun is shining over St. Jean on the River Arc where the wheels are going in two by two for to get out of the rain. Can't see watch all steamed up with rain and sweat but church clock strikes nine as I enter town. That's 64 miles in six hours which is good enough to get badge in this 1973 BRA and good enough to win the 1873 BAR, with apologies for punctuation because that's how it has been all 21 miles of it, no Full Stops, just a few commas but perhaps instead of , , , I should have put some . . .s which I mentioned earlier are called *points de suspension* in France and I've been in suspense all right and maybe a few * * *s and ! ! !s would tell tale better and a few ( )s too and talking of brackets I wonder how much water has got in bearings and I must check the brakes which did very well really, they are Mafac Racers which are centre-pull and the 'bars are Cinelli although personally I now call them Tenter Hooks which is what I have been on all the way down.

The Galibier

There was nothing to eat in the first café I came across, but a couple of black coffees worked wonders and *la patronne* didn't mind my bringing in a snack of a small packet of Graindrop cereals and a Bounty Bar. I took breakfast standing up with the cape still on, the tracksuit being too soggy to sit around in. A party of four BRA men were about to leave, the fifth remaining at the table unable to get up from his chair. He had fallen half-way down the *col* and slid on the wet road for many yards.

   Cape off and on the road again, a very famous road which figures large in the Tour de France history. It was along here, for instance (though in the other direction) that André Leducq was saved by the French team after his 1930 accidents on the Galibier which I related in the chapter on the old Touriste Routier, Benoît Faure.*

---

* *My 19th Tour de France*, Chapter VI, 'The Mountain Mouse'

Along that stretch of road in 1955 – the first Tour I followed professionally – we motored behind, in front of, and occasionally alongside a lone rider still virtually unknown to the French public, Charly Gaul by name. I knew him well, and so did young Shay Elliott from Dublin. The three of us had met earlier that year in the Simplex training camp in Monte Carlo, directed by Charles Pélissier, winner of eight stages in the 1930 Tour and organiser of the Leducq Rescue Operation just mentioned.

At the time Shay was considered something of a climber having, the previous year, won the Tourmalet stage of the amateur Route de France. In Ireland he was the best climber in the 1954 An Tostal 8-day race, the prize for which was a fortnight's stay at the Simplex Camp. Gaul was one of the few professional guests among two dozen amateurs from all over Europe. It was on training rides over the tough hills and *cols* rearing up from the Mediterranean that Shay Elliott first realised his limitations as a *grimpeur*.

"There he is, the murderer!" exclaimed Shay one day at lunch, pointing to another table where baby-faced Charly Gaul was sitting. "We went up into the hills this morning and the lot of us were strung out gasping for the air, and he just sitting there twiddling a little gear, whistling a tune and never once rising from the saddle. I'll never make a pro if they all climb like him."

No, Shay, they didn't all climb like Gaul, and you weren't all that bad really. What he did to you and the other amateur boys on that training ride, he was doing to the greatest pros in the business on that July day in 1955. Indeed Louison Bobet had the wind up properly for there was a real threat of the young Luxembourger ending his hopes of winning the Tour for the third year in succession.

Charly Gaul took his food bag at the feeding station at St. Jean de Maurienne. We watched him transfer the contents to his pockets and then have a leisurely meal on the "flat" road beside the Arc. He had all the time in the world, just how much we saw when a motorcycle drew up alongside with the pillion passenger holding up a blackboard for his inspection. A good one for the photographers. *Peloton à 8 minutes.*

All right. So a kid with a bit of a reputation as a climber among the amateurs and Independents has a big lead with 50 miles to go. But what comes next on the road? The Galibier. We'll call him a climber if he still has half of it left at Briançon. More than likely, though, he'll be caught and lose another quarter of an hour. All round us cynics were saying things like that, but I kept quiet because I was the new boy and didn't really know a thing.

But I did know Gaul, which was more than most of them could say, and as we drove past he gave me a large size in winks as if to declare: "I know what they're all saying, but I'm all right, Jock, and I'm going to enjoy myself on the Galibier." Charly did, romping up the "Giant of the Alps" on his 50 gear and winning the stage by more than 13 minutes. That night everybody in the *Salle de Presse* was calling him the Angel of the Mountain and I spelt the *col* as Gaulibier in my story. Gaul finished third in that 1955 Tour – and Bobet got his hat-trick.

In this Gaul memory I have described the 13 kms. between St. Jean and St. Michel de Maurienne as being "flat", and so it is compared with the *cols* that shoot off from the Arc Valley. In fact the stretch rises 500 feet, and I was having a nice steady ride on it, drying out and looking towards the snow-capped peaks to the south which was the way we would soon be going – I was thinking of past Tours when up from behind with a slap on my back and a cheery greeting came a BRA rider whose distinctive features would have been immediately recognisable by all students of the Tour de France history. Yesterday he had ridden through the back streets of Grenoble showing me a short-cut to the hotel. He was surprised, and pleased, to hear that his story is well known in Britain.

"Where have you been?" I exclaimed. "I expected you to be miles ahead by now. Did you stop back at St. Jean for a feed?"

"No – I overslept. Instead of starting with you at two o'clock I didn't leave until three. Tuck in behind and I'll take you up the *col*."

"No fear. Not with anybody, least of all you. Get on with it and *bonne route*."

"*Bonne route* to you as well," said Pierre Brambilla pedalling briskly away. Yes, the same Brambilla, Italian-born, who was actually wearing the *maillot jaune* when the first post-war Tour de France finished at the Parc des Princes track, Paris, in 1947. *Maillot jaune* – but not the winner. Brambilla had started that final stage Caen–Paris with 53 seconds lead over his team-mate Ronconi and 2 minutes 58 seconds on Jean Robic. It was the third man, Robic, who brought off the "Miracle of Bonsecours" by dropping the tiring Brambilla on the hill of that name just outside Rouen and taking 13 minutes out of him on the remaining 80 miles to Paris. Robic, who had not worn the yellow jersey during 2,800 miles on the road, pulled one over his shoulders to ride a 454-metre lap of honour as winner of the Tour.

"Hey – Brambilla," I yelled, but it was no good. The granite-faced fighter was away and miracles – such as catching him – are not in my line, even though my name is John and Arc the river I was following. I wanted to ask Brambilla to confirm the oft-told story that he was so upset at letting the Tour slip from his grasp that he buried his bike in the garden and didn't dig it up for years. Careless, Wadley, to miss that chance, and that might have been the bike he was riding now! But whatever the bike, wherever he dug it up from, 53-year-old Pierre Brambilla who suffered agonies in his professional racing days, was enjoying a *Randonneur* ride for a 50-centimes badge and maybe having an imaginary revenge over Robic at the same time.

I was nearing the end of the "flat" section when another local memory of the Tour slipped in. It was 1966, and again one rider was away on his own, although this time with only a one-minute lead which had been quickly built up after breaking away at the *zone de ravitaillement* in St. Jean de Maurienne. Curiously enough I made his acquaintance – although he was not there in person – at the same 1955 camp at Monte Carlo where I met Charly Gaul. To earn my keep for a fortnight at the camp I helped Charles Pélissier (who did not speak English) reply to training queries which Le Derailleur Simplex (London) had invited British club cyclists to send in. Some of the letters were, to say the least, rather odd. One, however, impressed me very much and I still have it among my souvenirs. The enquirer was 16, obviously intelligent, dedicated, anxious to learn and – so I judged from details of his racing career listed – with a touch of class. His letter was signed "Yours in sport, Thomas Simpson, Harworth C.C."

And Tom Simpson it was, the man who had broken away at St. Jean on the Bourg d'Oisans to Briançon stage of the 1966 Tour and he was wearing the Rainbow Jersey as professional road champion of the World. Tom had a plaster on his knee covering a cut sustained in a fall on the descent of the Col de la Croix de Fer which had been dry enough but badly surfaced. At the end of the 13-kms. "flat" at St. Michel de Maurienne his lead was a minute and a half, and there he turned right and was at the foot of the Galibier climb. I will be thinking more about Tom's audacious break as I follow in his wheel marks. For the moment, back to the BRA.

It was at St. Michel de Maurienne that my club-mate's wife was going to cook steaks and things, which perhaps would not have been the best fuel in the circumstances. I stopped at a general store to buy biscuits, cheese, chocolate, fruit and Coke to drink. I stood outside eating and drinking and watching BRA riders go by, returning to the shop from time to time for more supplies. I picked up what I thought was an old newspaper to wrap some fruit in.

"*Non, Non, Non,*" cried *la patronne.* "That paper is ordered. Please put it back."

"Come off it – it's a back number," I protested pointing to the headline announcing "Hoban winner of the stage". "This paper's ten days old at least."*

"*Non Monsieur. C'est le journal d'aujourd'hui.*"

Then I looked at the date. July 22. My birthday. Today. Yesterday Barry had won the stage finishing at Versailles and I'd been so busy with my own BRA preparations that I had completely forgotten the Tour de France which, incidentally, finished that same afternoon!

"Good old Barry. We'll celebrate that victory tonight with a drink from my birthday bottle of champagne, but for the time being let's have another Coke."

I had the money in my hand, but this Coke was on the house, thanks to The Boss who came into the shop after listening to the conversation from the back room.

"You English? Thought so. Hoban's well known around here. Won the Point Chaud prime down the road a fortnight ago. Fine sprinter. Isn't he the one who married Tom Simpson's widow? No – no money for the drink. On me. We often get British *cyclotouristes* through here with their big sacks strapped to the saddle."

"*Je vous remercie beaucoup Monsieur,*" I said raising the bottle, "*A votre bonne sante.*"

"Goot elt zir," was the carefully articulated response and (tilting forearm and extended fingers to 45) "goot up-ping on ze Galibier *montagne.*"

COL DU GALIBIER 34 kms. One of the magical signs of France. I had seen it often from Press cars and three or four times when arriving at St. Jean by bicycle, though I had never yet climbed the *Giant des Alpes.* I had been on my way to Italy to Milan–St. Remo

---

*On his transistor, by the roadside near Carcassonne, JBW had heard the live commentary on Hoban's win in the 15th stage at Argelès-sur-Mer.

(March) or the Giro di Lombardia (October) when all the high *cols* were blocked with snow, and had to take the train from Modane through the Mont Cenis tunnel to Bardonecchia. On those Spring and Autumn visits the Galibier sign had an additional line of information "*Col Fermé*" to warn travellers that the pass was closed. I heard of one young British club-man who learned the hard way the meaning of this important phrase for continental tourists. He toiled up the Galibier for three hours only to find the last two kilometres a solid wall of snow, and got very cold coming down in well under the hour. At St. Michel he met a C.T.C. man in a café whom he warned against making the same mistake.

"Thanks, but I'm not likely to do that," said the experienced tourist, "the sign makes it clear enough. *Col fermé*, closed."

"Oh is that it? I saw that sign and thought it meant it was a firm *col* and not one of those loose dirt roads."

COL DU GALIBIER 34 kms. Col Ouvert. Col in two half-stages. First the "step" to the summit of the intermediate Col du Télégraphe, followed by a short drop, then the real and longer dose of punishment to the Galibier tunnel.

Immediately after the crossing of the Arc the road tilted up and began wriggling its way with great ingenuity round the rock massif and up through the trees. After only a kilometre there was already a wide view of St. Michel's roofs and the valley. One BRA man had chosen this pleasant spot for a picnic lunch, although as I passed he was more interested in the upward view, pointing with mock despair to the old military fort perched on top of the green cliff we were scaling. "Doesn't look far, does it!" he called.

In a direct line the fort is only 2.75 kms. from St. Michel whereas the well-engineered road takes 11.5 to gain 3,000-feet elevation. I climbed for another *lacet* or two before taking off my tracksuit which was now thoroughly dry in the hot sun. I knew that corner. We waited there many times during the Tour. If the field was still together we would move off ahead until a substantial split allowed us to drop in behind the leading bunch. In 1966, I remember, we were there wondering if Tom Simpson really meant business.

At the foot of the Col du Télégraphe, kilometre 80, Tom Simpson, World Champion, has a lead of one and a half minutes over the peloton group, came the news from Radio-Tour.

In a few minutes Tom and his attendant Peugeot team-car and a few official vehicles rounded a distant, lower bend and was quickly lost behind a curtain of trees. Easy to take a time check from where we stood, and 1 minute 20 seconds later another lone figure briefly came into our view about 20 yards ahead of the disintegrating bunch. A light-coloured jersey he had. No prizes for guessing who.

Attack by No 7, Julio Jiménez, on leaving St. Michel de Maurienne. He leaves the peloton and moves rapidly upwards in pursuit of the leader, Tom Simpson, World Champion. (A nice touch, this, by the Radio-Tour speaker who always gives the Champion his due in communications. National champions, too, are treated with the same courtesy, even Luxembourg which often has only one title contender!)

We left our corner, cruising slowly ahead with frequent downward glimpses of the two leaders. Simpson losing ground, though still climbing faster than the main bunch from whom the Spaniard had now drawn right away.

Situation after five kilometres on Col du Télégraphe, kilometre 85. Leading, Tom Simpson, World Champion. At 20 seconds No. 7, Julio Jiménez. At 1 min. 30 secs. a first group of 20 men including several Spaniards, Anquetil, Poulidor.

By the time Tom reached us, half-way up the 7.25-mile climb of the Télégraphe he had almost been caught by Jiménez who wasn't the prettiest of climbers but, nevertheless, on his way to winning the Grand Prix de la Montagne competition for the second year running.

Now, like Shay Elliott before him, Tom Simpson had gone to seek fame and fortune in France with the reputation of being a good climber, having won the 1957 B.L.R.C. national senior hill-climb championship on Mam Tor. In a year or two Tom was to find that while he was as strong as any professional on hills, he was only moderate on what the French call the *haute montagne*. In the 1960 Tour, for instance, I remember his trying to stay with eventual winner Gastone Nencini on a *col* in the Pyrenees only to be left gasping well before the summit. Tom told me afterwards that he had learned his lesson. In future he would adopt the Brian Robinson method, keeping with the leaders until three-quarters of the way up, then dropping off voluntarily and trying not to be more than two minutes behind at the summit. Those two minutes could be regained by a fast descent. Brian learned this on his first two Tours in 1955 and 1956, telling me one night in his hotel room:

"On the flat you can hang on to a rider who is two or three miles an hour faster because you are in his slipstream and pedalling on air. But uphill you are going much slower and must overcome the same gradient as the chap you're trying to follow. On a high mountain in rarefied air you can get in trouble trying to follow a wheel that is only half-a-mile an hour faster."

"Ah yes – O.D.," says the well-coached reader. When Brian Robinson rode his first Tour de France the term "Oxygen Debt" was not in general use. Riders used to "blow up".

Well there was Tom about to be passed by a man who had gained one and a half minutes on him in under four miles. He reasoned (as he said later) that Jiménez was putting in a big effort to catch him and would then sit up for a breather. Probably the Spaniard did take it easy for a bit, going to the front to enjoy it. Even on the light pedal the tempo was basically too fast for Tom who hung on, mouth open, eyes fixed on the wheel of his pacemaker, hands in the middle of the bars and crouching with elbows out like a sprinter of the they-shall-not-pass brigade. He was "trying" hard while the leader sat relaxed with hands on the hoods. Incidentally, Jiménez was wearing a Ford jersey; the French division of the giant motor concern sponsored a professional team for a season or two (Simpson rode for Peugeot!).

It must have been close to the spot where Tom was caught that I was joined at great speed by another *Randonneur* who went by with not so much as a *bonjour*. I sprinted(!) after him, yelling.

"Sorcerer! That's a nice way to treat a club-mate. Don't you recognise my back view? You saw it enough at Easter!"

Roger Beaumann dropped back to apologise, wishing me a happy birthday again, and anxiously asked for news of our friend Duvivier who I had seen for a few seconds at the café in the clouds on the summit of the Croix de Fer. I said he must be ahead by now, probably having passed me when I was in the café or grocer's in the valley. Beaumann had started 30 minutes behind Duvivier and therefore one hour after me. We were about half-way, so the President of the Colchester Rovers was going to be screwed by the President of the Union Sportive de Creteil (section *cyclotouriste*) by at least three hours.

"But I haven't seen Jean-Pierre Gagneur," I gasped, naming the fourth member of our Flèche Velocio team.

"No – and you won't unless he's in a car. He didn't get through the torrent. There were scores riding back towards Grenoble. See you later."

The Sorcerer pedalled easily away on his 32 x 24 and sprints, while I urged roughly the same gear round (with wired-ons) in out-of-the-saddle sessions. Allowing for the stop to take off the tracksuit, I had covered 10 kms. in the first hour of the climb and still had 2.5 to go to the Télégraphe summit. I rode them behind a party of three who had stopped to fix a loose crank – a cottered crank which had been temporarily put back in place by a lump of rock. At the crest we were waved to a halt by officials operating a "secret" Control on the bend of the road where a short track goes up to the fort we had seen from the valley. Although a busy café looked tempting, I decided to carry on after a drink from the *bidon*, and ate a bar of chocolate and a banana on the five-mile drop to Valloire.

COL DU GALIBIER 17 kms., said the sign in Valloire, the mountain village where, in 1972, I saw Merckx beat Zoetemelk in the morning half-stage from Briançon after a crazy duel *down* the road which I was now sentenced to climb. The same road where, on July 7th, 1966, Tom Simpson and Julio Jiménez were still together. Radio-Tour was operating loud and clear but we were eye-witnesses of the drama.

Tom Simpson, eyes still down on back wheel. Julio Jiménez looking up to the distant snows. The Spaniard swung out allowing Tom to take the lead, then from the blind side sprinted away. Then 30 yards ahead he looked back at the damage, the World Champion head-nodding and thrusting harder on the left pedal than the right. Not surprising. Tom had broken the right thigh at the winter sports and although his comeback had been remarkable, this audacious attack on the Galibier after 14 days racing was paying him out. For a kilometre or so it was the formula as before, Tom hanging on, and we wondered how long it would be before Julio Jiménez jumped again. In fact the Spaniard knowing his opponent was groggy, did not bother to introduce surprise into his next move. He simply burned Tom off his wheel.

After Valloire a straight, rising road meets the Valloirette stream descending vigorously through an ice-hewn trough, a sort of neutral corridor linking the tidy wooded Télégraphe country with the wild rocky wilderness of the upper Galibier Pass. As well as the BRA *Randonneurs* toiling upwards there were walkers, too, packs on backs, off to explore the gorges slashed in the western wall of our trail. When one group called "Bravo" and "Courage" I felt the real *coureur*. When one youth cried *"Allez Grandpère"*, I felt my age.

"Allez Poulidor!"

That made me feel better; so did the glass of cool orangeade which the shouter supplied from a big plastic jug. I was the two-minutes guest of a family of holiday-makers picnicking in the sunshine. They had camped near Valloire since the day before the Tour came through and had a superb view of the opening phase of the Fuente–Ocaña battle.* Now they were having fun handing up drinks to "deserving cases" in the BRA. One such arrived as I was about to leave, but he waved aside the proffered drink with thanks and plodded on. A further boost to the morale came when I was up and passed him within a kilometre, especially as he was no more than 40 and on a stripped bike. The mountain, however, is a great leveller and curer of big-headitis, for almost immediately a grey-head of my own age on an oversized-tyred Rochet sailed by with a cheery remark about the splendour of the mountain scene.

Splendid was, is, and shall be ever more. A big moment in my cycling life. Alone on the Galibier. Like Georges Speicher in one of those copies of *Match* I took back to Colchester after my first visit to Paris in '33. Well, not quite like him. Georges was on the way to winning the Tour de France. *"Speicher seul sur le Galibier"* was the caption under the photograph that gave me my first touch of Tour fever. Since then I've seen hundreds of pictures of Tour riders pedalling up against the incomparable backcloth of mountain, snow and a multitude of cheering fans. Pictures in colour, black and white, sepia, blue, yellow. I've been up and down the *Col* a dozen times in Press cars, and often out of them on a thrill-packed kilometre walk to the summit clicking the camera as I went. That was great, so was the Speicher picture, but greatest of all was to be getting up the thing under my own power. Tough going but, as the man said, Splendid.

Brian Robinson once told me that the trouble with the Galibier was not its steepness, but its length. I can see now that the occasional 1-in-7 parts of the *Col* would be no bother to Brian who had learned his racing on the 1-in-4 staircases of Holme Moss and Sutton Bank, but they were beginning to bother me. If some joker had whipped out my saddle pin as I danced I don't suppose I would have noticed for another half-hour. The 36 gear was too high for me and I thought of the Condor Cadet lying idle at home, and fitted

---

* Ocaña v. Fuente – this was the essential struggle of the 1973 Tour.

with 28 x 28 bottom gear, which would have been just the job right now.

Still comparatively straight and following the river course, the road rose out of the trough on to a vast chaos of reddish rock reaching up to crinkled cliffs and snow-packed peaks. I couldn't be sure, of course, but it must have been somewhere about here that Jiménez dropped Tom.

So Jiménez was on his own, well away from Tom Simpson, now paying the price for his impetuosity. While watching the leaders we also had our ears on Radio-Tour which spoke of a gradually dwindling *peloton* until only three were left in front.

Huysmans loses contact with the leaders. Two men only now, Jacques Anquetil and Raymond Poulidor, riding one minute behind Tom Simpson, World Champion, and one and a half minutes behind Julio Jiménez.

We were just ahead of tired Tom, and looking over his head down the straight to a clutter of movement that announced the presence of the two great rivals of the Tour. Jacques Anquetil five times a winner and openly saying he wasn't expecting to make this one the sixth but was determined to stop Poulidor winning his first. Anquetil was in the same Ford team as Jiménez and according to the unwritten laws of cycle-racing entitled to "sit in" on Poulidor's back wheel and let him do all the work. There was, I suppose, a measure of sportsmanship and pride in Anquetil's refusal to do so, but also fear of thousands of Poulidor fans massed on the mountain who would be mad at seeing their hero so abused. Up the Galibier, then, they came towards us, side by side, Anquetil on the right just as they had been on the most bitter of all their battles on the Puy de Dôme in '64.

"Now," I said. The car stopped and I jumped out with the camera cocked and ready. One shot, a rapid wind-on, and another. See them in the September 1966 issue of *Sporting Cyclist*. Number one shows Tom Simpson, World Champion, head bare and bowed as if in prayer. Amen. So be it. Ten yards behind, Anquetil is out of the saddle, Poulidor is seated but leaning slightly to the east. Also present, team-cars, motor-cycle *gendarmes* and photographers. In the background a dull mountain mass streaked and blotched with snow. Number two shot, ditto, less Simpson. Anquetil now in saddle, gripping hooks, eyes on his front wheel; Poulidor, knuckles-up nine inches apart looking directly in front, and who could his gaze have been on but Tom. Far from having a killer "I got you" air of triumph,

Pou-Pou seems sad at the sight of a great rider in trouble.

The capture was out of lens range. Looking up the mountain road I had a distant back view of Tom briefly under distinguished escort, then left alone in his suffering as the two great French rivals powered in parallel away from him towards the snows.

The difference between this veteran *Randonneur* and his compatriot World Champion toiling up the Galibier in '66 was that I was riding an elevator with my finger on the button, able to get off where and when I liked, whereas poor old Tom was on a non-stop trip from basement to snow-covered roof of the Tour's most famous mountain home.

Unlike the ever-changing scene unfolding when climbing the coily part of a *col*, the Galibier north-side stage management does not go in for frequent changes of backcloth. The road is the crossing of a huge cyclorama of – so it seems to the cyclist – constant distance from the buckled rim of mountains. However, even a snail gets there in the end and well ahead, and still well up, was the bend I had been looking for, a point on the map marked Plan Lachat.

The Plan Lachat, often mentioned in Tour despatches from the Galibier front, is a strategic position in the wider sense, with a military road striking off to the east for a spectacular scramble over the Grande Parée massif. The main road turns and rears abruptly in the opposite direction to begin its own brutal assault of the higher Galibier wall.

It was just past 11 o'clock, the smell of tea drifting down the *Col* from the Plan Lachat Control. There, a long *Brevet de Randonneur des Alpes* banner was spread out over the rocks like a mountain giant's Long Johns drying in the sun.

"Eight kilometres to go," said the man with the rubber stamp, "and 600 metres to climb." Five miles and near enough 2,000 feet.

There, too, was the promised Vittel refreshment booth, surely the most splendidly placed, and one of the highest (6,000 feet) feeding stations in the world. I sat on a rock in the sun sipping tea and munching biscuits, pivoting full circle to devour the splendid view as well. What a contrast to the last official Control on the storm-lashed Col de la Croix de Fer only five hours ago!

During a ten-minute break I saw the arrival of two contrasting sorts who help to make up the world of the *Randonneur*. One who pedalled up serenely on a tiny gear, spent several minutes photographing the Control and panorama before having his card signed.

Then he collected a beaker of tea from the Vittel booth and a handful of biscuits, found a nice smooth rock and wrote postcards.

Up came another, all bustle and sweat, calling for a helper to hold his bike, another to pump the front tyre, like Gowland coming into the pits during a hard chase in the Skol International Six. He snatched two *bidons* from their cages, dumped them on the Vittel table, ordering tea with no sugar in one, plain Vittel in the other, had his Control card stamped, returned to the feedery for two quick cuppas, waved aside the offer of biscuits and a sandwich, disappeared for no more than 15 seconds behind a rock (one sweats a lot when climbing...), looked at his watch, peered anxiously down the road for a sight of the enemy who obviously was after his blood, and was off in under two minutes. With a *bidon* of Vittel-menthe for the voyage I got back on to the road, noticing that our gentle friend had finished writing postcards and was enjoying a quiet pipe and the view.

Fierce but manageable I found the first two kilometres after that break, then complaints began flooding in. Too old, the legs ... Too big, the gear ... Too high, the altitude and there may have been something in that because we were approaching 7,000 feet, a height where many a star roadman's engine has shown signs of wear. Too hot, the sun! Too bad. Then why not walk like so many others? I paused at a corner considering the suggestion.

Once again I said to myself: I have been here before several times. On the Tour visits it had been easy picking out the upward road by the crooked line of parked cars and people Z-ing up through the rocks and snow. The BRA doesn't attract that kind of crowd and, without reference to the map I just couldn't see which way we were going. Stopping hadn't been such a good idea after all, the legs aching from the first thrust. My troubles, however, were small compared with those of Tom Simpson in 1966.

After Tom was dropped by the Anquetil–Poulidor side-by-side tandem, I saw no more of him until the end of the stage. I was following as usual in the *Paris–Normandie* car, Anquetil's local paper, and it was plainly journalist Pierre Lardiere's duty to maintain contact with his famous neighbour. The second *Paris–Normandie* man in the car had a double reason for wanting to keep up with the action. Pierre Joly had just written a book on Anquetil with the title *En brulant les étapes* and was in the process of producing another on Poulidor which would be called *La gloire sans le maillot jaune*. I couldn't complain when they said I would have to be satisfied with talking to Tom at the finish of the stage.

Although accompanying the Anquetil–Poulidor elbow-to-elbow climb we got occasional backward-downward glimpses of Tom toiling on his own, latching briefly on to Huysmans who, it will be remembered, had earlier been riding with Anquetil and Poulidor. The Belgian had wisely dropped off from choice rather than necessity in order to tackle the Galibier at his own speed. Tom would probably have been just as strong if he had let Jiménez get on with it, too.

It was a late thaw in '66. Between giant banks of snow, spectators left only a narrow corridor for the two Frenchmen, but scattered in alarm before the following cars. Normally neither Poulidor nor Anquetil was interested in mountain points, but this Galibier summit was rather special, for here the annual *Souvenir Henri Desgrange* prime was on offer. Jimenez was already through the tunnel and beginning the descent with the £140 first prize credited to his Tour account, and (because Poulidor was his opponent) Anquetil put in a big effort to win the two-up sprint for the runner-up's £70. Soon we, too, were through the tunnel, now well behind the two arrivals speeding round the first bends of the Galibier descent. We pulled out wide to let the remarkable Huysmans pass, then followed in his wake listening all the while to crackling Radio-Tour which was never in good voice on horse-shoe mountain roads.

Here are the positions at the summit of the Col du Galibier, 2,556 metres, First Category counting for the Grand Prix de la Montagne, Trophee Chocolat Poulain, kilometre 114, Souvenir Henrié Desgrange. Leading: No. 7, Julio Jiménez; at 1 minute 30 seconds, No. 2, Jacques Anquetil and 26, Raymond Poulidor; at 2 minutes 30 seconds No. 85, Joseph Huysmans; at 4 minutes 30 seconds No. 74, Galera; 73, Gabica; 68, Mugnaini; 106, Schutz; 36, Janssen; No. 1, Aimar and Tom Simpson, World Champion.

The distance to the Galibier summit is getting shorter, my breath too. There is no snow of 1966 proportions, just a patch here and there with stick artists' POULIDOR, OCAÑA and (yes!) HOBAN in grey letters still showing faintly on the thawing page. Out of the saddle now most of the time, toe-straps tight but unable to use full power because I don't use shoe-plates. Another Tour souvenir stuck on a rock, one of those posters saying "Do not push the riders." I have in my time preached sermons on the text. Now the voice of the tempter is heard in the wilderness. How would I react if a strong arm suddenly grabbed the seat-pin to send me free-wheeling up the 1-in-7? Pulpit-blast the devil for falsifying the BRA or gasp a vote of thanks, and encore please? There's nothing in the rules about riding all the way. Indeed several are walking now. Three kilometres to go and who should flit by with a polite smile but my post-card writing friend of the Plan Lachat and with the bowl of a pipe sticking out of his back pocket? Well, it just goes to show. Would be nice to say I rode the whole thing. What would Col Collector Chanin say if he knew I walked, and me President of the Colchester Rovers, and all? Not all that amount of motor traffic but dangerous to tack across the road to blunt the gradient. Arms now aching as much as legs. Drip of sweat on end of nose, but no hand available for removal so snorted without decorum. An occasion for gritting teeth but also for opening mouth wide to gulp in air: Oxygen Debt? I'm nearly bankrupt. Tough, but not torture, because I can turn in any time I like; not suffering of the Christophe kind. Just a little private struggle. To work or to walk?

Earlier in the day I had a pleasant surprise on nearing the end of the Croix de Fer climb to find a gap in the mountains letting through a blast of air to blow me to the summit. Now another western gate had been left open and a beastly wind rushed out to hit me in the face. It wasn't all that strong really, and afterwards friends asked "what wind?" when I brought up the subject. Nevertheless it was the last straw that broke my resolution to pedal all the way, and to tell the truth those last two kilometres on foot were the most splendid of the day and took me half-an-hour. It was just 13h00 when I reached the summit of the Galibier having accomplished the journey from St. Michel at the remarkable rate of 34 kms. per 4 hours, or 5.3 m.p.h. I'd been called Poulidor and *Grandpère* and even Merckx on the way up . Now, hard by the sign *GALIBIER 2,556 metres*, my own name was being called by a familiar voice, Jean Bobet's.

I was only half surprised to find Jean and his wife a thousand kilometres from their Brittany home. Several times between Calais and Brive I had heard that he and his brother Louison would be riding the BRA, but they had not entered and nobody I spoke to at Grenoble knew how the story got around.

"No," said Jean after we had exchanged greetings, "we never intended riding the BRA, although it would have been great fun. Louison was afraid it would look like a publicity stunt. If he had entered the Press, Radio and Television would all have taken up the story. 'Ex-World Champion and triple-Tour winner rides *cyclotouriste* trial for 50-centimes badge', and all that kind of thing that would have attracted crowds following by car – something they could never do when he was racing. That is against the whole spirit of *cylotourisme*. But Louison was attracted by the idea of riding over the BRA course, so we did it yesterday when the weather was exactly the opposite to today's – it was fine on the Croix de Fer and wet here on the Galibier. I've heard all about the burst torrent. It was just an impressive waterfall when the four of us pedalled by yesterday."

"Four of you?"

"Yes, the other two were Pierre Barbotin, who you know, and an air-line pilot friend of Louison's, Paul Rochin. We were like four kids and had a prime here where we are standing now. The result was 1, Barbotin; 2, Bobet, L.; 3, Bobet, J. Me third at the summit of the Galibier, most impressive!"

Jean Bobet was speaking in excellent English. After graduating at Rennes he continued his studies at Aberdeen University riding with the local cycling club whose members were surprised to find him remarkably ignorant on such matters as the angles of Louison's Stella frame. Jean told them that Louison didn't even know what angles were! At the time Louison was doing well in the classics – in 1951 he scored the great Italian double by winning both Milan–San Remo (ahead of team-mate Pierre Barbotin) and the Tour of Lombardy – but had not yet won the Tour de France. In chilly Scotland young Jean received many letters and postcards from Louison, postmarked at some sunny spot in Italy or the South of France, which invariably included the suggestion that he should chuck up his studies and turn pro. At first Jean – who was a good-class amateur rider – did not even consider the idea, then suddenly decided to take the plunge. His old professor nearly collapsed on being told, Jean says.

"If I had said I was signing on as a pro. for the Rangers or Celtic, or Aberdeen he wouldn't have turned a hair – but to throw up an academic career to become a pro. bike rider..."

Jean Bobet never emulated Louison. He was an average performer in the professional ranks whose greatest moment, perhaps, was at the end of the 1955 Tour when, as a member of the French national team, he saw his brother ride a lap of honour, the first man to win the great test three years in succession. Earlier that year Jean

190

had won the week-long Paris–Nice and was third a few days later in Milan–San Remo.

After retiring from racing Jean was a journalist for a few years on *L'Équipe,* then became chief of Radio Luxembourg's sports staff. For the last five or six years he has been associated with Louison in the administration of the magnificently appointed Institut de Thalassothérapie at Quiberon on the south coast of their native Brittany. This modern health centre, based on the curative powers of sea water, leaves them only time to cycle locally. After his BRA ride, Jean was stopping in the area on holiday with his wife, while Louison flew back from Grenoble to Quiberon in his own 'plane.

"You're doing well," said Jean looking at his watch. "You've been gone 11 hours and have nine left to do the last 100 kilometres which are nearly all downhill. Come and have lunch with us in the sunshine at the café-restaurant over the road."

Invitation declined with regret, and Jean understood why. I couldn't let Beaumann better my time by more than three hours! I joined Jean and Mme in the café where they treated me to several cups of tea and half a large blackcurrant flan. I talked a lot with my mouth full, I'm afraid, for I hadn't seen Jean for years and there was a lot of news to swap. I wanted to know who were the British riders currently doing well in Brittany, besides Dave Wells, and Jean asked who was leading the B.A.R.! Jean and Louison were, with their wives, guests of the Road Time Trials Council at the 1954 Champion's Concert and Prize Presentation at the Royal Albert Hall, during which Louison presented Best-All-Rounder Vic Gibbons with one of the Yellow Jerseys he had worn in the Tour de France.

As for Mme Jean Bobet she wondered – as she cut me another slice of flan – if I had been to Brinetree lightly, meaning Braintree in Essex where, as a student, she spent a holiday, and by "lightly" she meant lately. She put playful stress on the *Brine* and the *light*, knowing that around Colchester we reckon that to be the correct pronunciation. Which led to more banter about getting wet in the rine, the pines in my leg and weren't it 'bout toime oi were bein' a-gooin'.

Jean and Mme supervised my dressing for the descent. Newspaper under jersey (like the *coureurs*), tracksuit top and bottom, yellow Alisian racing cape, light silk gloves.

"And don't forget," said Jean, "that although the profile shows the 60 miles from here to Grenoble to be all downhill, there are, in fact, one or two intermediate 'steps' which can hurt quite a bit. More important is the fact that the wind is going to be against you all the way. It usually is along the valley of Romanche in that direction. Don't do a time trial on your own. Get in with a little group. What was it your poet Herrick said: 'Take ye back-wheel while ye may, Old Time is still a-flying', or something of the sort?"

"Once more unto the breach, dear friends, once more..." was Mme Bobet's short but accurate quotation from Shakespeare, well knowing of course that it was Henry V's rallying cry to the English to set about the French!

The breach was, in fact, the dark tunnel through the black rock mountain, about the flattest 400 yards of the day's 150-mile round trip. First on the tourist's programme the other side of the tunnel is a short climb up the rocks for the view, and probably my placid friend was up there puffing his pipe and writing postcards date-lined *Galibier table d'orientation, 2,704 metres*. I was more attracted by something a little further on, part of which I had only seen fleet-ingly above spectators' heads from a Press car but now was all mine, the monument to Henri Desgrange, 'Father' of the Tour de France. Ten years before putting on his first Tour, Desgrange had set up the first world hour unpaced record of 21 miles 1,674 yards. The ride excited little comment. Who was interested in seeing one fellow tooling around the track on his own? Paced-racing was the thing, especially now that (in the 1890s) tandem, triplets, quads and quints were being used to boost the speed in hour-record attempts. Desgrange argued that anybody beating his own unpaced figures would be a stronger rider, whereas the man improving the paced distance would probably have had better organised shelter than the previous holder.

Henri Desgrange, Father of the Tour 1903, Man of the Hour 1893. As I stood by his monument on the Galibier summit I tried to think which riders had scored the "double" so near to his heart. I got three out of four, although not until I got back home was I able to fill in the actual figures.

In Desgrange's life-time (1865–1940) only one man won the Tour de France and held the Hour unpaced record – Lucien Petit-Breton whose real name was Lucien Mazan; he covered 25 miles 961 yards in the hour in 1905 and won the Tour in 1907 and 1908. Since the Desgrange memorial was erected in 1949 three riders have scored the double – and what champions! Fausto Coppi, Hour 1942 (28 miles 805 yards) and Tour 1949, '52; Jacques Anquetil, Hour 1958

(28 miles 1,099 yards) and Tour 1957, 1961, '62, '63, '64; Eddy Merckx, Hour 1972 (30 miles 1,234 yards) and Tour 1969, '70, '71, '72.

Jacques Anquetil changed his tactics on that 1966 descent of the Galibier. With few spectators around there was no fear of reprisals for tucking in behind Poulidor. There was, however, a better reason for letting his rival do the work. He had one Ford team-mate in front (Jiménez) and obviously would have no part in helping Poulidor get up to him. Such an action might help his arch-rival win the Tour. Horrible thought! Then down in the team-car raced *directeur sportif* Raphaël Géminiani, the old Tour rider with one of the most cunning brains in the business, bearing news that a third Ford man, and highly placed on overall time, Lucien Aimar, was making a spectacular descent and gaining on the Poulidor–Anquetil "tandem". Géminiani had no need to spell it out to Jacques Anquetil, who had won five Tours de France by using his head as well as his legs. By "sitting in" Anquetil knew there was a good chance not only of making Poulidor lose the Tour, but of putting Aimar on the road to winning it.

We were motoring just ahead of Anquetil–Poulidor having been ordered there with customary courtesy by co-race director Félix Lévitan who was determined to see the inter-group pursuit contested on a car-free road. We looked back at the snaking *col* behind us and had our ears on Radio-Tour.

Aimar making spectacular descent trying hard to get away from Jan Janssen who has a slight lead over him on classement general. Also in the picture are van Springel, Galera, Planckaert, Pingeon and Tom Simpson, World Champion.

We had already passed the Col du Lautaret, the cross-roads marking the end of the steepest part of the descent, and in no time at all there was the familiar sign "*Arrivée 20 kms.*" Time to get moving to the finish at Briançon. We drove fast past Jiménez in no danger now of being caught and moving well on the gradually descending road alongside the Guisane River.

Situation still the same. Leading, Jiménez. At 2 minutes 30, Poulidor and Anquetil in that order. At 3 minutes, Huysmans; at 3 minutes 45, the group Aimar–Janssen.

This was a routine Radio-Tour announcement by Robert Silva who incidentally is a journalist on the staff of *L'Equipe* who knows how to put over clear and concise information. Almost immediately Silva was back with a dramatic Flash.

Attention – Chute de Simpson …

No time for Christian names; no need to add "World Champion"; Simpson had crashed. Robert Silva the reporter no doubt wanted to stop and follow the story up, but Robert the Voice of the Tour had to carry on with the battle at the front, leaving the Race Doctor and police to attend to the high-ranking casualty. Not until we came to the notice *BRIANÇON – the highest town in Europe 1,326 metres*, did we hear that Tom was chasing on his own, with blood on his Rainbow Jersey.

Photo-finish evidence was not called upon to determine the stage placings at Briançon. First was the untroubled Jiménez, as if finishing a time trial knowing that nobody could touch him. Two and a half minutes later a two-up sprint which well-rested Anquetil won by several lengths from hard-worked Pou-Pou. A few seconds more and in came Huysmans, half a minute up on van Springel who finished strongly with one of his end-of-stage solos, trailed in by a disappointed Aimar and a grinning Janssen, the new race leader. Just under two minutes later Tom Simpson pedalled wearily over the line in 18th position, a long wedge of congealed blood running from a gash in his right elbow and disappearing into the wristband of the glove, an angry bruise scowling from torn shorts. Usually Tom had time to talk to journalists after a stage, but there was no Press conference today. He took a bottle of Perrier, lifted the Peugeot over a barrier with his good arm and climbed after it.

"Where's the ambulance?" he was demanding.

"Over at the far-side of the parking lot."

Ron White of the *Daily Express* and I ran with him as he pedalled across the gravel parade ground of the Champs de Mars. What happened?

"Stupid TV motor cyclist. Cameraman trying to get close-up shots of me, skidded in the loose stuff and brought me down. I was going all right and would have finished with Aimar and that bunch. Now it looks as if another Tour is over for me. I could hardly hold the bars downhill. Tomorrow's stage starts with a dirty great climb."

"What made you attack before the Télégraphe?"

"It was a gamble. I thought Anquetil would control the race as he usually does on the big mountains, and the main group would climb at club-run speed, with Jiménez and the other *grimpeurs* not budging until the last kilometre of the Galibier. Yes, I suppose I was stupid hanging on to Jiménez. If I'd let him go and recuperated a bit I might have been able to stay with Anquetil and Poulidor. Where's that ruddy ambulance?"

"Over there. I suppose you realise, Tom, that you aren't too popular with the Germans! Your team-mate, little Kunde, has lost the *maillot jaune* to Janssen. The Germans say he would still have had it if you had not attacked."

"If I rode a stupid race on the Galibier, Kunde rode a daft one on the Croix de Fer. I, at least, had to be aggressive if I were to make a show, but all he had to do to keep the jersey was to defend. Instead he was attacking. No wonder he couldn't follow them on the Galibier."

We left Tom in the ambulance. Several hours later, on leaving the Salle de Presse I saw Dr. Dumas who said that Tom had five stitches put in his arm at the local hospital. Would he be able to start tomorrow? we asked.

"There's nothing to prevent his starting the stage, but everything to prevent his finishing. Tom will virtually be riding one-handed."

Next day Tom gave us a tired grin when, just before noon, the riders assembled for the start of the 100-mile stage to Turin. He had been awake most of the night, he said. Tom limped to the official table, signed the Control sheet with his left hand, the bandaged forearm and elbow giving him the look of an Aussie trackie concerned only with his skin on the banking side. He took two *bidons* of drink, and Raymond Delisle helped him stuff a small sandwich and rice square in the back pocket of his Rainbow Jersey. He knew nobody would be around to help him take them out. Tom was resigned to a lonely ride.

The "dirty great climb" Tom had spoken of was the seven miles Col de Montgenèvre, with a second-category rating and beginning its 2,000-feet rise immediately on leaving Briançon. Tom was off the back right away and not a Peugeot man stayed with him, his right hand laying limp over the back brake-lever, the left firmly gripping the other hood. As the doctor said, he was virtually climbing one-handed. Senseless it would have been sacrificing a team man to nurse the helpless.

Take away the Rainbow bands from Tom's World Championship jersey and – but for bronzed legs and left arm – he would have been a study in black and white. Black and white Peugeot bike, white socks, black shoes, mostly-white *bidons*, whitish gloves, white bandages and gauze covering last night's hospital needlework, white PEUGEOT on black shorts, black PEUGEOT and BP on white jersey, black BP and black Peugeot domino squares on back-to-front white racing-hat with dark hair showing fairly short back and sides. A white face, too, for Tom was suffering and his dark glasses were worn both for protection against the sun and to hide the tears he knew were sure to come.

Peloton climbing Montgenèvre steadily. Only one rider delayed, Tom Simpson, World Champion, injured yesterday. At La Fontaine-Cretet, kilometre 5, he was 30 seconds behind.

Radio-Tour had opened the day's broadcasting.

Twenty-four hours before, one day, Tom was just shaping up for his audacious attack. One year before, almost to the day, I remembered, he had climbed into an ambulance, able no longer to stand the pain of the hand injured in a crash on the Aubisque mountain. It was in that ambulance that Tom planned his comeback into the big-time, and within two months he had made it, professional champion of the world. What was he thinking now, I wondered, as I watched him dropping further behind on the Col de Montgenèvre over which – historians say – Hannibal's elephant-paced army crossed the Alps into Italy 2,000 years ago.

As if in sympathy with Tom, the road writhed above the Durance Valley. The river was young and vigorous with a long adventure in store until its meeting with the Rhône at Avignon, but our wounded traveller's journey was nearly done. Three minutes down at the summit of Montgenèvre, encouraged by an understanding crowd of spectators. Three minutes ... Not the end of the world ... Get it back on the descent ... That would have been two-armed Tom's philosophy. In fact the descent was worse than the climb. He couldn't hold the back brake on, and sudden application of the front is not recommended on dusty mountain roads. Even if by some miracle – the whole field puncturing simultaneously for fantastic example – and Tom rejoined, what kind of future had he in that Tour? Immediately the Montgenèvre descent was over, the climb of the 1st-category Col de Sestrieres began and before reaching Turin the riders would have two 3rd-category hills to scale as well.

A mile or so over the border in Italy, where he had won Milan–San Remo and the Tour of Lombardy, Tom Simpson stopped. An official took his Peugeot, untied No. 46 from the frame and hoisted the bike on to the roof of the sag wagon. Another unpinned the linen 46 from the lower left corner of the Rainbow Jersey and an ex-rider of the 1966 Tour de France limped a few steps into the ambulance and drooped on to the bench, head down as if riding into the wind.

"Hard luck, Tom ..." What else could we say?

The Rainbow Jersey half turned towards us at the open door but the World Champion inside it did not speak or lift his eyes. He slumped over the table with forehead resting on the good left arm and we knew that Tom wanted to be left alone with his thoughts.

In the car we chased after the race. Radio-Tour came through weakly with a message which nobody wanted to hear.

From the back of the race the gendarmerie announces the abandon of Tom Simpson, World Champion, at kilometre 15.

Pierre Lardiere crossed No. 46 from the team-list stuck on the windscreen and I looked at the map. The nearest village to where Tom retired was Claviere, in Italy. Almost an anagram of the French word *Calvaire* which, although in common usage to denote worldly suffering, primarily means Calvary of the Cross. In just over a year, on Mont Ventoux, Tom Simpson would be making his last journey up the cruel hill.

"*Enfin.*" At last!

A group of three pedalled out of the Galibier tunnel, braked briefly for a glimpse of the Desgrange memorial which they had evidently seen before, called out a greeting to me, and were lost round a rocky bend. *Enfin.* At last. A long descent without a dirty great climb to follow. A minute later I was on it too.

In the ups and downs of life the mind's camera has a built-in filter which traps the grime of our experience and lets through the precious light. We remember army comrades with affection, forget the blasted Sergeant-major. In registering the ups and downs of the BRA my filter has gone into reverse. I remember every stumble of the drunken downhill waltz on the Croix de Fer, that black squirm through tunnels, cloud and flood partnered by a bicycle not quite right in the head and with a few screws loose in other departments as well – but I've forgotten everything about the first part of the Galibier descent except that it was a carefree frolic in the sun. Something, somebody, some voice – Jean Bobet calling through the tunnel? Desgrange whispering from his shrine? – something told me just to sit back and enjoy myself. I did, hardly realising the bike was under me and downing the kilometres like a hungry diner who in minutes gets rid of a meal that has taken all morning to prepare.

On that first five miles swoop I must have passed the spot where Tom Simpson crashed in that dramatic 1966 stage. Our N202 road joined the larger N91 at Lautaret Cross where modern Tourmen turn left for Briançon, whereas in Christophe's day they went right – as we were doing – for Grenoble. Wonderful mountain air on the Col de Lautaret! Just the mention of it has cleared my mind and memories start floating in ... A party of children romping in the grass and yelling *"Allez Pingeon"* at me. Now that was a new one. Where did they come from? From Lyon where the 1967 Tour winner began his racing career, or Maubeuge in the north of France where he lives now? I remember lush green pastures and sunlit slopes ablaze with anemone and lily, and the reappearance after the lunch interval of the fast-bowling west wind and having to pedal pretty hard downhill. I remember a thick cloud coming over the top of a mountain trench in a surprise raid and the irresistible counter-attack of the flame-throwing sun. Most of all I remember the glaciers, the furred-tongue hangovers of the 13,000 feet, three-headed monster of La Meije. I could hardly take my eyes off the great ice blocks, although I was forced to do so as N91 turned in a horseshoe bend on meeting the Romanche River, and again during the grope through the long black tunnel which followed when the road straightened out. I stopped in La Grave village in front of the hotel where we stayed during a Tour de France a few years ago. That was a short night for me! I was up at five o'clock scrambling up the mountain determined to get a closer look at the glacier.

During my short BRA breather I tried in vain to pick out the way I climbed that early morning. Then I began at the top and worked downwards, and it was easy. Like the stream whose course it copied, the path grew from a drip of melting snow, tumbled down through scree and boulder to tree and scrub and torn-out gully, ending with a half-mile grass track sprint to the white finishing-line of the foaming Romanche River. I looked at my watch ... Should I pinch an hour?

A group of six rattling through La Grave with a brisk *coup de pédale* brought me back to earth. Lift not mine eyes unto the hills but heed the word from the Book of Jobet and get myself a bit of back wheel. The idea had occurred to many others: within ten minutes I had picked up three non-paying passengers who claimed cramp, hunger and cold as excuses for their inability to do a turn of pacemaking. Cold – at two o'clock on a sunny mid-summer afternoon! He was, too, shivering with it. The ass had stopped, soaked with perspiration, at the Galibier summit, slept for 20 minutes in the sun and then made the descent without adding a stitch to his socks, shirt and shorts.

The road still dropping. I kept leg- and body-warmers on until after the tunnels skirting the Chambon Lake – a barrage across the Romanche River – where there was a sudden upward tilt followed by a plunge into the wild Infernet Gorge. Then I stopped hurriedly, looking back as I stuffed tracksuit, cape and gloves into the bag and plastic roll, and was back on the bike in no time, biting a banana and awaiting the arrival of a *peloton* I had spotted lower down the hill. Ever been had! They pulled up just behind me, unloading long loaves of bread and bottles of wine ready for a picnic meal.

After a mile or two I recaught the three invalids of whom only the cramped one stayed with me, although begging to be excused duty at the front. I heard him the first time, but moved over after a couple of kilometres just to hear him say it again. "*Non monsieur – vous êtes trop fort.*" I was too strong. Wonderful words! We left the contortions of the Infernet Gorge and were on the straight road leading to Bourg d'Oisans where, just before the little town, a signpost to the right said *Alpe d'Huez 13.5 kms*. Alpe d'Huez is a winter sports station where intrepid skiers and bobsleighmen descend at great speed, and up to which, in 1952, Fausto Coppi soared 3,500 feet in 8.5 miles in an epic climb which was the foundation of his second victory in the Tour

Although I was at the finish of that 1952 Tour in Paris, my spell as an official race follower had not yet begun. As usual I "followed" the race closely by radio and the French papers which in those days were on sale in London's West End at 08h30 on the day of issue (in some parts of France you couldn't get them until the evening!)

Coppi's Alpe d'Huez win gave him the yellow jersey by five seconds from a man who was very pleased to get rid of an embarrassment that had accidentally come his way the day before. The reluctant *maillot jaune* was Andrea Carrea, an Italian *domestique* who had been given a place in the national team for the sole purpose of helping Coppi. On the Mulhouse to Lausanne stage, with a third Italian, Fiorenzo Magni, wearing the yellow jersey the Swiss rider Diggleman broke away in the hope of doing a local-boy-makes-good on his home roads. Nolten (Holland) and Marinelli (France) went after him on their own initiative, and Carrea joined in because Coppi ordered him to do so – in the capacity of "policeman", of course. The Italian found himself towed along at great speed by the international triplet and building up a lead of five minutes over the main bunch.

At Lausanne, Diggleman sprinted to his dream victory and couldn't get to the podium fast enough to kiss the pretty girl and wave his bouquet triumphantly to the crowd. Far from overjoyed was the new race leader. Carrea had to be pushed up the steps and the *maillot jaune* pulled over his shoulders. An Italian Gregario Maglia Gialla in the Giro di Francia! What would Magni say? Worse, what would Fausto Coppi do? Throw him out of the team for betraying his master and collaborating with the enemy? According to many accounts I read of the incident poor Carrea, tall, rugged and sad-looking at any time, was the most miserable *maillot jaune* on record. This is how Pierre Chany recalls the affair in his book, *Le Tour de France*:

> At last the peloton put in an appearance, among the riders being Coppi and Magni. When the latter spotted Carrea decked in yellow he scowled and the new leader's teeth began chattering. Then Coppi slowly finished his ride. He pointed a finger at Carrea and burst into a hearty laugh. Not until then did the poor fellow start waving his bouquet and smiling at the photographers.
>
> Next morning Carrea was up early and began his day, as usual, by cleaning Coppi's shoes. Later in the afternoon the *campionissimo* overwhelmed the opposition on the Alpe d'Huez and very politely put everything back in its proper place.

After Bourg d'Oisans our BRA straight road kept almost north for another seven miles in the spacious (for these parts) Valley of the Romanche torn by a glacier of a colder age. Then N91 turned sharp left, with the river into narrow-gorge country again. *Grenoble – 42* said a big sign, and one on the other side of the road: *Croix de Fer – 30*. This is where we came in, back at Rochetaillée the circuit of the frying-pan course completed. Now for the return trip down the crinkly handle. So this was where we soaked and groped in the small hours ... those the hydro-electric and electro-metallurgical works whose roaring turbines scared us in the blackness of the night

... these, the rails (the *Rye!*) the girls told us to look out for ... those, the enormous cliff walls of the industrial corridor of the Romanche ... These, coming up behind the fellows who stopped to picnic back along the road.

My friend Cramp and I latched on the back, or nearly the back, that position being jealously guarded for some reason by a bearded *Randonneur* whose handlebar bag was thick with pinned-on badges and medals. We were 13 who rode the last 10 miles from Vizille to Grenoble, a biker's dozen of mixed Vets. and under-40s, all well inside the qualifying times of 18 and 20 hours, and frequent stops at traffic reds didn't worry us at all.

In the Anneau de Vitesse I had my card stamped and was presented with a small BRA brooch of the club-badge type. No times were taken but the presiding lady obligingly wrote *Arrivé 16h 50* on my card. Ten minutes under 15 hours for the round trip. Wish I'd known about this affair 20 years ago. I would have made a bit of a BAR jigsaw of the 150 Miles BRA, viz. 50 miles + 100 miles in 12 hours.

"Tea for Wadley! Trust him to arrive back at fyfoclock!" For half an hour my US Creteil club-mates and I swapped BRAvado stories. Beaumann went round in 11–10, Duvivier 12–20, while M.Rouhard's 14–30 was what I probably would have done had I not been so pleasantly delayed by Jean Bobet and Mme at the Galibier summit. Then two or three hours later we all met for a considerable meal which ended with the promised champagne to celebrate, as the Toastmaster said, *Le 59ème anniversaire de notre sociétaire Britannique, John Wadley.* I felt a great deal younger than early that same morning on the descent of the Croix de Fer. Then we had another bottle to celebrate Barry Hoban's Saturday win at Versailles. As the party broke up somebody said:

"By the way, I suppose Ocaña did win the Tour de France?"

Next morning's Dauphiné Libéré newspaper carried half a page of news and pictures of the BRA, headlined:

At Grenoble 1,200 candidates at the start of the Brevet Cyclotouriste des Alpes. A torrent barring the Glandon Road forced nearly half of them to abandon. The official figures: Entries, 1,200; Starters 1,100. Finishers 628.

During the morning I rode again to the Anneau de Vitesse where a reception was given by sponsors Liberia Cycles and the organising club, *Cyclotouristes Grenoblois*. In the crowded bar I could do no more than shake hands with Jo Routens, Grenoble's *Monsieur Cyclisme*, but in the afternoon I called at his lightweight shop for a chat. He knows the BRA better than anybody – ridden 26, fastest in 12 is his fine record. In 1938 a journalist on *L'Auto* wrote that amateur Routens was as good a climber as any French professional.

"The first BRA was in 1936 when the *cols* were surfaced with stones and gravel!" M. Routens remarked. "I see from the papers they reckon yesterday was the worst weather there has ever been. It was bad all right, but 1939 was the worst of all. Snow and hail on both the *cols*. Only 27 finished out of 250 starters."

"The next BRA will be held in 1975," I said, "and in the opposite direction. Some have told me yesterday's clockwise course is the harder, others think the opposite. You should know better than anybody."

"I prefer it the way we went round this year. Yesterday the last 100 kilometres were near enough all descent from the Galibier summit and the heat was no problem. But the other way round, the last 100 kms. start with that very difficult climb of the Croix de Fer. 'Feu' is more like it – Fire. Around 11 o'clock the place is like a furnace, and those who have forced themselves too much on the Galibier just collapse by the wayside. Still, it's all right if you are in shape. Last year J-P. Coulomb – your Creteil club-mate I think – put up a record 8 hours 54 minutes which is nearly an hour better than the fastest in the other direction."

"The best gears?" said Jo Routens. "Well, now you've ridden the BRA once you will have something to work on next time – and you'll be two years older, mind. Whatever you decide on, take my advice. Add another couple of teeth on the back just for luck."

The short ride from Jo Routen's shop to Grenoble station was really the end of my 19th Tour de France. I took a train to Paris, stayed a few days there, then returned by rail/sea to London.

"Didn't you feel depressed seeing your old friends following the race all the way?" my wife asked.

The answer was an underlined NO in bold letters. Indeed I felt sorry for them at times, even on the Tourmalet with the rain lashing down. They were in the dry. I was *in* the Tour de France at last. ...

My 19th Tour de France, 1974

On the road between Paris and Brest.

A Tribute to Jock

by Neville Chanin

Fourteenth of July 1981, Bastille Day, dawned with a clear blue sky and promise of a scorcher later on in the mountains. I was seeing my 21st Tour de France and had overnighted with my six colleagues at La Chambre in the Arc valley. Ahead of us, as we gazed from our hotel window, we could see the initial kilometres of the 22 which would raise us through 1,474 metres to the 1,924-metre summit of the Col du Glandon.

The previous day had been a 100-mile stage from Morzine, ending with a climb of the mighty Madeleine which, with its 1,600 metres of climbing in 26 kilometres, I consider to be one of the most formidable ascents in the Alps.

We dined well that night – but then we usually do. This meal was a special one: our table was laid for eight, yet fellow diners noted only seven lads present. They watched in silence as we drank a toast to the unoccupied chair at the head of our table. But our story begins much earlier in the year.

After Jock Wadley's funeral in March, his wife, Mary, expressed her wish that his ashes should be scattered on the route of the Tour de France – the race he had followed and reported on 23 occasions. Along with Jock's former asssistant editor of *Sporting Cyclist*, Roy Green, we discussed how it could be done.

Since my earliest visits to *La Grande Boucle* I'd met Jock on various Alpine and Pyrenean passes, in Normandy villages, on circuits and tracks. He would always spare time to answer my shouts, jump from his Press car and chat with us clubmen, take photos, before hailing a lift with other Press colleagues; there was always a touch of envy towards us, for we were soaking up the race atmosphere from the saddle whilst he was in a car. It seemed logical and fitting that Jock should attend his final Tour with a party of British clubmen.

And so Bastille Day came.

We – the seven of us – had each taken a turn in carrying the remains of our Sporting Cyclist over the mountain roads he knew so well and now Chris would carry him up the Glandon – two hours of real climbing.

I'd chosen a special spot on the Glandon because, in 1973 on his 59th birthday, Jock had climbed that pass whilst riding the Brevet Randonneur des Alpes.

Dave was first over the summit and had descended the 13 kilometres to locate the spot in the rocky Défilé de Maupas where the Torrent des Sept Laux comes crashing down from seven lakes higher up the mountain, forming a spectacular waterfall. He had already gathered a selection of mountain flowers and arranged them in a plastic bottle and was making a simple cross as I arrived. Chris followed soon after. The sky was without blemish and the sun shone strongly – what a contrast to that July day in 1973.

Our intentions had been announced that morning on Radio Tour, and the organisers had positioned a *gendarme* nearby to ensure that our scattering of his ashes was not interrupted. It was sad and silent.

(from *Bicycle Times*)